A HISTORY OF SOUTH INDIA FOR CHILDREN

From Prehistory to Vijayanagara

Dr Pradeep Chakravarthy is a graduate of the London School of Economics, UK, and JNU, Delhi. He has a PhD in history. An award-winning student, he has more than two decades of work experience, especially in learning and development. His mission is to help people understand present and future behaviour by understanding the past. Pradeep's corporate experience (TVS, Cognizant, Infosys and McKinsey) aids his consultations on helping individuals and organizations change behaviour, based on history. He has authored nine books with a focus on the culture of Tamil Nadu and how history can help us improve performance at work. He has published more than 200 articles in magazines/newspapers, mostly on history and its relevance to our lives today. He has recently opened 'Anantya in The Village', a heritage hotel in Alwar Tirunagari, Tamil Nadu. He conducts heritage immersion tours here for children.

Pradeep lives in Chennai with his teenage son.

A HISTORY OF SOUTH INDIA FOR CHILDREN

From Prehistory to Vijayanagara

PRADEEP CHAKRAVARTHY

Illustrations by Vibha Surya

hachette INDIA

First published in 2024 by Hachette India
(Registered name: Hachette Book Publishing India Pvt. Ltd)
An Hachette UK company
www.hachetteindia.com

6

ISBN 978-93-5731-417-6

Hachette Book Publishing India Pvt. Ltd
4th & 5th Floors, Corporate Centre
Plot No. 94, Sector 44, Gurugram – 122003, India

Typeset by Manmohan Kumar, Delhi

Printed and bound in India
by Manipal Technologies Limited

FSC
www.fsc.org
MIX
Paper | Supporting responsible forestry
FSC™ C043100

For Raghavan,
who constantly reminds me that history has to
be 'cool' like cars
and
for Aila, Ayaan and Saket,
who taught me that I can make history interesting
for children

CONTENTS

NOTE: The history of Andhra Pradesh, Telangana and. indeed, Karnataka, is often closely linked because of their geographic proximity and roughly similar geography; therefore, in this book Andhra and Telangana have been treated together.

BEFORE YOU BEGIN YOUR ADVENTURE IN SOUTH INDIA...

A NOTE FROM THE AUTHOR

South India is the region now composed of the states of Andhra Pradesh, Telangana, Karnataka, Kerala and Tamil Nadu. According to general estimates, together they not only house around 20 per cent of the Indian population, but they also contribute about 30 per cent of India's gross domestic product, forming a vital part of its economy.

All the states in the region have a rich and varied history dating as far back as the Stone Age. They boast long coastlines and, therefore, have maintained trade and cultural connections with the outside world over several centuries.

There are not many books for children (or even adults) that focus on the expansive history of the region, though there are many that focus on individual dynasties that ruled this ancient and fertile land. They include dynasties such as the Cholas who had one of the largest Asian empires because of their naval superiority, the Chalukyas who amalgamated Jain and Hindu religions in a harmonious way and built stunning temples, and the Kakatiyas who used temple building to drive the economy of their kingdom, among others. The region also houses Kerala, one of Asia's most international trading areas, and Hampi, which was one of the world's wealthiest cities in its heyday. The food, textiles, art and architecture of each present-day state in south India are as diverse as those of many nations in the world.

Of course, that doesn't sum it up. Many people are not aware of the diversity and depth of the region's history and polity. The curriculum largely lends itself to being more nationally focused (except that of some State Boards), with emphasis on north India.

Keeping this in mind, this book tries to:

- Present history as a subject that is relevant to contemporary times. While many things, such as technology, travel and lifestyle, are very different today, some things connected to the way human beings think, feel and act have not really changed. Gleaning insights from the past is a good way to understand the course of the future.
- Outline the broad history of the region and focus on the small details that breathe life into the subject, which is otherwise dominated by political history. Dates are given wherever relevant, but the approach is a 360-degree one rather than listing a long line of rulers and their achievements.

- Help understand the basic principles of structures, especially temple sculptures, and see how different they are from the rest of India. This region has the maximum number of art and architecture sites virtually untouched since the medieval times, and they give a rich understanding of that time in a visual way.

The Sangam period is roughly considered to be from the third century BCE to the third century CE. Several poems from this time, especially in anthologies like the *Purananuru*, mention kings, kingdoms and battles. These are considered to be historical sources for us to reconstruct the political history of that time. Sadly, we have no dates and, in some cases, we aren't sure whether it is the name of the king or a title. However, that does not take away from the rich source of historical information we have from these poems of the kings and kingdoms of Kerala and Tamil Nadu.

After reading this short book, you – the young reader – should be more knowledgeable about how south Indians really lived their life in the ancient and medieval times. And if you also enjoy getting to know all this, then this book will truly be a success.

Happy reading!

Pradeep Chakravarthy, PhD
Chennai, 2023

1

WHEN THERE WAS NO HISTORY

THE STONE AGE AND THE MARVELLOUS METAL AGE

Human evolution is the very gradual, 5,000,000-year-long and complex process of change by which people evolved from their ape-like ancestors. In hindsight, it is also seen as a process of advancement for the better. It enabled us to lead safer, healthier, comfortable and more enjoyable lives.

It is important, however, to not view this purely as a simple 'good' or 'bad' process, or say that only good came out of it. It is far more complicated and can be seen by different people in different ways. For example, urbanized humans living in cities are more comfortable with technology. However, those who continue to lead simpler lives, such as in forests and rural areas, are closer to nature and, perhaps, inflict less damage on it. This is possibly because their being so dependent on nature means that they need to protect it more fiercely.

Evolution is an ongoing process that has been unfolding for millions of years. We don't fully understand its complexities yet. We can learn only from the careful study of remains, such as old bones and fossils. For example, by examining the remains of an animal bone, scientists can conclude what kind of tools were used to cut the meat from the bone. Such evidence helps create a clearer picture, a kind of reconstruction of the past, and offers us clues to the process of evolution.

Evolution has to be studied in a social context as well. How did we learn to live together, find food and communicate? Simple things that we take for granted today – our parent tending to us if we are sick or even our ability to use language, are all incredibly complex actions and thoughts that we have learnt over thousands of years.

Going by some scholars who attribute this view to anthropologist Margaret Mead, the first sign of evolution was when a bone was discovered healed after a fracture because someone had taken the time and effort to tend to it. In the animal and plant world, if something is hurt, it is quickly eaten up, or dies because of lack of food and water. However, in the case of the healed bone from over 15,000 years ago, one is able to witness humanity. This, according to Mead, was the first sign of human evolution and civilization, and the core value that makes humans more evolved in comparison to other animals – the ability to feel empathy, as displayed in the willingness to care for the wounded.

As we learnt to communicate and live with others, human populations increased and moved in search of new and more fertile land, due to, perhaps, water and food shortage or even threat to life from conflict.

Then, some populations began travelling across land and a few landed up in India about 500,000 years ago.

This stage is called the Palaeolithic period, which lasted till about 12,000 years ago. 'Palaeolithic' means 'old stone' and refers to the earliest part of the period when human beings used stone tools, such as arrowheads and knives fashioned from stones, to help them hunt. They ate fish, plants and animals.

THE PALAEOLITHIC PERIOD

Tamil Nadu, Karnataka, Kerala, Andhra Pradesh and Telangana house many sites from which remains dating as far back as to the Palaeolithic period or the Old Stone Age have been unearthed. Since they are spread across each of these rather vast states, it isn't vital for us to know the names of all of them, but there are certainly a few that are worth taking note of.

On the following map, many Palaeolithic sites can be found situated close to hills and mountains. A popular site among these is Pallavaram, considered to be one of the oldest inhabited places in south India, now near the present-day Chennai airport.

Around 160 years ago, a British archaeologist and geologist, Sir Robert Bruce Foote, discovered old stone tools here and set up one of the earliest collections of what came to be known as the 'Madras Stone Tool industry'. Today, one can see some of these at the Government Museum in Egmore, Chennai. Another, less easily accessible, but certainly more beautiful location

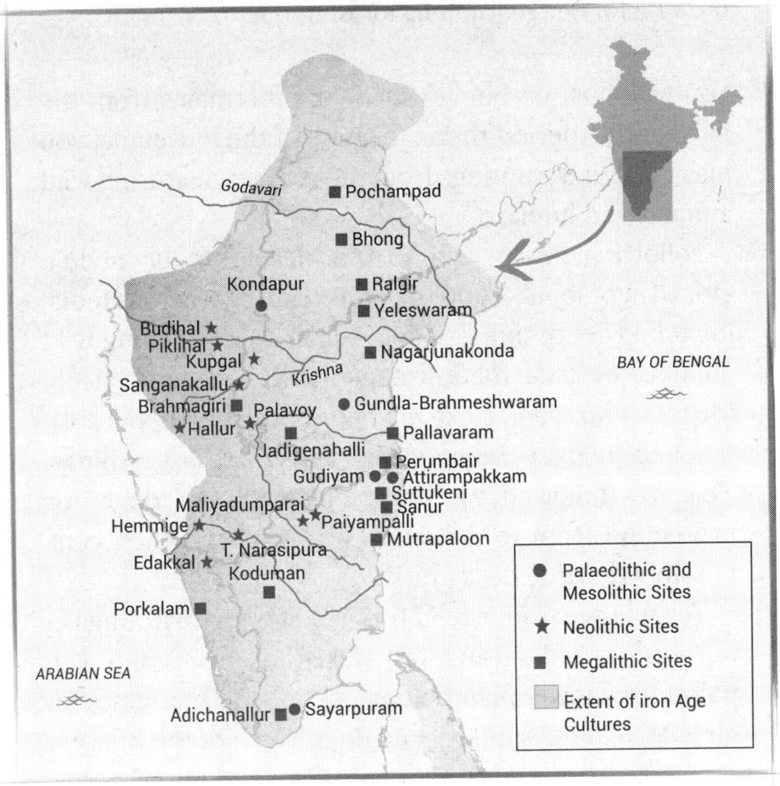

Map of main Stone Age and Iron Age cultures

of Palaeolithic remains is the site of the Belum caves in Andhra Pradesh. Some sites, like those in Hampi in Karnataka, started off being settled in and grew into big cities later.

In fact, there is a very good chance that the home that you live in might be located on top of such an ancient site. So the next time you visit any place in India, don't forget to check out the local museum or sites maintained by the Archaeological Survey of India.

You will most certainly chance upon remains from the Palaeolithic period there. In some of the museums, you may even find paintings from these times, featuring wild animals and humans.

Following this period, in the Mesolithic (or 'middle stone') age, about 8,000 to 6,000 years ago, across India, including south India, people began domesticating wild animals for their food. It began with cows and sheep, for milk and wool. Next in line was the horse, because it could help in transporting heavy and large things. This was followed by the domestication of dogs: for protection from wild animals at night. And then cats, possibly to catch pesky rats...

You will see evidence of this in some cave paintings in Kerala (Koodakkad) and Karnataka (Badami region). The paintings show a man holding a cup, and hunters with elephants, horses, bison, and deer. Some of the hunters are shown to be wearing conical caps made of leaves and are accompanied by some kind of dogs from about 6,000 to 3,000 years ago.

The typical tools of this period were tiny stone tools called 'microliths'. They were combined with other materials such as wood or bone to form compound tools like spears, arrows and sickles. Smaller tools helped in the hunting of smaller birds and animals.

THE NEOLITHIC AGE

About 5,000 to 3,000 years ago, human populations in south India had become smart enough to use stone weapons and to polish them. This is called the Neolithic (or 'new stone') age. The sharper stone weapons made hunting more precise and successful, so meat was a certainty for meals. And because hunting took less effort and time, the Neolithic people had more time to invest in farming and to improve it by adopting new techniques. The earliest grown grains in this period were corn and millets.

People made pots of all shapes and sizes during the Stone Age

Since farming needed water, humans began to move away from forests and caves to places closer to waterbodies. In several caves in the Palani Hills (in Kerala and Tamil Nadu) we find paintings of a community in the act of hunting and farming, featuring domestic animals such as cows, sheep, goats, pig and fowl, along with wild animals such as spotted deer and jungle cats. In some paintings you can also make out crops being grown, such as green gram, horse gram and millets. With the variety of food on offer, the Neolithic people were perhaps trying out newer recipes, given that fire had already been discovered during the Palaeolithic age.

As hunting and grain production increased, animals became increasingly important, not only as a source of food, but also for farming and hunting. Building shelters also became more important, especially during the rainy season. Caves were no longer comfortable enough, and sometimes these weren't close enough to the lands that were being farmed.

From 4,000 years ago to about 2,000 years ago, people started building shelters to protect themselves, their food and their animals. Excavations conducted in places such as Sendamangalam and Adichanallur in Tamil Nadu, and Brahmagiri in Karnataka show us that the houses from this period featured low walls of brick or were made using granite boulders. From some paintings we also come to know that roofs were made of wooden rafters and were thatched. Some houses even featured L-shaped roof tiles.

From archaeological remains we know that men and women had long hair that they coiled up over their head like a crown of snakes; they wore lots of bangles, pendants, beads and, sometimes, gold ornaments. They

Pieces of broken pottery with beautiful patterns on them have been found in Adichanallur

wore a piece of cloth around the waist. Kids played games such as discs made from broken pots – so we know that people were smart enough to recycle even back then.

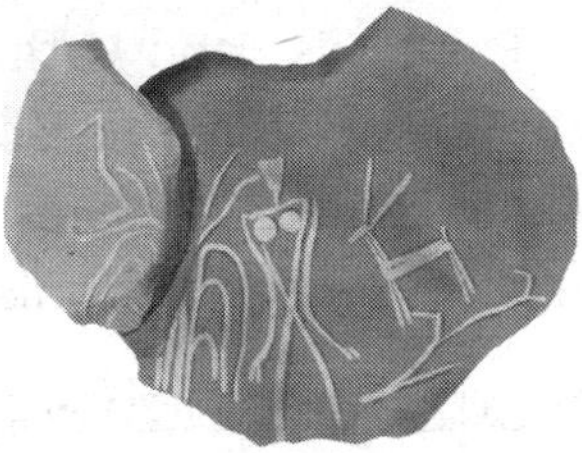

Bits of pottery (like this one from Adichanallur) give us clues about the crops grown and the animals around

WHAT BURIALS TELL US

Death was a scary thing and people died young, given that modern medical care didn't exist back then. We can infer this from the evidence of many skeletal remains of infants. Sad but true. Sickness and death were seen as mysterious, and healing was considered magical because people didn't understand the human body as well as we do today.

In places such as Sulimalthe, near Somwarpet town in Karnataka, dead people were cremated and a simple tomb was built with three flat stone walls and a slab on top. These are called 'dolmens' or 'cists'. In Adichanallur, in some cases, they buried the dead in unusual coffins, such as in the shape of an upright ram made from burnt clay. In other places, such as Kumarikalpalayam in Tamil Nadu and Pathekkar Hills in Kerala, they even erected menhirs, large upright stones, somewhat like the ones Obelix carries in the Asterix comics. In places, such as on the Nagaleru riverbank in Andhra Pradesh, they even made some cool carvings on the menhir – called petroglyphs – which are thought to be among the world's oldest engravings on rock.

Paintings and other artefacts recovered from these sites give us some idea of daily life. Evening time probably meant songs and dance and music from pipes and drums. Everyone ate and drank out

BURYING WITH LOVE

Today, we have good medical facilities that prevent or delay death. In the olden days, this wasn't the case and living even till the age of 30 was very rare. Couples had many children, and it was difficult for a child to survive their first birthday. But emotions were the same! From archaeological remains we learn that when some children were buried, their favourite toys, made of clay or game counters made of bone, were buried with them.

A typical burial: The pit usually went right down to the bedrock. The oval pot usually contained selected skeletal remains and teeth, along with grave 'furniture' consisting of different types of pots. It was covered with a lid.

SITTING LIKE A MUMMY?

As a child when I sat on the floor, hunched up my knees and put my arms around them, I was strongly reprimanded by adults. Can you guess why? It was a preferred posture for bodies buried in the Stone Age in some places. So, long after communities stopped that way of burying, that posture likely continued to be associated with death and was discouraged.

of pots and bowls that were red or black with artistic designs, composed of lines and circles and triangles. In paintings in Alambadi and Keelvalai (both in Tamil Nadu), you can see warriors on horses, big lizards in frames, and even an X-ray-like image of the tummy and intestines of a cow!

All these are more than 3,000 years old, and many are situated on the ceilings of caves. Looks like these people were superb rock climbers!

THE METAL AGE

Iron had been discovered and they made arrows, and even little goddess images in bronze, an alloy of copper and tin. They knew how to mix two metals, something which is difficult to do even today. A little Mother Goddess statue was discovered on the banks of the River Tambraparni (or Thamirabarani) in Adichanallur. The site was originally excavated around 1900, and

DECIPHERING DOLMENS

A dolmen is a megalithic (big rock) structure typically made by a large horizontal stone slab resting on two or more upright slabs, though shapes differ. This kind of stone monument has been found in different parts of the world. In India, archaeologists trace the majority of the megaliths to the Iron Age (1500 BCE to 500 BCE), though some sites go back to 2000 BCE. Megaliths are spread across the Indian subcontinent, though the bulk of them are found in peninsular India in the states of Maharashtra, Karnataka, Tamil Nadu, Kerala, Andhra Pradesh and Telangana.

These megalithic structures functioned as burial chambers or sites. In some cases, they were also places of worship. The megalith vary in size, but what is fascinating is the sheer size

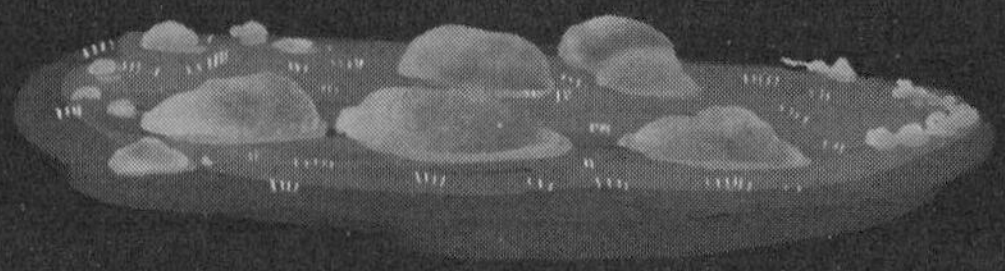

Dolmen cist type 1

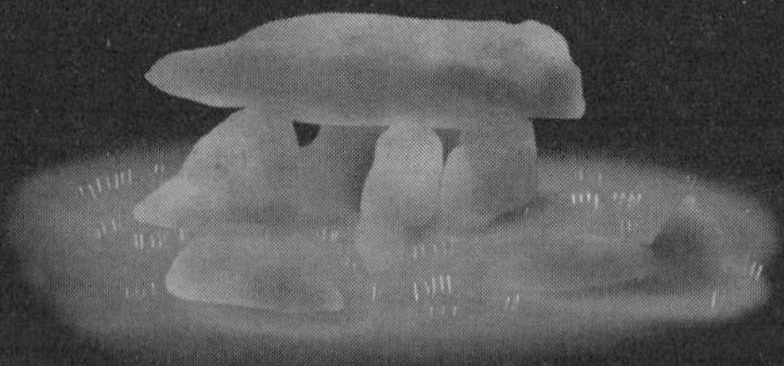

Dolmen cist type 2

of each. How such stones were moved and placed or what rituals were carried out around them remain a mystery. Sadly, sites like Marayoor (a small town around 40 km from Munnar, Kerala), famed for its cave paintings and picturesque dolmens, shows the neglected state of megalithic monuments in India.

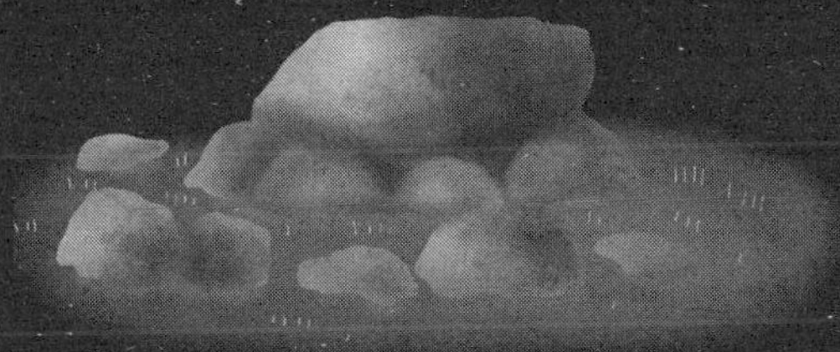

Dolmen cist type 3

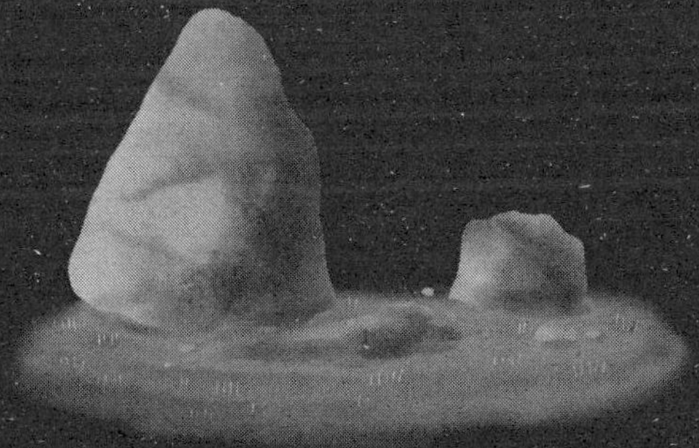

Menhir

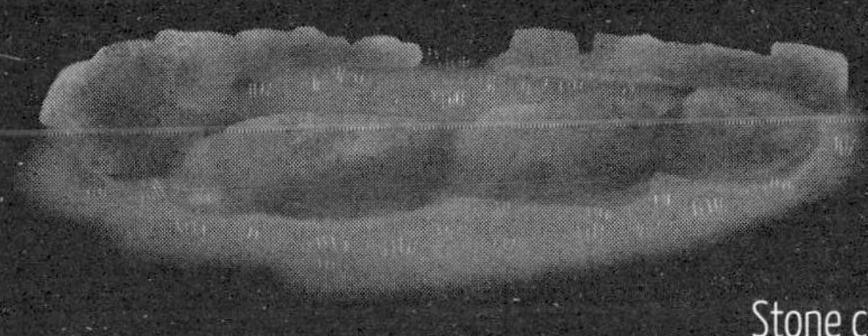

Stone circle

Mother Goddess figurine found in Adichanallur

several artefacts discovered, including gold jewellery. In the early excavations, only iron objects were found, such as arrows, daggers, knives, swords and many chisels. However, in later excavations in 2004, at the same site, archaeologists found items of iron and copper but no bronze or gold. These were found buried with paddy, a small dog-shaped toy and a small gold ring, leading archaeologists to believe that this might have been the burial site of a small child.

Broadly, the Bronze Age is dated from 2300 BCE to 700 BCE and the Iron Age from 700 BCE to 1 BCE. In western and central India, this demarcation is quite clear, with some village sites having only bronze and some only iron. In the south, it is not so clear-cut. In most places, we find both metals, which means that the places were continuously inhabited for longer and that people were slowly learning how to work with different metals, to melt them at different temperatures and to forge them together. Examples like this abound in south India.

In 2018, for example, very close to Hyderabad, a hand axe and a hammer stone dating back to about 3000 BCE were discovered in Athvelly. In some cases like near Regonda (Karimnagar district in Telangana), dating back to 10,000 years, metal slag was found, proving the existence of iron foundries back then.

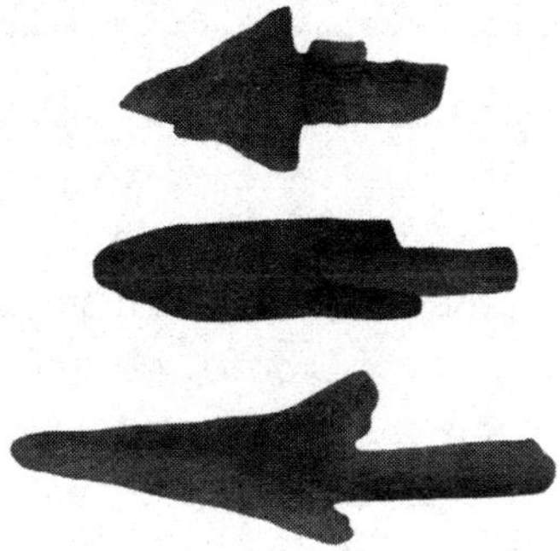

Arrowheads and spearheads of the Stone Age

In Kerala, megalithic monuments (2000 BCE to 2 CE) are either rock-cut caves, umbrella stones (unique to Kerala) and capstones – all found in the plains – and dolmens (eastern mountains), menhirs and stones are all found to have the same designs.

Menhirs and urn burials are found predominantly on the sea coast. In these sites, while complete skeletons have not been found, beads (that must have formed parts of ornaments) have been unearthed. Some of the beads were of carnelian (a semi-precious gemstone), found only in western India – which means that even as early as the third century BCE, Kerala was already trading with western India, especially Gujarat, where this stone is found.

In Karnataka too, metal age sites are aplenty, the most famous being Hirebenkal in Koppal district. Dated from 800 BCE to 200 BCE, this now remote location was in continuous habitation for over 1,000 years. The climb to the hilltop is tough, but the rare paintings there show warriors with metal weapons, and iron slag has been found too. The locally famous kettledrum is a hemispherical stone that, when beaten with a wooden or metal hammer, can be heard at least a kilometre away.

NO STAINLESS STEEL IN THE PUJA!

Stainless steel vessels are even now frowned upon in *pujas* (ceremonial worship of religious idols), but why? That's probably because many of the early Vedic customs came from the Bronze Age, before iron was used. Later, even when iron was used, it was only for agriculture or weapons. Which is probably why this preference for copper, silver or gold for the puja continues!

Maski near Hampi is famous for its Ashokan edict, etched on a rock-face of the gneissic outcrops, the oldest known rock on Earth's surface. Excavations show that it has been in habitation right through the Stone and Metal ages. Unlike in other areas, Iron Age societies in south India were not nomadic. In another metal age site of the same period called Koppa, in Chikkamagaluru district of Karnataka, grains of ragi and paddy have been found in the graves, revealing to us what people ate during that time.

As communities grew, more complex social and political systems were created, as you will find out in the next chapter.

2

A TIME OF AMBITIOUS KINGS

WHEN HISTORY BEGAN IN SOUTH INDIA

Most of what we know about south Indian history is from about 2,000 years ago. We have two main sources: books and inscriptions. The books may be of poems or stories, or religious texts, but they all offer us clues to how people lived and thought, and what was important to them. Temple inscriptions are somewhat like notices on your school website. In the olden days, all important announcements were carved into the stone walls of temples. With the help of these two sources, we can get a fairly accurate picture of the past.

By this time, the entire region had many small villages and towns. Villages may have had just a few streets of possibly 50–100 people living in them over a small area versus cities, which would have been much larger with more people living in them. It's difficult to pinpoint an exact number, but generally speaking, from the information available on new villages set up during the Chola rule, a village would have had less than a 100 people while a town would have had more. Cities may have had more than 1,000 inhabitants. In some cases, towns and cities flourished in places that had been continuously inhabited, right from the Stone Age times – for example, the area of Pallavaram in Chennai or the village of Hampi in Karnataka have been continuously inhabited for more than 5,000 years. In other cases, these were built, from the ground up, in new areas that people settled in as communities expanded.

As in most societies, villages were governed by one powerful family or a male individual. However, some scholars believe that many, if not most, ancient south Indian societies were 'matrilineal' (families were organized through their connection to the mother) or even 'matriarchal' (where key decisions were taken by the oldest female member of the family). Over the course of time, as agriculture developed and men began to spend more time on their farms, the system evolved to men being in charge and families being based on the relationships of the father.

Sometimes, a group of villages was ruled by a chieftain. When there was a shrewd, ambitious chieftain, he would fight and successfully conquer the land of other chieftains and become their 'ruler'. And it wasn't always that smart, ambitious and successful chieftains or kings had smart, ambitious and successful children of their own. So his kingdom could be wrested away from him by another king or chieftain. Very often, a powerful king would either have no children or have children who fought among themselves. Or, as he became older, he was not able to fight well or motivate his army, and a

An old painting of a Toda settlement

MATRILINEAL AND MATRIARCHAL SYSTEMS

In 1975, the matrilineal system was abolished by law in Kerala. Even till then, the Nairs and Ezhavas of Kerala, and the Bunts and Billavas of Karnataka followed either the matriarchal or matrilineal system. This meant that property and position passed through women, from mother to daughter; usually, the youngest daughter stayed with the parents and inherited the house. Husbands married and stayed with their wives rather than have the wives move to the husbands' homes. The Todas of the Nilgiri Hills and the Kottai Pillamars of Tamil Nadu also had a close connection to this tradition.

None of them follow much of this today.

more courageous and smarter neighbouring king would overthrow this one.

FAMILY AND DYNASTIC RULE

In the entire history of south India, there are only about 10–15 famous dynasties. The same ones, as if by rotation, kept coming to power, retreating to the background, and then coming back again for repeat performances. This depended on whether a particular king of the dynasty was ambitious or not.

Early kings of a dynasty would maintain a strong army

One can sense a pattern in dynastic rule. Generally speaking, the early kings of a dynasty were normally the ambitious ones who set up the foundation of their rule. They worked hard, fought and won wars, and looked after the needs of their people so that their citizenry was satisfied and their kingdom stayed united. The middle-order king, who had all the benefits

Middle-order kings invested in building and art

of land, wealth and organized systems, would start focusing more on the arts and on living a good life. So these kingdoms would then witness the construction of grand building projects, and artistic endeavours such as poetry, painting and sculpture would flourish. The later kings tended to overindulge in the finer things in life and ignored their kingly duties. The army became complacent, weak and lazy. This time was ripe for the king in power to be overthrown by a neighbouring state or by one of their smaller chiefs. And with this, the story would start all over again but with a different set of names.

Later kings were prone to overinduulgence, and neglected their army

GEOGRAPHY DETERMINES HISTORY

Where we live influences *how* we live. Much more than it does now, in the past, the geography of a region shaped the economic conditions and lifestyle of the people that inhabited it. For instance, mountains became defences and barriers for travel, and prevented the sharing of information. Rivers determined the amount of food production and, therefore, the prosperity of a place. Rivers connected to the sea and were pathways to seaports. Lands that were not fertile, such as rocky areas that could not have much agriculture, or areas with less water, tended to have kingdoms that sparred

THE CYCLE OF POWER

1. An ambitious, hard-working and focused soldier who motivates others, fights and defeats a militarily weak king.
2. Overthrows the weak king, sets up a dynasty and becomes King 1.
3. Strengthens his borders and administers well so people are happy and well-off.

4. His successor, King 2, copies his style and more prosperity results.

5. Life is good because there is lots of food and an efficient army.

6. Strengthens his borders and administers well so people are happy and well-off.

7. King 3 spends his time and money only on art and architecture.
8. King 4 mimics King 3 but neglects the army.
9. Local chieftains become more militarily powerful and start wondering why they should not be king.
   OR
   Ambitious kings from other kingdoms/ countries want to conquer the territory.
10. Local chieftain/ enemy king attacks.
11. Victorious local chieftain/enemy king becomes the new King 1.

over precious food and water. Therefore, these regions had smaller kingdoms and were often more frequently at war with each other. The Pandyas of Tamil Nadu are an example of this.

The Pandyas ruled a stretch of land (in present-day Tamil Nadu), which had only two main rivers, one of which had little water. The land was also in the rain-shadow region of the Western Ghats and received relatively less rain. Although they developed excellent systems of rainwater conservation, the smaller chiefs fought more viciously than most to resist subjugation. Once could assume that this was so since they had to work harder to secure the bare minimum of the scarce resources at their disposal.

Kingdoms that had control over a river and were able to harness the water for agriculture, were more prosperous. Owing to this, they had money to pay for a larger fleet of soldiers. One could say they were also more inclined to expand their empires through battles. The Cholas, who controlled the River Kaveri, or the Chalukyas, who held sway over the River Malaprabha, are classic examples of this.

However, this is not a one-size-fits-all formula! For instance, kingdoms that were located in present-day Kerala had many rivers, over 44 of them. Rivers, such as the Periyar and Pamba, have multiple tributaries, which are in turn fed by smaller streams. However, the large number of rivers and dense forests made it hard for big armies to move fast, so the region saw many smaller kingdoms, such as Trippappooru Swaroopam, Perumpadappu Swaroopam, Nediyiruppu Swaroopam and Kola Swaroopam, fighting each other, with very few being able to conquer significant parts of Kerala.

With so many conflicts taking place all the time, for land, water, and mineral resources, there was no exact division between ruling kings, dynasties and empires by way of time periods. It may seem fixed and linear in textbooks, as if one came after the other. In reality, however, there was quite a bit of overlap between ruling dynasties. Likewise, the boundaries of the kingdoms too constantly shifted as rulers captured new lands and added them to their kingdoms, or lost some in battle. Apart from this, the geography of the region too affected the way people lived. For example, the culture of Hampi in Karnataka was shaped by the nearest waterbody, the River Tungabhadra, and agricultural activities that sprang up owing to it. The kingdom's shape, size and culture evolved over its existence. It started off as a small village under the Hoysala kings. It grew to be the capital city of the very wealthy Vijayanagara kings, and then again reverted to being a small village after the Bahmani kings plundered it.

It can be said that tracing the course of a river system can help us understand the course of the kingdom located near it. For instance, the many rivers that flow through the mountains and forests of present-day Kerala kept the region relatively isolated from the rest of south India. Alongside, the long coastline that skirts the state offered an opportunity for establishing close linkages with the outside world, much more than what the other states of south India could boast of at the time.

Similarly, the Tungabhadra and the Krishna-Godavari rivers can help us better understand the history of Karnataka and Andhra. The Palaar-Kaveri river tells the story of the Cholas. The Pandya story is captured through the Vaigai and the Thamirabarani (Tambraparni) rivers.

WHAT ABOUT THE QUEENS?

Unfortunately, most of the political history we have is the story of kings. They were certainly supported by queens, but we don't hear much of them. What we do have are many stories of women who were famous for their expertise in the arts. There are two recorded instances of queens following a different religion from the king and able to maintain their position and power, which was unusual then.

One such queen was Angayarkanni (also known as Mangayarkkarasiyar), the wife of the Pandya king Koon Pandya. The king, who ruled in the seventh century, was a practising Jain. This was until he fell severely ill. To heal him, the queen – with the help of her minister Kula Chirayan and the boy-saint Sambandar – encouraged the king to adopt Shaivism because the king could be cured only by Sambandar using the sacred ash from a Shiva temple, and this warranted him to do so. It is believed that the goddess Meenakshi of the famous

Madurai Meenakshi Sundareswarar Temple, an avatar of goddess Parvati, is a deified (regarded as god) version of queen Angayarkanni. In fact, the Sanskrit meaning of the word 'Meenakshi' – 'one with fish-shaped eyes' – also happens to be a translation of the word 'Angayarkanni'.

Another story we have, this time from Karnataka, is of Shantala Devi, the wife of the Hoysala king Vishnuvardhana (1108–1152 CE). As a follower of Jainism, he was known as Bitti Deva. He adopted Hinduism under the influence of the saint Ramanujacharya. His wife, Shantala, however, continued to follow Jainism. Not only did she fund the construction of many Jain temples or '*basadis*' in Karnataka, but she also supported her husband's Hindu temple project in Belur. Many believe that she has been featured on the sculptures we see in Belur and Halebidu, for she was an excellent dancer, and possibly an equally acclaimed singer as well.

A sculpture of King Vishnuvardhana and his queen Shantala who followed Jainism

Legend has it that she died by suicide because she could not have a male child. What is more likely, however, is that she – like many old and devout Jains of the time – performed the *sallekhana* vow, where a Jain retires to a cave in a remote mountain and gradually gives up food and water as the final act of the mind overcoming the needs of the body.

Shantala Devi and King Vishnuvardhana seemed to have patronized different religions and still lived together. Was this common? No, it wasn't. We have an ancient Kannada poem titled the *Yashoda Charite*, the story of Yashoda (no connection to the mother of the god Krishna) who is a Jain queen married to a Hindu king. They are unable to have a child for a long time. In the story, the king's mother believes a sacrificial killing will fix the problem. The queen is aghast – how can she bring forth a child into the world with another being killed in its place? This went against the key Jain belief of *ahimsa*. The poem is an exploration of the circumstances that drive us to become violent in thought or action. In 1980, this poem was adapted into a gripping play titled *Bali – The Sacrifice* by well-known playwright Girish Karnad.

KERALA

Kerala is surrounded by the very tall Western Ghats mountain range with a few peaks as high as 8,000 feet. This meant that moving an army of soldiers, horses and elephants was not an easy task by any means. Even if they did manage to cross these mountains, the region was dense with forests and many rivers snaked through them. Not to forget that it rained most of the time, and during the rain, the army could not move at all. This meant that Kerala was left largely on its own while dynasties like the Pallavas and Hoysalas in Tamil Nadu and Karnataka fought with each other. Only the most militarily powerful kings like Rajaraja Chola were able to make inroads into Kerala through the Palghat pass (or Palakkad Gap) near Coimbatore in Tamil Nadu.

To the west was the sea coast and that was closer to the European trade route managed by the Arabs and Europeans. So, Kerala had much more international exposure to Arabia and Europe, and to their cultures and religions.

Although we have rock art from ancient times to help us understand the past, it is literature and inscriptions that offer us a more definite idea of Kerala from about 1,600 years ago. At the time, Kerala was ruled by the Ay kings in the south, the Ezhimala kings in the north and the Chera kings reigned over the central part of Kerala, which stretched into Tamil Nadu.

Malayalam had not emerged as a language yet, and everyone in the region spoke Tamil, an early version of what is spoken primarily in present-day Tamil Nadu.

MUZIRIS: A BUSTLING PORT

Somewhere around the town of Kodungallur today, not far from Kochi and Ernakulam, was the famous port of Muchiri Pattanam or Muziris. From about 3000 BCE till the 14th century, this was an active port with traders from Rome, Egypt and Arabia coming here to buy pepper and other spices. In the 14th century, because of the change in the course of the River Periyar, and perhaps earthquakes as well, the port faded away. Fortunately, in the last few decades, the Government has, through the Muziris Heritage Project, restored important buildings in the region to tell visitors the story of the international flavour the place would have had even 2,000 years ago.

On the banks of the Periyar was an ancient settlement from Iron Age times, and arrowheads and parts of farm tools have been recovered. By the seventh century, the region was controlled by the Pandya kings; later, the Chera kings conquered it in the eighth century. Today's Valapattanam, Kadalundi and Kodungallur were all important ports known

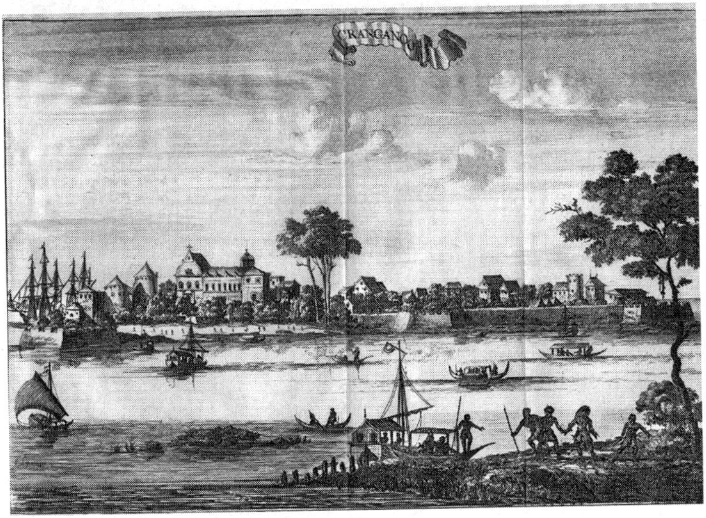

An old painting of Muziris

from Roman times. In this region, there is also the Cheraman Juma Masjid for followers of Islam, and the Paravur and Chendamangalam synagogues for the Jews (most of whom left for Israel when it was created in 1948). This was one of the earliest regions for Christianity to enter India, and museums in the area showcase the unique Syrian Christian community of Kerala. The Azhikode and Kottakkavu churches are particularly ancient. The Bhagavathy Temple and the Azheekal Sree Varaha Temple are all examples of the rich Hindu traditions from ancient times in this region.

Visiting the various sites and the museums, one gets an idea of how wealthy and cosmopolitan a place the entire region would have been in that time.

Kerala had five broad divisions based on geography.

Name in the Old Days	Because...	Ruled By
Venad or Velnad	'Land of the Vel chieftains'. The 'Vel' is a spear associated with Murugan, the god of war.	Ay kings. who later became the Chera kings and in 1755 came to be the most dominant rulers of Kerala.
Kuttanad	*Kutta* means a pond or a lake.	The Cheras
Kudanad	The 'western' land (west of Kongunad, which is now Coimbatore in Tamil Nadu)	
Puzhinad	The marshland, further up north	Ezhimala kings
Karkanad	Means 'remote and difficult to pass'	Ezhimala kings; later, the Mushika king Nannan was a great ruler in the Tamil Sangam times. Ezhil Mala or the 'Beautiful Hills' got distorted to Eli Mala or 'rat mountain'.

Time Period	Today, They Are...
From the first century CE to the ninth century, they organized themselves and in the 18th century CE became very powerful, especially under the ruler Marthanda Varma.	Thiruvananthapuram (Thiruvaramcode in the olden days)
One of India's oldest dynasties from the second century BCE. Their fame dipped from the third century CE but revived in the ninth to 11th centuries CE under the Kulasekhara kings. After their defeat in the 11th century CE by the Cholas, smaller kingdoms like that of the Samuthiri evolved.	Ernakulam and Kottayam Trichur, Palghat and Malappuram
From the third century and in the 11th century CE, they supported the Cheras of central Kerala and became smaller chieftains. By the 12th century CE, there were many rulers in this region, the Kolathiri being the most important. In the 17th century CE, there were ten kingdoms that were eventually conquered by Tipu Sultan and then the British.	Kasargod and Kannur; Mountainous region of Wayanad

We have a huge collection of stories of these kings from a set of poetry texts collectively called Sangam literature.

Many of the poems talk about war. Some also capture the ruler's idiosyncrasies. One Chera king, Utiyan Cheral, became famous for hosting big feasts and honouring poets who sang about this. His son Nedum Cheralatan won a battle against the Yavana (Greeks) about 1,700 years ago. Legend has it that he poured a tonne of ghee on the head of the enemy and forced him into a walk of shame on the roads of his capital. Please don't try this at home unless over a hot *idli*!

In another example, Adu Kottu Pattu Cheralatan, a fierce king from the Sangam times, would, after defeating his enemies on the battlefield, perform a rather scary dance while brandishing his sword.

Around the ninth century CE, the Chera kings united with branches of the Kongu Cheras (rulers of Coimbatore in Tamil Nadu) and ruled over almost the whole of central Kerala. According to some scholars, the word Kerala comes from the word 'Chera'. They first ruled from Vanchi, which is called Kodungallur/Muziris today and is believed to have been an important port until it was flooded in the 14th century CE. Thereafter, Kochi became the new port of the kingdom.

From the ninth century CE, the Kulasekhara (meaning 'jewels of the clan') kings ruled from Kodungallur, then called Mahodayapuram. The first of their kings was Kulasekhara Varman. He was a devotee of Vishnu and is considered a saint. In 1000 CE, one of his descendants,

Arrival of the Jewish pilgrims in Cochin in 68 CE

THE JEWS IN KERALA

About 2,000 years ago, a group of Jews fled the Middle East to avoid persecution and reached Kerala, They were welcomed by the king of the Kulasekhara dynasty, Bhaskara Ravi Varman. They lived as a distinct community and were allowed to build synagogues and own property without conditions attached, for as long as 'the sun and the moon exist'. The reference to the sun and the moon is a poetic way of saying 'forever' as these two will always be in the sky. It is believed that these Jews introduced the *appam*, a staple bread in Malayali cuisine, and vinegar made of raisins. Even today, the pastel, their deep-fried pastries with assorted fillings are popular in Kochi.

Bhaskara Ravi Varman, gave a land grant to Joseph Rabban, the leader of the Jews seeking refuge in India after fleeing the Middle East. This wasn't the first time they had done that. The first group of Jews are said to have come to Kerala in around 70 CE when they were persecuted by the Romans.

The Jews, by 1000 CE, had established an important place in Kerala's society. By trading mostly in pepper and horses, they had amassed an enviable fortune.

In those days, traders went from coast to coast transferring or selling goods. The trading rights were given to a body called the *anjuvannam*. They worked in organized groups called 'guilds', which were very diverse, with traders from different religions and regions working together. Besides doing business, they also donated substantial amounts to temples and through that to the local people.

By about 1000 CE, the Kulasekhara king was defeated by the army of Rajaraja Chola, who ruled from Thanjavur in Tamil Nadu, and had the courage and ambition to cross the forests and rivers of western Tamil Nadu to enter Kerala from the east where the mountains are relatively lower. He also defeated the Kerala kings in a naval battle by coming around the southern Indian peninsula – quite an achievement for his first campaign of conquest. For the next century, the Cheras were completely under the control of the Cholas.

The Kulasekharas never recovered from this defeat. However, the Venad kings of the south managed to overthrow the local king, and from the 12th century CE onwards they ruled most of Kerala for about 200 years. We know from an inscription that one of them, Ravi

Varma Kulasekhara (no connection to the earlier one), even donated a huge vessel made of solid gold to the Padmanabhaswamy Temple in Thiruvananthapuram. Imagine that!

Kollam became his favourite place, and he ruled from his palace there. Over a period, the Venad kings became less vigilant and less powerful. They did not maintain their army and were given to luxuries. You can guess what happened next.

Smaller kingdoms, about 35 of them, once controlled by local chieftains or ambitious and wealthy individuals, grew bolder. Many of these were called '*swaroopam*' (meaning created on its own). Many were not very friendly with one another, which made it difficult for them to survive in the face of frequent conflicts.

THE PORTUGUESE AND VASCO DA GAMA

A number of foreign travellers came to Kerala by the sea route, bringing glass, wine, horses, gold and silver. In return, they took back more gold, ivory and whole spices to their countries. Everyone flocked to India, as she had much more to offer to the West than the West had to her. Although the Indian subcontinent could not be considered a single political entity back then, it impressed many of those who visited it. These travellers and traders were impressed with the beauty and wealth of the land, but what they wanted most was Kerala's famed pepper and cardamom to add flavour to their food. They were desperate to find a way to get to Kerala quickly and buy these spices at the cheapest prices possible. They were willing to go to war for it!

The route at that time was controlled by the Venetians (from present-day Italy) and Arabs (from present-day Middle East). It snaked through Venice, Egypt, the Red Sea and then across the Arabian Sea (using its winds) to reach Kerala. This was the short route but expensive, since the Arabs and Venetian merchants multiplied the tax (for travelling through) many times over. European countries were keen to find a route around Africa. It would be longer but cheaper.

The following explorations created a new approach to south India for Europeans. Till then, traders had no political ambitions, and their intention was to trade and go back and make a profit in Europe. Now, with the Portuguese, Dutch, French, English and Danes trading in the same ports for the same goods, competition increased and their rivalry in Europe spilt into wars and rivalry here as well – for example, the French and English fought in Tamil Nadu, and the Portuguese and Dutch in Kerala. To safeguard their warehouses, they started owning land in south India. To protect their trade and land, they played off one king against another and rapidly got involved in the politics of the region. They also allowed missionaries to come into their region to preach Christianity. This was also the birth of colonialism in India with the English eventually coming to rule India.

South India became a favoured place for European travellers to visit and travellers like Domingo Paes from

DISCOVERY OF DISCOVERED PLACES

The period between the 15th and late 18th centuries CE is called the 'Age of Discovery' in Europe and it affected south India tremendously. By the 15th century CE, besides pepper and cardamom, the Europeans wanted the textiles of Asia, the silk of China, and gold and ivory from Africa. Much of this came from China via the land route called the Silk Road, but the Mongols and Turks had blocked it. European countries also realized that Venice, which held the monopoly of trade to India through the Arabs, was making high profits and they wanted to find ways to get to south India for its textiles and spices.

Besides, the Christian kings of Europe had now lost Constantinople – the centre of Christianity – to the Muslims and they wanted to find ways to spread Christianity in the world. The push came with King Henry of Portugal. A good student of geography, he wanted to find a southern route to attack the Arabs and used his money to fund ships to reach China and India by going around Africa.

After Portugal, Spain too joined in and when Christopher Columbus became the first European to find America, more and more European countries started funding ships to find new places to build trade. This is called the 'Age of Discovery', reflecting a very Europe-focused way of looking at history, because many of these places had already been discovered by people in the past.

Portugal have left us lengthy descriptions of what they saw, which help us reconstruct the life of those days. One such explorer, Vasco da Gama, landed in Calicut in 1498 CE. From accounts about him, we know that he

A painting of Vasco da Gama landing on the coast of Calicut

was strong, healthy and ill-tempered! Though not well educated, he was loyal, fearless and persistent. He had a close childhood connection with the king of Portugal. So much so that when the king wanted to expand his trade to Asia, Vasco da Gama was his first choice to explore this. The Portuguese had a strong navy and they were rich. They had amassed this wealth from their trade in slaves and ivory with Africa.

They were, until then, buying their spices from Venice, but buying them directly from India would mean they could buy much more for less money. So, the new king of Portugal needed a tough guy like Vasco da Gama to make this happen and do something no one had ever done before – find a way to get to India using a brand new sea route. He started off with three ships and a crew that included interpreters who spoke Arabic and many Bantu dialects of Africa. He felt that going around Africa would get him to India. He was delayed by the weather and eventually took a route around South Africa. He continued to follow the coast of Africa till he reached Malindi (present-day Kenya), where he found a Gujarati navigator who knew how to reach Calicut. Sure enough, in 23 days, the coast of India was spotted.

Here, Vasco da Gama met the Samuthiri or Zamorin, the monarch who ruled over the Raja of Kochi and the Kolathiri kingdom, in May of 1498. The Samuthiri insisted that the Portuguese obey the laws of the land, but Vasco was not keen on this. The Samuthiri was not impressed with the cheap goods da Gama was dealing in. They may have been precious in Africa, but in Kerala all that mattered was gold.

Da Gama had to return soon after. He ignored local advice to not travel in the monsoon, when the winds blew in the opposite direction, it took him over three months to return. This caused heavy losses for his crew. On his second voyage to Kerala, he reached out to the ruler in the neighbouring Kolathiri kingdom, who agreed to Vasco da Gama's terms. Finally, the Portuguese's dream was fulfilled: a formal trade agreement with an Indian kingdom for their flavourful spices!

Further trips from Portugal under Vasco da Gama's guidance were successful, but the Arabs, who monopolized the trade routes, were not happy about the competition. Bitter sea wars were fought between the Arabs and the Portuguese. This was over who would have exclusive trading rights with the various kings of Kerala. The kings themselves were not united either, so they were manipulated into taking sides.

The Samuthiri was supported by the *kunjali marakkar*, a succession of four marine merchants of Arab descent. They organized the defence of the coast with their ships and were able to defeat the Portuguese navy. To work with the Samuthiri, they chose their bravest, who became admirals of the Calicut fleet and experts in naval guerrilla warfare. This meant that they divided their forces into smaller groups to efficiently fight against a larger army.

The Raja of Kochi had never been happy to rule under the Samuthiri and welcomed an alliance with the Portuguese army to fight the Samuthiri. He was successful, but it came at a price as more and more of his kingdom began to be controlled by the Portuguese. The battle of Cochin (in 1504) saw a small army of 150 Portuguese, along with the help of the Cochin royal family, defeat an army of the Samuthiri, numbering more than 19,000, over five months. The Portuguese were helped by an efficient spy network and always kept their strategies a secret. They took local help to understand the tides and monsoon winds, and use them to their advantage. Alongside this, the Samuthiri's armies suffered from cholera and other diseases that tremendously weakened their forces. Their defeat made the Portuguese the undisputed rulers of Kerala.

As the Portuguese control over land increased, the Portuguese king began to appoint 'governors' to rule the land on his behalf. These governors did not care about the welfare of the local people. Their only concern was maximizing profits from the spice trade. While they became very unpopular rulers in Kerala, they were too powerful to be challenged by the local armies, which were not as well equipped as the Portuguese forces.

Seeing the wealth gained by the Portuguese by obtaining spices directly from India, the Dutch also sought direct trade links with Kerala. They were also funded by their government and very quickly defeated the British – first in Kerala (1795 CE) and then in Sri Lanka (1796 CE).

THE ENGLISH, THE DUTCH AND THE COLONIAL ERA

In Kerala, the Portuguese and Dutch were the main European nations. In other parts of India, especially Bengal, Andhra and the Tamil coast, the English were gaining a foothold. The then English kings did not have the money to fund expeditions like the Portuguese rulers. The English East India Company (EEIC) was formed in 1600 CE to trade in cotton, silk, spices, indigo dye, and saltpetre (used for making gunpowder). The English were able to defeat the Portuguese in 1612 and obtained trading concessions from the Mughals. Much of their operations were in Bengal and the eastern coast. The first EEIC factory in India was set up in Masulipatnam on the Andhra coast in 1611 CE.

With their base in Masulipatnam, the British had to protect their trade in textiles, spanning the east coast of south India and the spice trade along the west coast in Kerala. Soon, the EEIC began to interfere in local politics. Local kings fighting with each other called on the English to take sides.

In 1619 CE, the Dutch allied with the English and, in 1663 CE, snatched Kochi from the Portuguese. The new Samuthiri realized that unless the local kings united, the Dutch would continue to conquer and control the land. So he began making friends with the smaller kings, but slowly faded away after he was defeated in 1755 by the Venad king Marthanda Varma. From this time, the Venad kings who ruled from Travancore (renamed Thiruvananthapuram) became the dominant rulers of Kerala.

Marthanda Varma had already defeated the Dutch in the Battle of Colachel of 1741. Travancore earned the distinction of being the first Indian kingdom to have won a war against a European power. In 1748, Marthanda Varma signed a treaty with the Dutch, where they promised to not disturb the English trade or their factories in Kerala. They also assured their neutrality

King Marthanda Varma

in any of Travancore's future wars. Soon after, Dutch power declined in Kerala and India.

The treaty also led Marthanda Varma to become close to the English. The Venad rulers originally ruled south Kerala and western Tamil Nadu but were, under Marthanda Varma, the rulers of south and central Kerala. The northern part of Kerala at that time was occupied by Tipu Sultan. When Tipu challenged Marthanda Varma, the English supported Varma. Tipu was defeated in the battle and all kings in Kerala – including Marthanda Varma – realized the power of the English.

In the 18th century CE, as tea became popular in England, it was added into the mix of traded goods. Meanwhile, the English shifted the centre of their activity to Madras, the lease of which was granted to them by the local king in 1639. They built a fort around their factory, called Fort St. George. From then, Madras and Calcutta became the centres of English trade and the seats from which their rule extended to the rest of India. With tea estates in Kerala along with the spice trade, and tea estates in the Nilgiri hills (in Tamil Nadu), Madras helped keep a close watch on Kerala. As the English trade in India grew, and they became richer, the EEIC began interfering more and more in local politics.

In 1800, Kochi came fully under the control of the EEIC. In 1805, the latter's treaty with Travancore took away all independence from the king. After 1857, the EEIC was dissolved and the English government took over Indian territory until India's independence in 1947.

KARNATAKA

In the past, present-day Karnataka was referred to as Kannada Desa. The people continue to be known as Kannadiga and the main language spoken here is Kannada. We don't know for sure the root word it came from, but some believe it is from *kar* in Sanskrit, which means black, indicating the black soil of the region. This soil is very fertile owing to the Tungabhadra and Kaveri rivers. The region had more than sufficient food-grain production in the past and its ambitious kings were able to fund large armies due to this abundance.

THE EARLY PERIOD

Karnataka is close to the Vindhya mountains. It is also close to central and north India. So, unlike Kerala or Tamil Nadu, and more like Andhra Pradesh – it had deeper connections with central and north India, and not the world at large.

As the Metal Age progressed and farming became more prosperous, Karnataka would have naturally had many landowners and kings connected to farming, but we don't know much about them.

After the Iron Age, in the north, towards the Gangetic plains, the first great ruler to emerge was Chandragupta Maurya (350–295 BCE), followed by his grandson Ashoka (c. 268–32 BCE). The Mauryan Empire stretched from present-day Afghanistan to West Bengal. Because of the vast and challenging terrain it was spread over, control was probably not uniform or absolute. Still, Ashoka left 33 inscriptions in stone, recording his thoughts and decisions. These are the first of their kind, where a king publicly put down information about himself. They are valuable as they show his respect for Buddhism and, by mapping their locations, we get a sense of the important parts of his kingdom. He also mentions south Indian kings, such as the Pandyas, Cholas and Keralaputras (Cheras).

In south India, his edicts are located in Karnataka. This was possibly the boundary of his empire.

Ashoka left eight inscriptions or edicts on large expanses of stone in Karnataka. These are located in:

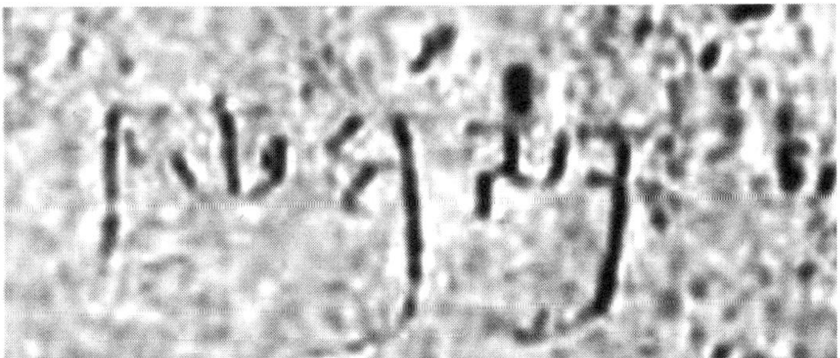

The word 'Ashoka' in the Kanganahalli inscription near Sannati

- Palkigundu and Gavimath, Koppal district
- Brahmagiri, Chitradurga district
- Jatinga-Rameshwara, near Brahmagiri
- Siddapur, near Brahmagiri
- Maski, Raichur district
- Nittur, Bellary district
- Udegolam, Bellary district
- Sannati, Kalaburagi district

The last of these was discovered as late as 1986 when the Chandrala Parameshwari Temple in Sannati (on the banks of the River Bhima in north Karnataka) collapsed. It was found here that the deity's pedestal had a slab with an inscription of Ashoka. This inscription, like the others, is carved on the rock face. It gives instructions to the people on how they should behave and conduct themselves in life.

After the Mauryas, this region was ruled by the Satavahanas and then the Pallavas of Tamil Nadu, who were overthrown by the Kadambas.

The story goes that the Kadamba king, Mayurasharma, overthrew the Pallavas because he was humiliated as a young man and sought revenge. As a youth, he was called Mayura Deva and was studying in Kanchipuram, the capital city of the Pallavas, near present-day Chennai. One day while he was bathing, the Pallava king's horse trampled his clothes. He objected to this and when he tried to seize the horse, the accompanying warriors got into a fight with him. Mayura Deva wanted revenge for being treated this way by the guards. Determined to learn to be a fighter, he went to Kurnool and learnt guerrilla warfare. Patiently and intelligently, he built up more support for himself, defeated the Pallavas and installed the Kadamba dynasty as Mayurasharma.

His descendants followed the smart-to-complacent pattern and were eventually replaced by the Chalukyas, the first great dynasty of Karnataka, which ruled for 250 years.

THE CHALUKYAS

We do not know the exact origin of the word Chalukya – some say the root of the word in Kannada refers to a plough. So, maybe they were farmers who became kings. Their royal insignia was the boar, symbolic of the *varaha* avatar of Vishnu.

Like Vishnu, the Chalukyas believed their reign would save the world. There were primarily three families, which ruled in different parts of the Karnataka–Andhra region.

They chose their capitals: Badami, Aihole and Pattadakal respectively, which were all close to one another. These locations were chosen for two practical reasons – soil security and fertility. These three present-day villages, which were big cities during those times, were well protected by the surrounding sandstone mountains. The black soil and the waters of the River Malaprabha made the land very fertile, so they had a good run at food production. This was used to pay the soldiers.

Pulakesin II is considered the greatest king of this dynasty. His uncle, Mangalesa, ruled when Pulakesin II was a small boy. He had also sneakily tried to steal the

Pulakesin II, as depicted in a statue in Badami

HARSHAVARDHANA AND PULAKESIN THE GREAT

Harshavardhana ruled from 606 to 647 CE. His capital was Kannauj in present-day Uttar Pradesh and his kingdom stretched across most of north and north-east India. By Harsha's time, the kingdom established and created by Ashoka had collapsed and fragmented into small kingdoms. Harsha's had been one of these smaller ones. However, owing to his military skills, Harsha was able to conquer the remaining ones. Soon after, they declared him as their maharaja in 606 CE. The Chinese pilgrim Xuanzang visited Harsha's court, and sang praises of him and his kingdom. He also mentioned that Harsha was unable to defeat Pulakesin II. It is possible that this took place around 619 CE, based on an inscription of Pulakesin II.

To paint a picture: Pulakesin's elephants possibly cleared the forest ground and his foot soldiers circled Harshavardhana's army. Many of the soldiers were killed with arrows fired from behind trees and then the soldiers engaged in close combat. Pulakesin's elephants must have had swords tied to their trunks. As they stampeded through Harsha's army, they would have inflicted further injury on their opponents.

Banabhatta, Harsha's court poet, wrote the *Harshacharitra* that speaks of Harshavardhana's life and times. From this we learn that at the height of his reign, the number of elephants in the army was supposed to have increased from 5,000 to 60,000 and the cavalry from 2,000 to 100,000. In addition to this, there were many foot soldiers as well.

In spite of such a vast battalion, if he was unable to defeat Pulakesin, the latter must have been a truly admirable warrior and general!

throne from young Pulakesin. To prevent this, Pulakesin II had Mangalesa killed and became king. Historians believe that Mangalesa could have been Pulakesin's father's stepbrother. This would, perhaps, explain the reason behind the animosity between the two.

Pulakesin II began to expand his empire in the present-day region of Andhra, Karnataka and Maharashtra. He sent his ministers to China and Persia. He even defeated Harsha, the king of the Vardhana dynasty. At that time, Harsha was considered a great king because he had a vast, efficiently managed empire. This defeat prevented Harsha from crossing the River Narmada and extending his empire. Pulakesin also defeated the Pallava king Mahendravarman I. The oldest cave temples in Tiruchirappalli and the five *rathas* and the lighthouse in Mamallapuram (present-day Mahabalipuram) in Tamil Nadu can all be credited to Mahendravarman I's vision.

Mahendravarman's son, Narasimhavarman I, ruled from 630 to 668 CE. He continued the *rathas* and was a great wrestler – or 'Maha Malla'. Mamallapuram is named after his title. He defeated the Chalukyas and took control of their capital. However, another Chalukya king, Vikramaditya I, defeated the Pallavas and occupied their capital, Kanchipuram. Here, the Chalukya kings were very impressed with the Pallava's style of temple building and began to use it in their own capital city, Pattadakal, in Karnataka.

The Chalukyas were replaced by the Rashtrakutas in about 740 CE. The Rashtrakutas are known for having built the magnificent Kailasa Temple in Ellora (in present-day Aurangabad, Maharashtra), which was adroitly cut into one massive stone mountain face.

They were followed by the Hoysalas who ruled for almost 317 years.

There is a legend from around 1,100 years ago about why the dynasty was called 'Hoysala'. Nripa Kama II, an early king, is said to be known as Sala. One day he was attacked by a tiger, and understandably, Sala did not want to be killed and eaten up just yet. His guru, a Jain teacher called Vardhamana, possibly egged him on and in a show of support exclaimed, 'Poy, Sala!', where '*poy*' could mean 'fight, man!' or even 'you can do it, buddy'. Sure enough, Sala won the wrestling match, killing the tiger. Thereafter, he decided to call his dynasty 'Hoysala', a play on his teacher's encouraging words.

Why not 'Poysala', you may wonder. No one knows, but this is the story repeated in the inscriptions of the greatest king in this dynasty – Vishnuvardhana, who ruled from 1108 to 1152 CE.

There are several temples from the Hoysala period in Karnataka and some inscriptions in Tamil Nadu that mention them. We know from the ones in Tamil Nadu that they variously invaded or supported Tamil kings, such as the Cholas and Pandyas, over the 500 years they ruled.

The Hoysala dynasty was most famous for its temples, where every inch is covered with sculptures, such as

A stunning Hoysala sculpture, Belur

those in Somanathapura and Belur. Here, during the Rathotsava festival, verses from the Quran are recited as well, revealing the area's syncretic spirit. Some of these temples were Jain too, since the region's queens followed that religion, while the kings were devotees of Vishnu.

MALIK KAFUR IN THE DECCAN

The Hoysala kings were defeated by the army of Malik Kafur, a general of Alauddin Khilji, the sultan of Delhi. In 1311 CE, Malik Kafur, an intelligent and fearless warrior came far down south into Tamil Nadu. He was invited by Sundara Pandyan, who wanted his support to fight his stepbrother for the throne. Malik had already defeated the Hoysala king by 1311 and occupied the Hoysala capital Dwarasamudra.

Malik saw the vast wealth of the south and began a systematic campaign to take away riches from temples and palaces.

After defeating the Hoysalas, Malik Kafur entered the Pandya kingdom, benefitting from the infighting between the Pandya brothers Vira and Sundara. During the months of March and April 1311, he ravaged and plundered Pandya territory, including their capital Madurai. He failed to completely subjugate the Pandya king, but carried away a large booty. This included elephants, horses, precious metals and gems.

He occupied almost all of Karnataka and central Andhra, and even north and central Tamil Nadu, by the time he died in 1316.

THE BAHMANI SULTANATE

An artist's impression of Malik Kaur (left)

The Karnataka and Andhra regions, known as the Deccan region back then, was ruled by different kings. Deccan comes from the Sanskrit word *dakshina*, which means south. It refers to the land south of the Vindhya mountains, and between the east and west coast. Although geographically it stands for the entire southern India, in the study of history, this region is generally considered to include present-day Maharashtra, northern Karnataka and northern Andhra Pradesh.

The area, especially the part closer to the west coast, was a part of the Bahmani Sultanate. It was probably named after 'Bahman', a mythological figure from Iran/Persia, from where these rulers came. The Bahmani Sultanate was founded by Ala-ud-Din Bahman Shah in 1347 CE after defeating Muhammad bin Tughlaq of the Delhi Sultanate. The Bahmanis ruled from 1347 CE to 1527 CE.

By 1518 CE, the rulers had become more reliant on their viziers (prime ministers) and had neglected to keep direct contact with their army. Due to their inability to sense the mood on the ground, the kingdom began to break up into factions. It eventually broke up

A panoramic view of Bidar Fort

into five smaller kingdoms, with the former governors of these provinces calling themselves sultans.

These five kingdoms of Ahmednagar, Golconda (Hyderabad), Bidar, Berar and Bijapur kept their peace with the more powerful ruler Krishnadevaraya, who ruled from Vijayanagara.

VIJAYANAGARA

Further south on the banks of the River Tungabhadra, another great kingdom was taking shape as the Deccan sultans were carving out their independence from Delhi. Two young chieftains, Harihara and Bukka, took advantage of the confusion after the invasions of Malik Kafur.

They worked as a team, treated people with respect and were able to unite them to establish the Vijayanagara kingdom. It soon became an empire with its capital at Hampi (derived from Pampa, a name for Parvati) from around 1336 CE.

At its height, under the great king Krishnadevaraya, Hampi was believed to be larger than most big cities in the world and was among the richest as well.

The Delhi Sultanate was defeated by the Vijayanagara kings and, at that time, Tamil Nadu was ruled by them through local kings called Nayaks. There was a Nayak king in Madurai and another in Thanjavur. They were not related to each other and were not even friendly, but both owed their power to the Vijayanagara kings in Hampi. From the poems of the time, we know what they ate, the music they enjoyed, and how good they were with composing riddles and playing games. At one time, the Vijayanagara kings were able to rule all of south India except Kerala.

Although we see them as one dynasty, there were actually four dynasties – the Sangama; the Saluva (meaning hawk in Telugu); the Tuluva; and the Aravidu. They were all connected through marriage. Together, they ruled the region for around 310 years. This was a golden age of art and literature. Their capital city, Hampi, although in ruins today, is still a very impressive sight.

Sadly, as time passed, and with the onset of every successive generation, they became less vigilant. They also lost opportunities to bond with their armies. So much so that many of their army members became spies and worked actively to overthrow the empire.

The northern Bahmani kings united and fought with a weakened Vijayanagara king. In the Battle

An artist's impression of Krishnadevaraya, the famous king of Vijayanagara

KRISHNADEVARAYA AND VIJAYANAGARA

Krishnadevaraya (1471–1529 CE) was the greatest king of the Vijayanagara Empire. In his time, Hampi was one of the world's biggest and wealthiest cities.

Duarte Barbosa, a Portuguese trader, visited Vijayanagara during the time of Krishnadevaraya. According to Barbosa, the kingdom comprised cities and large townships. It was very rich, and well-supplied with provisions. He talks about the seaport of Bhatkal on the western coast of present-day Karnataka. The exports packed here included iron, spices and myrobalan leaves (to flavour wine and seafood). The region imported horses and pearls. The governor of Bhatkal was Krishnadevaraya's nephew, who lived in a 'great state and calls himself king, but is in obedience to the king, his uncle,' Barbosa adds.

Leaving the sea coast and going inland, Barbosa passed upwards through the ghats, entering the city of Hampi. Here, he says, it was very populous. On one side, a very sturdy wall covered it. On the other side, there was a river. The third side was covered by mountains. Barbosa describes the city where the king of Narsinga (Vijayanagara) resides in a splendid palace. The houses of common folk were covered with thatch roofs, and the streets and city squares were very large. He goes on to describe the city as one comprising crowds of all nations and creeds, and says that infinite amounts of trade took place in this city. In his account, Barbosa says that many jewels were brought from Pegu (Myanmar) and Celani (Sri Lanka), and that there was a diamond mine located in the kingdom of Narsinga and another in the kingdom of Dacani (Deccan). He also talks about the trade of pearls and seed pearls from Ormuz and Cael, along with silk-brocades, scarlet cloth and coral.

Barbosa goes on to say that the king deliberated with his governors and officers upon the affairs of the realm. The king kept a herd of 900 elephants; over 20,000 horses; and more than 1 lakh foot soldiers. He also adds that the king of Narsinga, with the support of the king of Otira (Odisha), was frequently at war with the king of Dacani, who had wrested away much of his territory.

of Talikota, around 450 years ago, the Vijayanagara army was mercilessly overthrown. Sadly, the Bijapur armies plundered the capital city, and Hampi became a ghost town. The fall of Hampi was an opportunity for many smaller kingdoms to declare their independence.

One of them was Mysore under the Wodeyar rulers, which eventually grew to occupy most of Karnataka in the 18th century CE. One of the generals of the Wodeyars, Hyder Ali, a smart, courageous and brave general in the Mysore army, became the *sarvadhikari* or de facto ruler of the Mysore kingdom. He left his son, Tipu Sultan, a large kingdom bordered by the River Krishna in the north, the Eastern Ghats in the east and the Arabian Sea in the west. Finally, Tipu was defeated by the British, who took over all of the region known today as Karnataka.

The Bahmani rulers, meanwhile, were constantly at war with the Vijayanagara kings. In 1527, Krishnadevaraya defeated the last sultan. The region comprised today's Hyderabad in Telangana, and Bidar and Gulbarga, both in Karnataka. When the sultanate collapsed, it fragmented into five small kingdoms, which were not really controlled by Krishnadevaraya, but kept in check by him. These were Ahmednagar, Golconda (Hyderabad), Bidar, Berar and Bijapur. The former governors of these provinces now styled themselves as sultans. While they constantly quarrelled among themselves initially, in course of time, they came together to defeat the mighty Vijayanagara Empire in 1565.

One of the most courageous rulers among them was Malik Ambar (1548–1626 CE) of the Ahmednagar Sultanate. This can be located in present-day Karnataka/Maharashtra. Malik was able to keep the Mughals at bay. By this time, the five kingdoms had united and defeated the Vijayanagara kings in the south and were fighting the Mughals from the north. Malik used guerrilla warfare techniques to outwit the Mughal army. Mughal emperor Jahangir was so angry he could not conquer Malik that he had a painting commissioned which featured him beheading Malik.

Unfortunately for him, this never became a reality. Malik also built the city of Khirki, later called Aurangabad by Aurangzeb. This city was famous for its very innovative water management techniques. Malik taught his warfare techniques to all his generals, one of whom was the grandfather of Chhatrapati Shivaji Maharaj.

TAMIL NADU

Tamil Nadu's history broadly covers three areas:

1. The southern part of the banks of the River Vaigai and River Thamirabarani house the oldest settlements, such as Adichanallur and Keezhadi (Keeladi). This was the kingdom of the Pandyas, who ruled continuously for almost 1,700 years. Quite possibly the longest ruling dynasty in India and the world, their symbol was a pair of fish.
2. The central part on the banks of River Kaveri, including places such as present-day Tiruchirappalli, Thanjavur and Nagapattinam, was part of the Chola kingdom. Their symbol was the tiger, probably representing the way they saw themselves: a brave clan.
3. The northern part on the banks of the River Palar, near present-day Chennai, was fed by a complex system of ponds and lakes to store rainwater. This area was ruled by the Pallavas, who came from present-day Andhra Pradesh. Their symbol was the lion or the bull for fearlessness and vigour.

THE LANGUAGE

Tamil, which is more than 2,500 years old, is the oldest language spoken in south India. The earliest inscription we have in Tamil is situated in the Puliman Kombai village on the banks of the River Vaigai. Here, you will find several memorial stones, celebrating the death of a hero in battle, in the village's fields but with a few damaged words. The script on one of the hero stones says that it was erected in memory of a person from Koodal, who died in a cattle raid. This is perhaps a reference to the city of Madurai, which is still known as Koodal in Tamil.

It is due to the efforts of Dr U. Ve. Swaminatha Iyer, Tamil scholar and researcher, that a large group of 2,100-year-old Tamil poems and epics, collectively called the Sangam (group of) literature, were introduced to the world. From these we get to know about the lifestyle, food, music and even wars fought in this region, which included all of present-day Tamil Nadu, Kerala and the southernmost parts of Telangana and Karnataka.

One of the poems by a Pandya king called Arivudai Nambi, written more than 2,000 years ago, is likely to be a useful one for young readers like you. He writes:

You may have lots of money,
Give even God a lot of things,
Eat and party with many others,
But
What's the point of living,

if you don't have kids?
Kids who run sounding like 'kuru kuru',
Reach out with their tiny palms for a little bit of ghee and rice,
And then make a big mess with that!
Tell me, what is the point of living?

So the next time round when you are mischievous, remind your parents of this poem!

HERO STONES

Stone is one of the most indestructible materials on Earth and is therefore connected with permanence and age. In the olden days, death was a mysterious and frightening thing. When people died, just like today, others grieved for them and thought they had joined the world of spirits. People who lived on were anxious that those who had died should not be forgotten. The best way to remember them was to erect a stone over the place they were buried. As you have read in the previous chapter, in the prehistoric period, dolmens, cists and other stone monuments were probably erected.

Sangam poems from 2,000 years ago tell us that people continued the practice of erecting a stone monument in the memory of the dead. It was also a way to remember what had made them famous and for others to live up to that. For instance, if a warrior had died fighting thieves, every time people saw his hero stone, they would remember his sacrifice and feel motivated to be just as brave as him. Even today, as part of death rituals, for ten days after the cremation, many communities place a tiny stone as a representative of the departed person and perform rituals around it. This is followed by finally casting the stone off into a river.

Most hero stones were for men who had lost their lives in battle, and since they were erected by the local villagers, the local battles were likely cattle raids. Hero stones have some sculptures of the event and then a short inscription, so by looking at them you can get a sense of how people lived. The Government Museum in Chennai has a large collection of such stones. Many are from Andhra Pradesh as well. In the western region of Tamil Nadu – called the Kongu region – thick forests and very few stone records have been found.

The Dharmapuri Museum in Tamil Nadu has a hero stone of a warrior who sacrificed himself to the goddess of war before the battle began. Death while hunting for wild pigs were also common as seen from many hero stones of hunters. In many ways, hero stones give us very important clues about the region's history.

A hero stone, now in the Dharmapuri Museum

THE DYNASTIES – CHOLAS, PANDYAS AND CHERAS

Till about 1,800 years ago, the three main dynasties in this region were the Cholas, the Pandyas and the Cheras. The Pallavas, who were based in present-day Andhra, had not come down to Tamil Nadu yet. These three dynasties were supported by many smaller chieftains, who left behind cave temples with beautiful sculptures in hills amidst scenic landscapes. Some places you can visit are Namakkal, Thirumalapuram, and Boothapandi. Other locations, such as Arittapatti or Samanar Malai, make for great trekking trails and picnic spots.

FROM BUDDHIST NUNS TO INCREDIBLE BALL GAMES

'*Mekalai*' is an ornament women wore on their waist and '*mani*' means gems, so the story *Manimekalai*, a Tamil epic, literally means 'the jewelled waist ornament'. Composed in about sixth century CE, it tells the story of a lady called Manimekalai (born to the dancer Madhavi and a trader called Kovalan), who lived her life as a Buddhist nun. Kovalan was the husband of Kannagi – their love story called *Silappadikaram* ('the story of the anklet') ends in tragedy with the death of Kovalan.

Generally speaking, Jain and Buddhist texts preach about how to lead a noble life, but in a Jain text called *Perun Kathai* ('big story'), there is a whole chapter called '*Pandhadi Kandathu*' ('where we saw them playing ball').

Here, women challenge one another in ball games. A lady named Rasanai both caught and kicked the ball. Another lady called Kanchanamala hit a ball into the sky and then hit that ball with another and similarly made 1,500 such consecutive hits! Then another lady, Ayirapathi, hit the ball with her palm and the back of her hand while simultaneously adorning her hair with flowers and applying a *pottu* (bindi) on her forehead; this she did about 2,000 times. Viswalekai hit the ball with a stick. Finally, Mananikai was the best player of all. These women are described in fine detail – as they spun around, their hair coming loose, growing tired, their waistlets loosening, the *sandu* dots on their foreheads smudging, and the collyrium in their eyes too!

Then, from about 1,500 to 1,800 years ago, the Kalabhras, originally from Karnataka, ruled all over Tamil Nadu. It is likely that they were strong believers in Jainism and Buddhism. Therefore, while we have no intact buildings from their times, we have literature from the period, which is again mostly Jain. Sadly, since Buddhism nearly disappeared from India by the ninth century, not many Buddhist texts have survived.

Then we had the Pallavas in the north, marked by the Tirumala Hills; the Cholas in the middle, around the River Kaveri; and the Pandyas in the south, below the River Vaigai. They were constantly playing musical thrones with each other in the region, so all of them kept coming into and falling out of power.

NORTH TAMIL NADU – CHENNAI TO TIRUCHIRAPPALLI

In the seventh and eighth centuries CE, the Chalukyas from the north fought with the Pallavas and conquered their capital, Kanchipuram. The Pallavas took revenge and conquered Badami.

Although these kings fought with each other, when it came to art and architecture, they were constantly learning and getting inspired by one another. For instance, the Chalukyas were so impressed by the Kailasanathar Temple in Kanchipuram that they adopted some of that design in their city of Pattadakal in Karnataka. The Chalukya cave temples of Badami and the Pallava cave temples of Mamallapuram inspired each other.

Eventually, the Pallavas were conquered by the Cholas from central Tamil Nadu.

THE CHOLAS – TIRUCHIRAPALLI TO MADURAI

The Cholas were an ancient kingdom from more than 2,000 years ago, but they had small kingdoms near the River Kaveri. The word Chola probably comes from the word *chezhipu*, which in Tamil means fertile. (If you can't pronounce the 'zh', check how to say it online and try harder. 'ழ' is a letter found only in the Tamil language.)

Vijayalaya Chola captured Thanjavur around 850 CE. From then on, the Cholas were busy fighting the Pandyas in the south and the kings of Sri Lanka. The Pallavas had died out by then.

In the 11th and 12th centuries CE, the Chola Empire was at its peak. Rajaraja Chola and his son Rajendra Chola established the supremacy of the Cholas. They conquered not just most of south India but also west India and spread their (indirect) rule across South-East Asia up to as far as present-day Malaysia. It is believed that Kedah, the name of a state in Malaysia, for example, comes from the root word '*kadaram*'. The word is possibly a combination of the word *kadal*, which means sea, and *aru*, which means river. So, it denotes a place where the sea and river meet.

However, it is important to remember that although they conquered this land, the Cholas ruled it by a lot of delegation of power. Their army was well trained, had many elephants, and the kings personally fought in battles. They had a navy as well. Sadly, apart from single-line references to naval battles in literature, we have no information about them. We know there were texts on shipbuilding, but none have survived. Sculptures of ships in temples like Tirukurungudi (near Tirunelveli) date back to the 17th century onwards. Scholars believe that the navy may have been composed of smaller ships that traders used in those days. These wooden ships would have had sails and were managed by skilled persons who had excellent knowledge of the

A detailed painting of Rajaraja Chola

A line drawing of the Brihadisvara Temple painting of Rajaraja Chola

RAJARAJA CHOLA

Did you watch the movie *PS-1*? It is the story of how Rajaraja comes to power. His name was Arunmozhi Varman and he ruled as Rajaraja Chola from 947 CE to 1014 CE. He made the Chola dynasty really famous.

In the Brihadisvara Temple that he built in Thanjavur, we have a painting of him with his queens, praying to his favourite god – Nataraja or the dancing Shiva at Chidambaram. Rajaraja Chola is shown as dark, thin and muscular, with a luxurious beard, moustache and long hair that he knotted up on one side. In this painting, he is only wearing a loincloth tied up at his hips. This is probably out of respect to the god. Usually, he must have been decked out in a lot of jewellery, silks and weapons. His queens are shorter and dressed similarly. Sadly, the painting is damaged and you can't see all the intricate details.

So, why is Rajaraja called 'great'?

He never saw defeat in any battle he fought and he was able to not only expand the Chola kingdom but also train his son Rajendra to be an even more courageous king than him. Rajaraja is not just known for being an able warrior; he also had a remarkable ability to plan and consider even the minutest details. For instance, he made sure that every gift – even the smallest – that was given to the Brihadisvara Temple was meticulously recorded. In his time, he was able to revive and modernize the canal systems in the River Kaveri. More canals meant more water to more parts of land, and that meant more paddy, which in turn meant more money to expand his territories and take care of the needs of the people. During his reign, everything that one needed from the government was given by the local temple, so it was a very decentralized system, which was efficient and easy to implement.

wind direction, monsoon patterns, navigational sense and the sea at large. In effect, the boats would have been simple, but the people steering them were very knowledgeable, committing all of it to memory.

The Cholas administered their land well. After a king died, succession to the next king was smooth without any fighting among claimants to the throne. However, the same story of complacency repeated itself, and after Rajendra Chola, the Chola kings became more relaxed, preferred to enjoy life in the palace, and were eventually defeated by the Pandyas.

PANDYAS – MADURAI TO KANYAKUMARI

The Pandyas are India's longest ruling dynasty. Their name figures in the Sangam poems and they ruled till the 17th century. Even later, branches related to them ruled in southern Tamil Nadu as zamindars or landlords. Among the three ancient dynasties of Tamil Nadu – Chera, Chola and Pandya – it is a common surname even today. Scholars think that Pandya comes from the Tamil word *pandu* or very old. Their symbol was the carp fish. Their floral symbol was the neem flower (the Cheras wore the palm flower and the Cholas the fig).

The Pandya kings were always fighting with the Cholas in the north. In the south were the Sinhala kings of present-day Sri Lanka and in the west were the Cheras. With them, the relationship was more complex – at different times they were friends or enemies. To make it even more complicated, at many times there were two or three Pandya kings with similar names ruling around the same time, so dating them is very difficult. However, the greatest Pandya king, Maravarman, who ruled in the 13th century CE, brought fame to the kingdom.

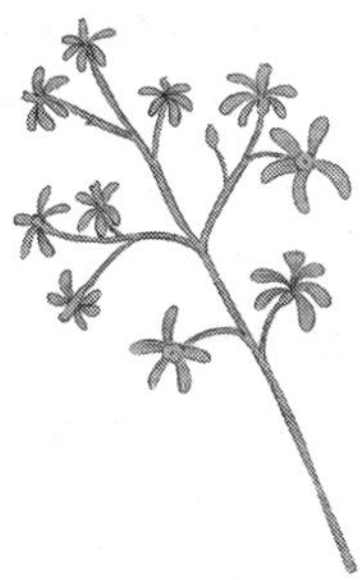

Dynasties in Tamil Nadu had floral symbols too; the neem flower was the Pandyas'

As a young boy, he was able to unite the local warriors and lead an army that rebelled against the Cholas, who were ruling the Pandya region. He then marched with his army northwards to the Chola kingdom and fought with the Chola king Kulotunga III, who had earlier conquered and humiliated Maravarman's uncle who was then the Pandya king. Maravarman demolished the Chola capital, and is said to have razed all the buildings to 'the height of a blade of grass', then got a donkey to plough the palace and planted the *kavidi*, a weed that grows so fast that very soon there were no traces of the palace to be found. However, he gave back the Chola territory when the Chola king met him and promised to name his son after Maravarman and accepted Maravarman as the lord of the Chola kingdom. Diplomacy at its finest, some may say.

Maravarman was succeeded by other powerful kings. One of them, Jatavarman Sundara Pandyan I, was so victorious in his wars against the Hoysalas of Karnataka, the Kadavas of Karnataka and the Kakatiyas of Warangal (although they won their land back quickly) that he used the gold he earned from his triumphs to plate the roofs of both the Nataraja Temple in Chidambaram and the Sri Ranganathaswamy Temple in Srirangam.

Much later, in the 14th century CE, a Pandya king, also called Sundara Pandyan, who was cheated out of his kingdom by a stepbrother, invited Malik Kafur to help him. Kafur had other plans. Taking advantage of the disunity among the Pandya ruling family, Kafur decided to capture the wealth of the Pandya kingdom and take it back with him to Delhi.

The Delhi Sultanate was defeated by the Vijayanagara kings, as mentioned earlier, and Tamil Nadu was ruled by them through local rulers called Nayaks, in Madurai and Thanjavur. When the Vijayanagara dynasty collapsed, each of these small kingdoms became independent. The Thanjavur Nayaks were defeated by the Marathas, under a stepbrother of Chhatrapati Shivaji Maharaj. who established the Maratha Empire.

COLONIAL ERA

Ever since the 1600s, the British had started trading in India for spices and textiles. Since they had to export their goods via the sea, they began establishing trading centres in Bombay, Madras and Calcutta, all along or close to the coast. They were in competition with the Dutch who were dealing in the same items. The British traders at that time had no support from the British government, unlike the Portuguese or the Dutch. They found the spice trade expensive, but the textile trade was cheaper and highly profitable. Indian textiles were so beautiful and there were so many types that there was something for everyone to buy back home in Britain.

However, the British traders began to find it difficult to deal with the weavers. The weavers would take an advance for cloth and promise to have it ready in a few months. However, when they went to the village, the weavers would have migrated from there. The British, therefore, thought it a good idea to keep a few weavers

INSCRIPTIONS OR EPIGRAPHS

Today, if you want to know more about your favourite sportsperson or about a college you want to study in, you will visit their website. Websites and the internet have made important information easily accessible. This same need to make information available to the entire community has existed ever since humans began to live in communities. In ancient times, people used palm leaves to write down important information, but they were easily degradable. So, what if something needed to be permanently available? Sheets of thick copper were used, but these too could be melted or hidden away. Stone walls were the most permanent and easily accessible. In the olden days, people lived in houses made of mud walls, or at best bricks. Stone was very expensive to

The inscriptions at Mangulam near Madurai are the earliest known Tamil-Brahmi ones (this is a model)

A wall inscription in Tamil

cut and build with and, therefore, it was used only for temple building. These stone walls became an ideal place to record important decisions, since everyone in the village who was affected by the decision would visit temples and thus come to know of them.

These 'written' records on stone or metal are called inscriptions or epigraphs.

The state with the maximum number of inscriptions – more than 50,000 of them – is Tamil Nadu. Although they are found on temple walls, sometimes on irrigation sluices (a type of rock gate), and other sundry rocks too, they have nothing to do with religion or philosophy. All of them either record gifts given to the temple or capture important decisions on farming, irrigation and crime. The oldest inscriptions are from the time of Ashoka – his rock edicts. Till the 15th century, the handwriting is in perfectly parallel lines with no spelling errors. Some are very long, each line being even 50 to 60 feet. Later, letters became larger and a bit messy with errors and finally, by the 17th century CE, as paper became more common, inscriptions became just commemorations of important events.

under their control and build a warehouse to stock the textiles. This made more financial sense.

The EEIC was searching for land on the east coast near the Andhra region where there were communities of weavers. The Nayak, Venkata III of Chandragiri (a descendant of the Vijayanagara kings) gave them a small piece of land on the beach, which they called Fort St. George, located in present-day Chennai. Trade in textiles was profitable, and they were slowly able to grow their trade and fund an army to protect their interests. Using this army, they fought and defeated the French and the Danes in India. Under the leadership of Robert Clive, they were able to subjugate many of the local kings and take over their kingdoms. Some of the kings fought back hard but failed against the sophisticated guns of the British armies. With the occupation of Thanjavur in 1855, most of Tamil Nadu came under the EEIC. Local landlords too had to submit to them.

ANDHRA PRADESH AND TELANGANA

The region now called Andhra Pradesh was called Andhaka in earlier times, its language being Telugu. The first known book in Telugu, Nannayya's *Mahabharata*, is about 1,000 years old. However, inscriptions from before that time feature words in Telugu. This proves that the language is older than we thought.

The region, which includes both present-day Andhra Pradesh and Telangana, we will refer to as Andhra in this book. It had some of the oldest communities that lived in forests and caves, and then moved to villages. Such groups lived there in relative isolation even 100 years ago. At that time, much of the region was inhabited by tribes such as Chenchu, Yanadi, Koya and Savara, who have been around from more than 2,000 years ago. They climbed very tall and steep cliffs using thin ropes, and taught both their boys and girls how to quickly climb up a tree and gather fruit.

EARLY PERIOD: THE MAURYAS

The region is mentioned as Andhra Desa in the Mahabharata. Ashoka's inscriptions are found here from about 2,200 years ago. Yerragudi in Kurnool district has one where Ashoka asks people to be kind to their slaves and servants, and stop killing animals, but also warns those who live in the forest and thereby do not follow the rules of kingdoms and villages. Scholars are not in agreement on whether Ashoka actually ruled this entire region or if this was just a far-off colony he controlled nominally. It appears, however, that at this time, in this region, there were no large dynasties and much of the region was populated by tribes.

During the reign of Ashoka and after, more and more areas came under farming here. This area was rich in copper and iron, and the region between the Godavari and Krishna rivers was very fertile. This made it an ideal place for farming and the metals mined here helped in the making of farming implements.

Being on the path of the trade routes from the north and south meant that the region was open to influences from both sides.

Megasthenes, an ancient Greek historian, emissary and explorer, mentions in extracts from his book *Indica* or *Indika* that in the Andhra region there were 30–40 fortified towns, and the rulers maintained 1,00,000 foot soldiers, 2,000 horsemen and 1,000 elephants.

As the Mauryas moved southward, like Ashoka, they also allowed traders from the north, especially from present-day Bihar and Madhya Pradesh, to come and trade in this region and become rich. These traders were known as *sethi*, from the Sanskrit word for a distinguished wealthy man – *shreshti*. Many of the traders at this time followed Buddhism.

As they moved southwards, they were accompanied by Buddhist monks, and Andhra became a place renowned for Buddhism. The Satavahanas who ruled Andhra at that time supported both Buddhism and Hinduism. They also let the traders support whatever religion the traders wanted to. Since there were many traders in Andhra, Buddhism flourished. The fertile soil of the Krishna and Godavari rivers meant paddy, cotton and gingerly (for oil) were important goods for trade. The coastline of Andhra allowed trade with South-East Asia and China. Apart from this, along with the help of Tamil ships and caravans, they went into Karnataka and Kerala as well. Konasamudram and Elgandala villages in Andhra were centres for the prized Wootz steel, which was used in Europe to make swords and other weapons. Traders made a lot of money from this and gave rich gifts to the many large Buddhist schools and buildings in Nagarjunakonda and Amaravati (which had a life-size statue of Buddha made in real gold!). Both were centres of Buddhism.

Most of Andhra is very fertile, watered by the River Godavari, among others. But the difference in prosperity in the two areas of Andhra between the Godavari and Krishna rivers, and the Rayalaseema region is very sharp. Rayalaseema is a rain-shadow area and receives very little rainfall. The two important rivers that flow here are the Tungabhadra and Krishna. Both these rivers are

HOW DID THE BUDDHISTS BECOME FRIENDS WITH THE TRADERS?

In Hinduism, there are six *darshana* or ways to interpret the philosophy. One of them is Mimamsa, in which a lot of importance is given to rituals. At that time, the dominant group of Hindus were people who believed in this interpretation.

Traders, who constantly travelled in uncertain conditions, found these rituals difficult to follow and were more comfortable with the teachings of Jains and Buddhists. Merchants who travelled along the western sea coast took Jainism from present-day Gujarat to Karnataka and from there to Kerala and Tamil Nadu. Others who travelled from central and eastern India took Buddhism from there to Andhra and further south to Tamil Nadu and Sri Lanka. From the east coast, Buddhism spread to other parts of Asia as well.

heavily used in Karnataka, and don't have much water left in them as they enter Rayalaseema. As a result, even today, this is the next most arid region after Rajasthan. So, in Andhra it has always been important to study who had ownership of most of the fertile land and which king these landowners supported.

THE SATAVAHANAS AND THE KAKATIYAS

In parts of Maharashtra and Karnataka, the Satavahanas became kings around 2,100 years ago. Their most famous king was Gautamiputra Satakarni. Coins featuring his bust show him to be a stern-looking man. He ruled all of present-day Maharashtra and Andhra, and is said to have had a very powerful army comprising elephants, horses and about 100 spies. From available inscriptions, we know he worked hard to keep his land safe for traders who paid a tax for this and made the kingdom wealthy. He even created a new Hindu calendar based on the Shalivahana Saka year.

His mother and his wife were important people in his life, and we know this because of inscriptions that mention his mother supporting him to become the king and his wife being the guardian for his sons when they would become kings.

A coin of Gautamiputra Satakarni

The Satavahanas started encouraging local people, who were intelligent or physically powerful, to own more land and become a *kutumbin*, or one with a large family. In this case, it meant a person who owned a lot of land and had farmers working under him (whom he would – hopefully – treat as one large family). It was his responsibility to pay taxes to the king for the land he owned, based on the crops he cultivated.

Being supporters of Buddhism, the Satavahanas even repaired the Sanchi stupa. Around this time, Buddhism started to lose popularity and the simplicity that had helped it form a connection with ordinary people. Soon, Hinduism began to see a resurgence – there was a spirit of reform with fewer rituals, vegetarianism and closer relationships with landowners. Successive Satavahanas began to support Brahmins more, giving them land and making them landlords who would collect taxes on their behalf. This also contributed to wealth flowing into temples rather than Buddhist monasteries. The decline of the Roman Empire meant less trade and this also affected Buddhism. This was possibly because traders could not donate as generously as they had before. Also, the Buddha began to be thought of as an avatar of Vishnu, and many Buddhists adopted Hinduism.

A beautiful sculpture from Amaravati, showing the veneration of the Buddha

By 180 CE, the last great king of the Satavahanas, Sri Yagna passed away. He was succeeded by a series of weak kings, who were not able to control the many local *kutumbins*. By about 225 CE, the *kutumbins* had declared independence from Satavahana rule.

WOMEN POWER – SHAKTA AND TANTRA

In the sixth to 13th centuries CE, Andhra, like many other states in India, had a powerful tradition of worshipping female energy. Traditionally, ancient Hindu systems had accorded respect to men and women as equally important for life to be created and nourished. However, over time, males and male energy came to be seen as more important. As a means to address this and influenced by the old Mother Goddess worship (that existed since the Stone Age), female energy and power were exclusively worshipped by male priests called Shaktas (from Shakti or female energy). They did not worship the main gods but created a female form of them – Brahma became Brahmi, Vishnu became Vaishnavi and their Mother Goddess was a ferocious one – Chamundi (a skeletal form with a skull head and demons all around).

These goddesses were especially patronized by the Eastern Chalukyas of Vengi as their goddesses of war and victory, to inspire soldiers. Animal (and even human) sacrifices were common. Even today, most villages in Andhra have an Ellamma Temple where goddesses carry the names of old Shakta goddesses, the *sapta matrikas* or *yoginis*. Srisailam, Alampur and Pithapuram were popular centres of such worship.

Goddess Ambika leading the Matrikas (top row, from left) Narasimhi, Vaishnavi, Kaumari, Maheshvari, Brahmani. (bottom row, from left) Varahi, Indrani and Chamunda or Kali against the *rakshasa* Raktabeeja

Different parts of Andhra were ruled by the respective region's locally powerful families, such as the Ikshvakus in present-day Nellore and Guntur, the Pallavas in the Tirupati area, and the Brihat Palayanas near the coast, among others.

Important ports on the coast, such as Dharanikota, Kalingapatnam, Kothapatnam and Masulipatnam, continued to flourish. Textiles were the major commodity of trade. Beads and roof tiles from India were in demand across the world, and India brought porcelain and wine from South-East Asia to its shores. In Motupalli, an inscription records how traders would be protected and the taxes they had to pay.

After the collapse of the Chalukyas in Karnataka, till about 1,000 years ago, the family of the Chalukyas ruled from Vengi (now called Pedavengi). In the early part of the fourth century CE, the Pallava rulers became more powerful and pushed the borders of the Vengi Chalukyas to the north of the River Godavari. The Pallava rulers expanded their kingdom from the region between the Godavari and Krishna rivers all the way to Kanchipuram and then further to the River Kaveri in Tamil Nadu.

The Pallavas had also been small *kutumbins* under the Satavahanas. Although the Pallavas are famous in Tamil Nadu, the first inscription that mentions them, dated to 320 CE, is not located in Tamil Nadu but in Manchikallu in Andhra's Guntur district. It mentions a Pallava king called Simhavarman who gave gifts of woollen carpets and food to the local Shiva temple. From then on, till

Coins of the Pallavas of the Coromandel Coast

the end of the Chola dynasty of Tamil Nadu, the Andhra region was a part of the kingdoms of the Tamil Nadu rulers. However, 800 years back, the greatest dynasty of Andhra, the Kakatiyas, conquered them from their capital Orugallu (now Warangal). Goddess Kakati was an avatar of Goddess Durga, whom they prayed to for giving them courage and victory in war. It is possible they named themselves 'Kakatiya' after her. The Kakatiyas are remembered not just for their magnificent temples like the Ramappa Temple and the *torana* (or gateway), but also for their administration and irrigation systems.

Inscriptions and literature from the Kakatiya times give us an indication that land was the important source of income for the kingdom. They had to improve the cultivation of land by enhancing and expanding water facilities and administration. They also had to bring new land (earlier heavily forested) into cultivation. So, they relied on giving land as gifts to military and civil officials, probably as rewards for loyal and efficient service.

Apart from this, land was also gifted as '*agrahara*' gifts to Brahmins. *Agrahara* is a Sanskrit word that means 'necklace of houses', referring to the houses on the four streets around the temple where Brahmins lived. Very often, these land gifts were in forested areas so as to

Ramappa Temple, Warangal, Telangana, was built by the Kakatiyas, and is a rare temple named after its sculptor

bring them under cultivation. The Brahmins had to make the land cultivable and, in return, did not have to pay a tax initially. However, as time went by, land that had been cleared by them but used by others was taxed – usually one-sixth of the yield had to be paid to the temple, from where it was distributed as salaries to the village administrators and others employed in the region by the king.

From the Chalukya times to the Kakatiya period and then to the Vijayanagara times, the number of words connected to taxes increase, showing how the system of taxation became much more complicated. The Kakatiyas had about 19 types of taxes; in the Vijayanagara times, there were 27 or more. Local bodies would also ask for their own taxes. Sometimes, certain professions were taxed. Any taxes on the sale of grain and cloth – the most important goods traded – went to the king. To encourage farming, people who built ponds or dug canals were allowed to pay fewer taxes, were given gifts, and were allowed to collect user fees as well.

RUDRAMMA DEVI

History, in general, is unfortunately dominated by the stories of men in power. We know little of the many brave women who supported the men or, in rare instances, came to power by themselves. Rudramma Devi, a Kakatiya queen, who ruled from 1262 to 1289 CE, is one such example.

The Kakatiyas were true Telugu kings who created the Andhra of today. One of their most important kings was Ganapatideva, who established the independence of the Kakatiyas from the Chalukyas as they weakened.

He had no male heirs and used an ancient Hindu *putrika* tradition where a father could, if he had no sons, appoint his daughter as his heir, equal to a son in all respects. He must have encountered a lot of opposition, but he stuck to it and ruled with her jointly for some time.

Rudramma also rose to this role – against all odds – and learnt the skills needed to command respect – education and military strength. In his accounts, the Venetian traveller Marco Polo admires her skills as a ruler.

Using income from diamonds, textiles and agriculture, she made the Warangal Fort even stronger and encouraged a rare dance for warriors called *Perini Shiva Tandavam*. Even till she was 80, she was in fighting form and died in battle.

An artist's impression of the warrior-queen Rudramma Devi

The Kakatiyas were very focussed on their armies and forts and had four kinds of forts. Gandikota and Hanumakonda were *giri* or hill forts; Kandur and Narayanavanam were *vana* or forest forts; Divi and Kolanu were *jala* or water forts; and Warangal and Dharanikota were *sthala* or land forts. In a rare instance, they even had a strong queen, Rudramma Devi.

Sadly, most inscriptions of them were on temples that were destroyed in attacks by the Delhi Sultanate.

Ruins of Warangal Fort

It was during the siege of the Warangal in the 1300s that the Kohinoor was moved out of south India to Delhi. It was believed that the diamond – which was mined in that region – was fixed as the left eye of Goddess Kakati's idol. When the Delhi Sultanate armies invaded Warangal, they took away precious items, among them the Kohinoor.

The location of the Kakati Temple is a mystery. Some believe it was fully destroyed. Others believe it exists as a small temple in Dharanikota near Amaravati.

Prataparudra, the Kakatiya king, was captured and taken to Delhi but killed himself on the way to escape indignity. The Kakatiyas were replaced by the

Vijayanagara kings, and after that, by the Bahmanis in the part that borders Karnataka today, the Reddis in present-day coastal and central Andhra, and the Gajapatis in the northern parts bordering present-day Odisha.

Even as these political changes were happening, local rulers were still supporting trade on the Andhra coast. Much of the trade was carried out by Tamil traders. In 1358 CE, the Reddi king called Annapota (or Anavota) Reddi issued a royal order for fair treatment of traders from foreign nations in Tamil in the port of Motupalli (near Ongole).

The order mentions that traders would be given freedom to stay where they liked, transact business freely and could bequeath their property to others without taking approval from the king. They were not required to pay taxes on gold or silver; however, they did have to pay a tax on sandalwood. The practice of asking them to pay by yards of cloth instead of money as taxes was also abolished. Tax rates for ships and boats coming from the south (Tamil Nadu, Sri Lanka and South-East Asia) are listed. Items mentioned were pearls and cloth. Far-off lands (*dvi pantaram*) had a special rate as well.

Similar edicts to give traders concessions were issued by other kings, including those from Vijayanagara, as traders helped the economy of the kingdoms.

The Vijayanagara dynasty's last remnants survived in a place called Chandragiri, where the ruler Venkata III gave land to the EEIC to establish their factory.

THE MUGHALS AND THE COLONIAL ERA

The rest of Andhra was ruled by the Asaf Jahi rulers from present-day Hyderabad. The Jahis were originally from present-day Uzbekistan and found employment with the Mughals, serving them so well that they were allowed to rule this region provided they recognized the supremacy of the Mughals.

Their main seat was the famous Golconda Fort. The fort (with its unique 'whispering' gallery) was originally built as Mankal Fort by the Kakatiyas. Then the Vijayanagar kings and, after them, the Bahmani sultans occupied it, before they were defeated by the Mughals.

When the Mughals became weak after Aurangzeb, Asaf Jah declared himself independent as the Nizam of the Asaf Jahi dynasty. The Nizams were very wealthy; the last one – Osman Ali Khan (1886–1967) – was one of the richest men in the world.

The EEIC was quickly able to conquer Andhra by 1800 CE. The smaller rulers were wiped out, the tribes who resisted were ruthlessly supressed and only the Nizam was allowed to continue to rule from Hyderabad after agreeing to accept the authority of the EEIC, and then the British rulers.

3

RULERS AND THEIR COURTS

LIVING LIFE KINGSIZE

If you ask adults who work in an office what the most difficult thing about working in an organization is, they will likely tell you that it is getting people to do what they should when there is no one to check whether they are following instructions and rules. In your school too, you may have noticed that sometimes children don't follow guidelines, and what happens as a consequence. This problem hasn't changed since the olden days. Today's elected rulers have tools, such as CCTV cameras, mobile phones, email and quick means of transport to keep a check on things. But imagine how the rulers in the past did this without means of connectivity and surveillance. They would also have to make regular visits to different parts of the kingdom to see how things were faring.

Clearly, ruling a kingdom was hard work.

The king had a lot of power, money and a position of great importance in society. But it all came at a cost. The rulers constantly faced the threat of internal rebellion by their own scheming ministers or external aggression by neighbouring rulers. To prevent such attacks, they had to keep their army happy, so they had to pay them well.

For this, he relied on taxation and income from farming vast tracts of land. Most salaries were paid as grain and not in currency, so collecting and storing grain – usually rice, in south India's case – were critical.

There were different kinds of taxes, including those collected in coins – mostly copper ones but sometimes gold and silver too. These had to be stored away in the treasury.

All of this without the help of technology!

So, to be working in the king's administrative system, you had to have a good memory, great writing and fast-paced reading skills, and the willingness to travel to different parts of the kingdom to make sure that it was running like a well-oiled machine.

GETTING TO KNOW WHAT WE KNOW

We get to know how the courts and administration of the kingdoms of southern India were organized from three main sources.

The first is literature, where the poet or writer would write about the ruling king and his court. Many Tamil poems dating back to the Sangam times comprise guidance offered to the king, telling him what an ideal king should do. For instance, in Thiruvalluvar's *Tirukkural* – a Tamil anthology of 1,330 rhythmic couplets or *kurals* – there is a chapter titled 'Greatness of Kings'. Its couplets explain the duties of a king. Among the many listed are words of advice, such as speaking pleasantly; sharing ones' wealth; not sleeping too much;

lifelong learning; being brave; and caring for the welfare of others, to mention a few.

Apart from this, there are also several texts on how kings (applicable to general folk as well) should conduct themselves. These include the *Manasollasa*, an early 12th-century Sanskrit text by the Kalyani Chalukya king Someshvara III, who ruled in a region of modern-day Karnataka, and the *Raya Vachakam* – a kind of diary recording the day's events, written by Krishnadevaraya, the monarch from Karnataka.

Copper plate inscriptions of the Eastern Chalukyas from the 10th century CE

The third kind of sources are the many royal orders inscribed on the stone walls of temples. Similarly, they were inscribed on copper plates, bunched together and fashioned to look like the rotating card files of today. Temples or even homes would house them. And these usually contained information, such as records of land gifts or important judgements passed by a king.

Based on these sources we come to know of two predominant styles of administration across south India.

One, a decentralized style, in which power and responsibility were distributed across the lower levels, such as to village-level officers, meaning that local problems were addressed locally. For any major issues, they used to report back to the king. The king used to rule from afar, and collected taxes to maintain the army and provide security to the citizens.

All other decisions were taken at the village level. For example, we know from sources that each village was free to decide how it would elect their local government. This was recorded in inscriptions such as those located and found in Manur and Uthiramerur in Tamil Nadu.

The second system of administration, a more centralized one, was one in which the king held more power when it came to making laws per se, but the task of making sure that the people followed these laws was left to local governors and landowning nobles. These lower-level officers also collected taxes on behalf of the king.

A king's style of ruling the kingdom across all of south India can be slotted somewhere between these two kinds of administration, depending on their personality and power, and that of their nobles. Strong rulers like Krishnadevaraya preferred the second system of control as did the Kerala kings who ruled smaller kingdoms. The Chola kings preferred the former system since they had a very large area to rule and it worked better to give more power to the villages.

In the Manur and Uthiramerur temple inscriptions, we get an idea of elections for village assemblies. Rules for contesting in elections were far more stringent than today and age alone was not a criterion. The candidate

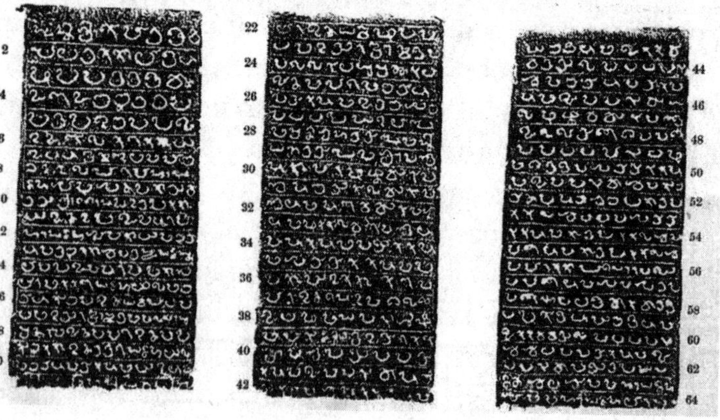

Old inscriptions are a good source of information about land grants and other actions by rulers and their courtiers or families

had to own land in the village and have educational qualifications. They had to have done good work if they had been elected in the past and could not have relatives in office. We cannot be sure if the same rules applied in all villages in south India, but membership to village administration bodies was restricted to landowners. In Karnataka, at the same time, we hear of village assemblies being under the headship of *gavundas*, *urodeyas* and *settis*. Some of these titles still survive as surnames.

Certain items, such as a peacock-feather fan, were signs of honour from the ruler

Some headmen were honoured by the king, who allowed them to use symbols of higher office like a white umbrella, or a gold fan made of yak tail hair, a flag, warrior's drums and peacock-feather fans. Among the most important work of the village assemblies was creating new irrigation systems, keeping current ones in good repair and finding ways to persuade the governor of the area to reduce tax on farming income.

Regardless of the area under a kingdom, a few common themes emerge:

- The king was the most powerful person in the kingdom, but there were ways to ensure he did not let it go to his head. As the heir, the ruler was taught a variety of texts from a young age, including those that helped him see different points of view. He was expected to be guided by learned ministers and was constantly reminded that his power existed only in the context of his subjects being happy. This does not mean that all rulers were ideal ones, but there was clarity on how an ideal ruler should behave.
- The ministers and the departments that supported the king were well organized. Merit was an important criterion for selection, though preference was also given to well-qualified sons of ministers to take their father's position. There were also cases of less privileged people making their way up the ranks in the court, but this was a rarity. For instance, if they revealed their prowess in battle, they were promoted very quickly.
- The king's court consisted of the king and his set of ministers, in turn supported by officials.

HOW THE KINGDOM WORKED

1. The king's job was mainly to protect people from external/internal war and enable them to live in peace for them to grow food and enjoy life.

2. For this, he needed an army to fight enemies.

3. Money was needed to pay the army. Taxes were mostly paid in foodgrains and not money.

4. Food was money, and new villages meant new land for cultivation and more income.

5. More land under cultivation led to more disputes.

6. The king did not have enough time to travel across an expanded empire.

7. More local power was given to those who knew the law. Thus, time was saved for the king to focus on his job.

This same system of the ruler being advised by ministers was followed by the local governors, who in turn reported to the king. The basic unit of administration was the village, which was managed by an elected body of landowning people. The level of autonomy, especially at the village level, was much higher than it is today, which means that they could take decisions at the village level without having to ask anyone else for permission. The village was answerable to the king only for the payment of taxes and for providing soldiers.

WOMEN IN THE KINGDOM

The role of women in the kingdom's administration was minimal. However, the wealthier ones, particularly those who were part of the royal family, had a better standing within the system of administration and in society in general. Queens, for example, had access to their own income, and were free to give gifts to temples and fund public community projects like building or renovating water sources and hospitals.

It was not unheard of for the queen to practise a different religion from that of the king, as in the case of the Hoysalas of Karnataka where the king was Hindu and the queen a Jain. In the villages, the *devadasis* (women who dedicated themselves in the service of the temple) were well-versed in music, dance and philosophy, and could own and spend their money as they pleased, but they were not allowed to marry. Many important welfare projects, especially related to water irrigation, were funded by *devadasis*. The respect the community largely had towards the *devadasis* changed during the colonial era.

Sadly, since all these sources of information were controlled by the communities that owned land, we do not have information about the poorer sections of society. Their stories and traditions in songs or other oral traditions have also been lost in time.

TEMPLES: AT THE HEART OF THE COMMUNITY

Temples played an important role during these times not only as religious centres but as administrative ones as well. The local temple was the institution through which the kings collected taxes and carried out public benefit schemes for the local community. Each temple complex had a designated space for this. Sometimes there may have been two – one for the god Shiva and one for the god Vishnu, and they would have either worked together or functioned as two separate entities.

Despite the importance of Hindu temples in the day-to-day lives of the people, a few rulers, such as the Chalukyas of the Karnataka and Andhra regions, gave specific instructions to their governors to allow all religions to be practised without interference.

Temple projects were also a means of employment and income generation. The Kakatiyas of Andhra smartly used the construction, renovation and enlargement of temples to create a kind of 'temple economy'. The temple helped generate local income for workers while being constructed, and helped the temple itself, post-construction, by attracting many visitors to it. Such projects provided employment and also opportunities to implement mass feeding programmes across the community.

THE KING'S PALACE AND COURT

The king had a large and complex administration system. The Kalyani Chalukya king Someshvara III's *Manasollasa* lists 66 different departments. You will see that some of these are part of administrations across the world even today. This exhaustive list comprises departments such as the navy, finance, prisons, messengers (postal services), weaponry, wildlife, education and learning, and musical instruments. There were others too, such as wrestling, customs, caste relations, and precious stones. There was even one dedicated to the king's white umbrella. Yes – you read that right – a whole department to look after royal umbrellas!

This system survived till the Maratha kings of Thanjavur – they were descendants of Chhatrapati Shivaji Maharaj's half-brother Venkoji (Vyankojirajah Bhonsle), who was from the Bhonsle family, to which Chhatrapati Shivaji belonged. In the 19th century, Serfoji (Sarabhoji) II Bhonsle of Thanjavur also had various departments called *khanas*, which included those for managing water supply, weapons, cultivable lands, equipment needed for shipbuilding, and medical institutions.

The administration of the palace was managed by *mahals* or departments. There were different *mahals* for managing food stuffs and medicine, the cattle farm, the throne room and palanquins. Handmade paper was used to write down the king's orders and for documentation, and these were also managed by a department.

We have detailed records and transactions of how the king checked each department's functioning. For example, Serfoji II, in a surprise inspection, noted that when a judge was late to court, he was fined, based on an attendance registration system.

Keeping ministers under check was an issue for all kings. The *Yasastilaka*, a Jain text, relays the story of a spy employed by a king, and how he found and caught a corrupt minister who would demand bribes. He was forcing people to work on his fields and collecting taxes even before the crops were harvested. The text advises the king to punish him, for the main duty of rulers was to eliminate evil and do right by their subjects.

We have many accounts of how kings spent their workdays. Foreign visitors, such as the Portuguese traveller Domingo Paes, left an extensive account of his time spent in the court of Krishnadevaraya.

ADVISERS TO THE RULER

The king was the ultimate boss – he could pretty much do what he wanted. If the king was a wise person, he would do the right thing: whatever helped him and others around him, and even the animals of his kingdom were bestowed with his benevolence. But if he was ill-disposed, things could go wrong very quickly. While kings were all-powerful, there were systems, checks and balances, which prevented the king from taking poorly thought-out and hasty decisions. Kings had a

THE COURT OF KRISHNADEVARAYA

Like Domingo Paes from Portugal, many visitors from Europe came to the court of Krishnadevaraya, Here is a paraphrased account of what they saw during one such visit.

We were made to wait a while before the king's elegantly dressed staff came to respectfully escort us into the palace. They carefully counted how many of us were there and led us into a small room with a courtyard that had a smoothly plastered floor with walls of the same finish. Everything was bright and shining.

At the end of the courtyard was a pair of gates. One led to the king's residence and the other to his offices. A pair of brightly painted life-size sculptures adorned the gate. We were informed that one of them represented the king, and the other his father, who was stouter in comparison to the king. Both sculptures featured jewels and fine cloth, all of which were painted in minute detail with many colours.

At this point another headcount was taken and in hush-hush tones we were told that we would be going to visit the king's living spaces, an honour that was reserved only for the highest ranking individuals. The king's living chambers were like a smaller mansion within a large courtyard. One room had steps covered with 'chasing' (a method of using metal to form fine designs). It led to a pillared porch with railings decorated with heart-shaped rubies, uncut diamonds and pearls. Another chamber, situated nearby, had a large bed with a gilded canopy, surrounded by another set of railings decorated with pearls. The beds had a black satin sheet and a pair of cushions.

There were many other rooms. One entranceway had stone pillars supported and framed by lintels, and topped with richly adorned minute carvings of roses, lotuses and other flowers in ivory. The work was so fine, it was out of this world.

The walls of the mansion were painted with frescos, mostly featuring scenes from the court. We even found images of us being depicted. We were told that in this way, the women of the palace household would know what was happening in the court.

We then moved on to see many other rooms in the mansion. In one building, under many arches, was a small room with a small door locked with many large, thick padlocks. This was the treasury of one of the former kings. We were not allowed to see it but were told of the fantastic jewels and gold rumoured to be inside it.

One of the courtyards seemed to be designed for animal hunts, a type of entertainment sport involving hunting and killing of wild animals held in royal captivity. This arena featured painted pillars of wood, and cross beams gilded with copper. After this, we passed by many more houses, and climbed many steps. One of them featured finely carved stone pillars. This was a temple, but it was used only when the idol from the main temple in the kingdom was brought here during festivals to grace the palace. At that time, the idol would be covered with many jewels and dressed in expensive cloth, and was carried here accompanied by a group of priests, who would conduct rituals. The idol's procession was also flanked by many women whose duty it was to dance and sing for the idol. We were told that the golden throne for the idol was one of the finest in the world and was inset with several precious stones including diamonds.

In another room past a few stairs, we were greeted by huge vessels of solid gold, large enough to fit a cow! Finally, we arrived at a huge hall where the king and his subjects enjoyed shows put up by dancing women. The walls and pillars of the room featured paintings of elephants, deer and other fantastic beasts; there were also paintings of women in dance poses as if they were prompts to help the dancers. We were later taken to the mansions of the female members of the royal family. Any man, other than the king, was forbidden from entering these. So we retraced our steps, a headcount was taken again and we were escorted out of the palace gates.

Krishnadevaraya and the *ashtadiggajas* or 'great scholars and poets' of his court (a model)

bevy of ministers to counsel them. And they came from different fields.

For instance, during the Sangam ages, poets were the conscience keepers of the kings. They travelled from place to place, reciting their poems, which were sometimes harsh truths, put across in a tactful manner. This meant the king couldn't take offence. Famous poets such as Avvaiyar and Kapilar, were particularly good at this.

An artist's impression of Avvaiyar, a legendary poet and adviser to kings

Once, Avvaiyar heard from her dear friend King Adhiyaman who ruled from Tagadur (Dharmapuri in Tamil Nadu today) that the king of Tondaiman (located in present-day Chennai) was planning to wage a battle against him.

'What a waste of effort and lives!' she remarked. Determined to stop this, she travelled to the Tondaiman kingdom, and the king invited her to see his weapons. She only remarked how new and well-oiled they are compared to those of Adiyaman, whose weapons are all old, rusty and worn out.

As a poet himself, the Tondaiman king knew that Avvaiyar's words always held a deeper meaning. He realized that what she was really getting at was that Adiyaman was a more experienced warrior, given his well-used weapons. He called off the battle and presumably focused on administering his kingdom well rather than conquering Adiyaman's.

A proverb of Avvaiyar's that is useful for everyone, including you, dear reader, goes as follows: *What we know can be compared to a fistful of sand. What we don't know, and need to learn, is comparable to all the collective deserts of the world.*

Now, about the poet Kapilar, who was a dear friend of King Pari of Parambu Nadu (in ancient Tamil country). When Pari was defeated in a battle, Kapilar took care of his daughters Angavai and Sangavai. Kapilar too averted many battles for Pari, and his final resting place, called Kapilar Kundru, is on a small island on the River Ponnaiyar near Tirukoilur in Kallakurichi district, Tamil Nadu.

You can see this tradition continued with Tenali Raman (or Ramakrishna) who, using his common sense and humour, was able to help Krishnadevaraya rule wisely. In many chapters in this book, you will come across works of literature composed in the reigns of various kings, many authored by the kings themselves.

Many tales like those of Mahabali and Narasimha are about kings who could not control their ego – another reminder for kings to rule wisely with the help of advisers. Many old texts featured stories from the Ramayana and the Mahabharata, which reminded the king to fulfil his duties. From these two epics, we get

IT'S A KING'S LIFE!

The king would wake up before daylight, around 4.00 a.m. He would drink a large vessel of gingelly oil. He would also rub himself with this oil, and tie a small loincloth around his waist. This was followed by a workout comprising lifting *mudgars*, which were weights shaped somewhat like baseball bats and made of stone or metal. Alternatively, he would practise sword fighting till he sweated out the oil.

After a bout of wrestling with his wrestlers, he would gallop on his horse till daylight broke. Once the sun came out, he had a bath and performed a series of rituals dedicated to his ancestors, and prayed. Then, he went on to the business of governing the kingdom with his ministers. Giving them instructions, problem-solving, and reading reports from different parts of the kingdom were all part of his workday. According to Paes's record of Krishnadevaraya, the king's favourite minister was Saluva Timma, also known as Timmarusu or fondly as Appaji.

A workout with 'mudgars'

According to his account, the governors also followed a similar regimen in the morning, though one is unsure if all of them woke up so early in the morning and exercised!

A version of this routine was also adopted by local landlords. Tamil scholar U. Ve. Swaminatha Iyer, in his autobiography, describes the daily routine of the landowning class (known as zamindars) of Ootrumalai. Iyer captures the life of a Hridayala Marudappa Thevar, who lived in Veera Keralan in Pudur, near Tirunelveli. Iyer stayed there in the 1890s as a visiting guest. Of course, a king would have had far grander and more elaborate ceremonies than the zamindar Swaminatha was privy to.

Routinely, Marudappa Thevar woke at 4 in the morning. After completing the morning chores, he had a glass of milk and went out at 6:00 a.m. for a stroll with his support staff.

He would inspect his elephant stables, the horse stables and the cattle shed. He would walk through the town under his charge. He had planted avenue trees on either side of the road. The gardens were well laid out and cared for. On his return from his rounds, he would study both ancient and new texts with a scholar from 8 a.m. to 10 a.m.

The scholars in his court hailed from intellectually gifted families and composed literary works.

At around 10 a.m., he would go to the court hall and attend to administrative matters. This would be followed by a bath and meals. At 2 p.m., he would settle down again to study Tamil literature, and attend to state matters. After 6 p.m., he would grant an audience to those seeking to meet him. He would examine the grievances and complaints of citizens, which they would present to him on a palm manuscript. He would review them and produce the verdict the next day. Visitors were always received with courtesy.

He also mentions that every night, the zamindar was given a glass of boiled milk mixed with honey and flavoured with saffron to end his night on a sweet and healthful note.

some very good advice not just for kings and ministers but common folk like us too:

1. If you want or take away from another what does not belong to you, be prepared for violence, which in the end does not help anyone.
2. If you hide behind rules when you see a person being unfairly treated and do nothing to help, be prepared for violence, which in the end does not help anyone.
3. When we tease someone or wound their self-respect, it comes back to hit us.

Administration moved to a more centralized system with the gradual expansion of British rule. More and more decisions began to be taken from the seat of British power in Madras (now Chennai). Post 1857, however, after the First War of Indian Independence, all important decisions began to be taken in London.

4

A HARVEST OF TASTE

PLATES OF THE PAST

Would you believe that people of south India didn't even eat potatoes, carrots and beans, up to 1,000 years ago? The region is today famous for many dishes made of these. They did have rice though – lots of it. In fact, people believe that the word 'rice' itself is derived from the Tamil and Malayalam word for it: '*arisi*'.

Around 2,000 to 1,500 years ago, we have information from Sangam texts on what people ate in Tamil Nadu and Kerala. During those times, they mostly ate what was locally available, so there is a good chance that the same was the case in Karnataka and Andhra too. Around 2,000 to 400 years ago, we also have poems and stories composed in or about palaces, which mention food or sometimes gifts of food or offerings made by the kings and devotees to temples. These have been recorded on inscriptions on the stone walls of temples.

Kerala's entire history is connected to food. The climate of the region is conducive to growing spices, such as pepper and cardamom. Besides, the long coastline and relatively calm waters of the Arabian Sea, and its proximity to the Middle East, and further on to

Europe, made it an ideal destination for Arab traders to load their ships with spices and take them back home. The Arab traders made so much money from this that slowly every European country wanted a piece of the proverbial pie. So they began to send their own ships to buy spices from Kerala directly. Owing to this, the food and cooking techniques of Kerala were heavily influenced by Middle Eastern and European countries.

Cardamom was one of the most wanted items on traders' lists

Many of the poems of the region and time were composed by the *panar*s, a group of folk singers. Their songs included references to the food and drink of those times. We know from the literature of the time that most people ate millets and wealthier people ate rice (not the polished rice of today but hand-pounded rice) as the staple. Of course, many people ate meat too. The Sangam poems keep telling us that food is fun and tastes so much better when we have it with friends and family. Wouldn't you agree?

Pepper was worth its weight in gold (well, almost!)

TAMIL NADU, KERALA AND SOUTHERN PARTS OF ANDHRA AND KARNATAKA

There were broadly five zones in this region, based on the environment. Each region was named after a local flower/tree, and everything that people did – what they ate, what they sang and how they danced – was connected to the local plants, animals and weather conditions.

People who lived in the mountains or the Kurinji region (named after a flower species, one of which blooms only once every 12 years) ate jackfruit, honey and *punsei tinai*, a kind of millet. They would have something similar to the modern-day biryani, cooked with the meat of wild pig or *udumbu* (a monitor lizard), among other animal meat. Another favourite was the red-coloured *moongil arisi* or bamboo rice, which was cooked with sour mango, jackfruit seeds and buttermilk. To drink, they had *theral*, a juice made of honey, among other juices made from local plants and flowers. Sounds yummy!

Jackfruit, ripe or raw, and its seeds too were popular ingredients

In the forests, called Mullai, named after the jasmine flowers found there, people were fond of a sweet called *kummayam*, made by mixing *thinai* (foxtail millet), *varagu* (kodo millet) and *avarai parruppu* (a variety of beans) mixed with jaggery. *Kanda chakkarai* was another favourite delicacy made with rice along with jaggery and camphor. *Karamani* (cowpea) and *cevappu avarai vidhai* (reddish-green spinach) mixed with tamarind water made a delicious soup, somewhat like the tamarind-based *rasam* of today. They also liked very fine rice cooked with lamb meat or mutton, often complemented with a side dish of *thinai mavu* (millet flour) and honey.

One of the poems refers to a *panar* enjoying himself at a tiffin shop, a small roadside kiosk dealing in small snacks, called *nedungadai*. Here, he ate a very thin *adai* (a dosa of rice and mixed dals) along with *eral*, a freshwater fish or shrimp roasted and cooked in honey. Apart from this, they made *modak* or *kozhakattai*, dumplings as big as coconuts, made of beans and millet flour. They also enjoyed a sweet *appam* (a lacy, fluffy pancake made with rice batter thinned out with coconut milk or jaggery syrup).

The 'fruits of the sea' made their way into south Indian cuisine naturally due to its coastlines

The *idiappam* of today was then called *ezhai soozh vattam*. Of course, our favourite *dosas* and *idlis* would have been around at this time, but they were probably called something else until they got these names about 1,000 years ago.

The third 'zone', Marudam (named after a tree) consisted of farmland and rice fields. The people of these areas liked their rice with freshwater crabs, fish and hen meat. Many fruits like mango, banana and jackfruit are mentioned along with lotus stalks and tubers (not potatoes). Some vegetables were cooked in milk. A special dish was pomegranate

Bananas and plantains are used in many different ways in the food of southern India

porial in which the pomegranate seeds, along with curry leaves and a spicy powder were fried in ghee.

A version of today's *sambar* was known as *kayam* in those days. Bird meat was often roasted in ghee. *Pookamazh theral* was a drink made with saffron and flowers. Vendors would sell pickle made with tiny mangoes or *mavadu* in big jars imported from China. Pickled gooseberry and tamarind were popular too.

The Neithal region, named after a lily, was the seashore where fare from the sea, like *eral* (prawn) and steamed turtles, was popular. The juice of the coconut and palm were favourites with rice. A cylindrical fish – perhaps an eel – was roasted in ghee and eaten with rice. They used to fatten pigs with rice and eat them too.

Coconuts, its by-products and oil are synonymous with the southern states

Vegetables were cooked in tamarind water. Deer meat was very popular as well. Meat was also salted and dried for future use. These cured meats were skewered and eaten like a kebab. Saffron was brought down south all the way from Kashmir. People chewed areca nuts and betel leaves (the *paan* of today) in those days as well.

When there was a drought, these regions would become Paalai or the desert. Food was hard to come by, but people continued to be hospitable to guests.

Around 1,000 years ago, we have many inscriptions, especially in Tamil Nadu, of food donations to temples.

Puttu – a steamed breakfast dish popular in Kerala, *iddlipadi (idli)*, *dosaipadi* (dosa) and a sweet called *adhirasam* were popular gifts. Some inscriptions even mention recipes and what honours should be mentioned as the food was carried to the deity from the temple kitchens.

One inscription dating to 900 years ago, found on the walls of a Shiva temple in Piranmalai, gives us an idea

EPIC FOOD

Around 2,000 years ago, many people in south India were followers of Jainism. In the epic text *Silappadikaram*, a Tamil epic by Ilango Adigal, we have a few verses on a special '*savaga nonbu*' meal that Kovalan, the hero of the story, is served by his wife Kannagi before he leaves for Madurai. The meal included jackfruit, long, curved cucumbers, tender pomegranate, mangoes, bananas and red rice along with milk and ghee. All of this was served on young banana leaves.

of the pantry of those days. The merchants who sold certain items to the temple paid a tax to the temple and some of these lists are available to us. See how many of these you can spot in your home's pantry: salt, paddy (unhusked rice), rice, green gram, flat beans, *tuvar* dal, castor seeds, areca nuts, pepper, turmeric, dried ginger, onion, mustard, cumin seeds, gooseberry and honey.

About 900 years ago, the important ports in Kerala were Kollam, Kochi, Kozhikode (Calicut), Kannur,

Areca nuts were also a top trading item

Anchuthengu (Anjengo) and Tanur, among others. Most of the trade was in foodstuff – of which pepper was the most important and fetched very high prices. Pepper was literally worth its weight in gold. Other 'most wanted' spices included dried ginger, cinnamon and areca nuts (which the Dutch sold in Malaysia and Indonesia in exchange for textiles). The import of sugar was widespread. Ma Huan, a Chinese traveller who came to south India during 1421–22 CE, mentions the impressive coconut and pepper farms of the Samuthiri, the ruler of Calicut, and marvelled at how the sellers made complicated calculations using their fingers and even their toes!

Some idea of what people in Kerala ate around 1,000 years ago can be formed from the food served in temples today. Kerala temples are of two types: the Kshetra temples – looked after by the Namboodiri and similar groups of Brahmins, and the Kavu – the family-run village temples. The food offerings in the former are vegetarian while in the latter, meat (and sometimes even liquor) is included. Kerala cuisine is dominated by rice, fish and coconut. A lasting influence came from the Arab connection (Mappila food), as well as from the Portuguese and Dutch merchants. An example of the Arab connection reflected in Mappila food is the *aleesa*, a traditional meat porridge with the Mappila-Kerala influence being in the added coconut.

Several food items were introduced by the Portuguese traders and travellers to south India

About 700 years ago, the Portuguese introduced potatoes, chillies, tomatoes, guavas, papayas, cashew nuts, *mosambi* (from Mozambique in Africa!), pineapples and custard apples, among other fruits and vegetables.

The Mappila make a sweet called *mutta mala* (egg necklace), similar to the Portuguese *fios de ovos* (egg threads). Cheese must have made an entry into India at this time too. It is believed that *puttu* (steamed cylinders of rice layered with coconut, sometimes with a filling) and the popular stew called *kadala* curry came from the Portuguese army who used *puttu* in place of bread and made stew in large quantities for their travelling soldiers.

Unlike the rest of India, food influences from north India were slow to come to Kerala, which was isolated from the north due to the Western Ghats and the seas. The main food influences came from foreigners who arrived via the Arabian Sea.

Over time, delicious foods from Tamil Nadu became popular around the region. Soon, Maratha kings, such as Serfoji II Bhonsle (Sarabhoji II Bhonsle) even wrote recipe books focusing on foods for better health. His *Sarabendra Paka Shastra* and *Vaidya Ratnavali* had recipes from the royal kitchen, which were both

TASTY TIMES IN TAMIL NADU

From the 16th and 17th centuries CE, we have more information about Tamil Nadu, then ruled by the Nayaks, representatives of the Vijayanagara kings. The Telugu-speaking Nayaks of Thanjavur began a practice where a son would write a long poem to honour his father. It would describe a day in the father's life. The *Raghunatha Adbhudayamu* is one such text on a day in the life of King Raghunatha Nayaka of Thanjavur, written by his son, and mentions the king's food from 600 years ago:

> 'Seated in a chair above a *ratna kambalam* (embroidered carpet), he has before him cups and gold and silver jugs fashioned into parrots and peacocks. These are laid beside more humble ones made of leaves. Ladies and men sit facing each other in the long room and a screen of silk with gold embroidery is drawn in front of him. Dishes are served in *gangalams* (large metal bowls) along with rice. The first dish is *pachadi*, then *kadiyam*, followed by *paruppu* (ghee); an assortment of vegetables, *papads*, and six varieties of chicken, one of them flavoured with pepper. Then come many kinds of *payasam* (sweet porridge), including those made with *jeera* and *sooji*; roasted fish; *beeranji* and *vadiyam*, two kinds of *rasam* (one with lime and the other with salt); *peni* and *mande* (sweets). *Kajjayam* and *managu poolu* (a spicy savoury) are among the savouries. *Adhirasam* and *laddu* are more sweets. Types of *vada* (*vadala*) include those served with a curry or with curd. Several dishes of rice such as tamarind rice are also served.

King Achyuta Deva Raya (1529–42 CE) from Vijayanagara gave a gift of a grand feast to the Kanchipuram Varadaraja

Temple. He dedicated 14 villages, and the entire income of all these villages, for the *maha neivedyam* [the 'grand dinner']. The dishes were: *panagam* (a drink of jaggery and cardamom); *vadaparuppu* (an uncooked lentil snack); *kari-amudhu* (fried vegetables); *dadhiyodhanam* (curd rice); *dosaipadi (dosas); adirasapadi* (a deep-fried sweet of flour and jaggery), *appapadi* (*appam*); *vadai; sukiyanpadi* (a sweet) *with chukka* (dried ginger); *puliyodarai* (tamarind rice); *ellorai* (rice with gingelly seed); *kadugorai* (rice with mustard); *pongal* (mildly spiced rice), *iddali* (*idli*) *and akkaradisal* (a milk sweet).

A typical traditional south Indian meal is served on a tender banana leaf

therapeutic and delicious. They were a combination of Marathi, Telugu and Tamil cuisines. He even had an English kitchen to toast bread and boil eggs!

NORTHERN PARTS OF ANDHRA AND KARNATAKA

Both Andhra and Karnataka, and most of Maharashtra, were ruled by the Satavahana kings around 2,200 years to 1,800 years ago. From their time, we have a book of poems, authored or complied by the Satavahana king Hala, called the *Gathasaptashati* (700 verses in the

Gatha or 'storytelling' form, meant to be sung), one of the world's oldest collections of poetry. Composed in Maharashtri Prakrit, similar to Sanskrit, it is set in central Andhra and Karnataka. Some poems in it mention food cooked by the wife for the farmer to take with him to the field. The staple menu was rice and pulses. They liked honey a lot. One poem mentions a *modak, a* sweet dumpling that is popular even today.

From the 15th century CE, the *Kreedabhiramam*, a play in Telugu written during the Kakatiya rule, contains a description of the menu in an eatery in Warangal. It served well-cooked white rice; another kind of long-grain rice like basmati; wheat-based dishes; a dish made of green gram – perhaps a *sambar* of some sort; sweets; cow ghee, honey, *payasam*; arrack; ripe bananas; and different types of betel leaves. So, it appears that traditional food hasn't changed much in Andhra.

In Sri Nathudu's *Sri Kasi Khandamu*, from the same time period as above, there is a story of a spoilt child called Gunanidhi. We hear of his mother feeding him *va dapindiyalu* (preserved mango pickle), *perugu* (curd) and *vantakamu* (cooked rice).

In another book, called *Kasi Kandam*, the writer who lived about 600 years ago, mentions an array of dishes served at a temple festival: sesame cake; oil; green gram; millets; tamarind rice, lemon rice, curd rice and pepper rice served with a curry using mustard powder; vegetables fried in oil and garnished with coriander leaves; and another gravy dish, made using ivy gourd, split pigeon peas and dollops of pure cow ghee. He also mentions grape juice with sugar; and sweets, including those made with bananas. Much of what we know about food in these parts comes from Telugu literature of the Vijayanagara Empire.

Our information on food in Hampi comes from the descriptions of Nunez and Domingo Paes, two Portuguese travellers to the city. They talk of the kingdom being abundant in rice, wheat (eaten only by the Muslims), other grains, Indian corn, barley, beans, pulses and horse gram.

The palace alone had about 200 cows to meet its requirements of milk, curd, butter and ghee. The king had 10 cooks, and ate out of gold vessels studded with precious stones, and even used a finger bowl to wash his hands! Even today in Hampi you can see long rows of plates and bowls carved in stone. They flank a sunken path, built in such a way that those serving the food could do it without having to bend too low.

In the *Amuktamalyada*, the book Krishnadevaraya wrote on Andal, the great saint he was devoted to, he says that dishes changed from season to season. Those listed as seasonal ones include young green mangoes (*vada pindelu*), black lentil chips (*vadiyamulu*), stir-fried vegetables (*varugulu*) and sweet dumplings (*rasavalulu*).

Whew! Isn't it amazing that the dishes we eat now have been around for so long!

DOMINGO PAES SAYS

This Portuguese traveller visited Hampi, the Vijayanagara ruler's capital, around 1520 CE. It was ruled by Krishnadevaraya, the greatest king of that dynasty. His accounts are very detailed and give us a good idea of daily life in the prosperous and bustling city. We know very little of Paes's life except that that he was a trader of horses and his handwritten manuscript was sent to Portugal and circulated but never published as a book. His descriptions have been verified by archaeological excavations that indicate his accounts of most places are true.

Agriculture seems to have been important for him because many of his notes are connected to that – about how the fields around Hampi were planted with 'rice and Indian corn, grains, beans, and other crops that are not sown in our parts; also an infinity of cotton.' As an important visitor, it is likely that he was just shown the most prominent places in the city by someone from the palace, so his account is limited and selective.

An old Portuguese painting showing workers in a pepper plantation

5
WARS AND PEACE

GORY STORIES OF BATTLES

In your textbooks you would have often come across a list of battles and wars. You may have had to memorize the dates as well. Historical records are rich in vibrant descriptions, so we have enough information about battles and armies to bring them to life, just as in video games and movies! But before we get into all the colourful details, let's understand why we fight at all even now. It is not very different from why people waged wars in the past.

Simply put, a conflict can occur because you like something you have and want more of it; or you don't have it and you want to take it away from those who do. It can also happen when you are trying to protect what you have or believe is yours. In the past, this was land or ports, or even roads vital for the basic needs of human beings – food, water and shelter. When these needs were threatened, people did not hesitate to fight.

TAMIL NADU: THE THREE STAGES OF WAR

What is unusual about conflicts in the ancient days in Tamil Nadu is that battles were fought in stages; at each

BIG FISH, SMALL FISH

Under the law of the jungle, the seemingly beautiful forest or ocean is a place of constant war. Whether it is insects or the bigger animals, every other creature is either a predator or prey. Ancient Indian philosophy talks of this in our scriptures as well in the principle of *'Matsya Nyaya*[1]*'* – the logic of the bigger fish eating the smaller fish: that the strong devour the weak (first recorded by Chanakya in the fourth century BCE, but a concept older than that). With predators, animals either fight (like a tiger) or run away (like a deer) or freeze (like a camouflaging chameleon). Humans used these techniques too, when they lived as hunter-gatherers.

The alternative to this is coexisting in society with other human beings, where everyone feels safe and isn't in constant fear for their lives. This is called 'Dharma', a very ancient Indian concept that is mentioned in the Rig Veda. Dharma in its basic form recognizes that we have to live with others to stay happy and to get what we want. For example, only because we live together can we eat the food others grow for us, or drive the cars others make for us. If this has to happen, we have to make sure the needs of others are met as well. So, Dharma is when we think, speak and behave in a way that our and the needs of others are fulfilled. This means that there is a greater chance for everyone to be happy without being worried about conflict or revenge. Battles and wars were waged frequently in history, and our epics and accounts were ways to remind everyone that violence may be a logical way to respond to certain situations that are not easy to resolve, but it only begets more violence and is harmful for everyone in the long term.

stage, there was an opportunity for the warring sides to have a dialogue and stop the war. War was seen as the last resort. This sequence is evident in Sangam poems.

STAGE 1: *VETCHI*

This started with the announcement that war was about to begin: Wearing the white flowers of the *Ixora pavetta* or the torch tree, the side that would like to start the battle would steal the cattle of their enemy. Cattle were symbolic of wealth; in fact, in Tamil the word used for cow and Lakshmi, the goddess of wealth, are the same!

South India abounds in hero stones in villages and fields to commemorate those who died defending cattle.

STAGE 2: *KARANDHAI*

The second stage of the war was when the people whose cattle were stolen would wear a ring of purple flowers known as *karandhai* (*Sphaeranthus indicus*) on their heads, and steal back their cattle at night. This would be an indication that the war had now begun.

STAGE 3: *VANJI*

Warriors from the attacking side would charge forth, carrying a flag with the symbol of a bow and arrow that would represent the king. These warriors would wear the *vanji* (*Salix tetrasperma*) flower and would pray to Kotravai or Kali before entering the battlefield.

During the offensive, if the other side decided to ask for peace and return the cattle or agreed to be ruled over by the other side, the victorious side would wear the *kanchi* (*Trewia nudiflora*) flower and the battle would come to an end.

Finally, if the peace meeting did not go well, the fighting would begin. Care was taken to fight on open land so that farmers, farmland and forests did not get harmed. As the battle progressed, the forts would be the first points of attack. These forts were built with mud walls, but the mud was bound and reinforced

with jaggery made from palm tree juice (which made an excellent binding material), making them as strong as stone forts. While attacking or defending the fort, warriors would wear the *nochchi* (*Vitex nigundo*) flower.

Can you guess what would increase the chances of a side winning the battle? It's the number of elephants they had. Sometimes, the war would spill into the villages as well. When that happened, people would take refuge in temples or temple complexes, which is why their doors had pointed and sharp iron finials to scare away elephants from battering them down. In the frenzy of battle, both sides would wear the small white flower called *thumbai* (*Leucas aspera*).

When victory was achieved, the winning faction would wear the *vaagai* (*Albizia lebbeck*) flower on their head. To celebrate his victory, the king would organize a grand ceremony with feasting and music.

ACCOUNTS OF BATTLES

The main battles in south India from 2,000 to 700 years ago involved the Chola dynasty that ruled in Tamil Nadu. How do we know of these battles? Well, many of the kings had a court poet compose a song that described major battles; such poems are called *barani*. The *Kalingathu Barani* by the poet Jayamkondar in the 11th century CE is one of the oldest war poems known in India.

The poem describes the battle fought between Kulotunga Chola and Anantavarman Chodaganga, the king of the Kalinga Empire, which could be situated in present-day Odisha. It is a mix of actual events embellished with imagination.

The poem starts with all the ghosts or *pishachas* who would feast on the dead bodies in the battlefield after a day of fighting. Some of these are tall and some fat, while some are thin. Some others have holes in their teeth and one even has a hole in her stomach, from which food keeps falling out, keeping her hungry forever. There has not been a big battle for a while and these *pishachas* amuse themselves and others with tricks, which includes making elephants and horses appear magically, and fight with each other. Once they feel happy, they feel hungry too!

When they are talking about how ravenous they are, a *pishacha* arrives with the news that the Cholas have defeated the Kalinga armies and the battlefield is littered with the dead. The *pishachini* then describes the battle as they all go to the battlefield to eat the dead bodies.

While describing the scene, the *pishachini* says that the fighting elephants are like mountains and when they ram into each other, it is just like immense clouds clashing with thunder and lightning. As their tusks grind, they ignite sparks that fall on the flags that fly on the backs of the elephants and set them ablaze. The burnt flags fall on the ground, like the tears of a weeping sky.

The horses charge as if to destroy the whole world. In one instance, a horseman is fighting one opponent and then another. As another horseman comes galloping from behind and beheads him, his head falls to the ground but the body with the sword continues to fight. Behind them are archers, who look like they are throwing an entire fence of arrows on the enemy army.

In the end, as the battle ends with the Chola army winning, he describes the gruesome battlefield in a contradictory yet poetic way: the blood on the ground was flowing like a river, and the heads of the fallen elephants floating in it looked like lotuses, with the two ears of the elephants seeming like lotus leaves.

What an imagination!

What we can infer from the poem is that the army was highly trained, and the soldiers well equipped with spears, swords, bows and arrows and other weapons, and that elephants were essential for victory. There is also a sense of how the greatness of a king hinged on territorial expansion.

A king in battle

Clues about battles can also be found in inscriptions. The Cholas, for instance, not only fought with the Kalingas in eastern India but also the Chalukyas who ruled present-day Karnataka. On

25 May 2010, when the Kailasanatha Shiva Temple in Thiruindalur was being renovated, workers stumbled upon a secret chamber at a depth of 12 feet. In it were found 85 copper plates from 2,400 years ago.

These thick sheets of copper, weighing a total of 150 kg, were gifted to the temple by Rajendra Chola II, a king who ruled from 1051 to 1063 CE. One of these plates mentions a battle fought between Rajendra Chola II and Someshvara Chalukya or Someshvara I, who was called 'Ahavamalla' ('an expert in war'). The inscription on the plate says that the Chola army was so large that the dust of the army almost blinded Someshvara Chalukya. Finally, it says that Rajendra won this battle in a village called Koppam.

The Chalukyas never quite recovered from that decisive battle and were soon replaced by the Hoysalas in Karnataka. The battle was led by Rajadhirarja I (father of Rajendra Chola II) when a Chalukya warrior killed him with a spear, he fell off his elephant and died instantly. Rajendra II was crowned as the new king on the battlefield itself to lead the Chola side.

A BATTLE AND THE MAHABHARATA

Clues about wars are hidden in the most unusual of places – such as in Pullalur, a tiny village near Kanchipuram in Tamil Nadu. Here, an inscription in both the Shiva temple and the Vishnu temple records a gift of a large tract of land to a group of people who had to read and tell the story of the Ramayana and Mahabharata every day to the villagers. This was to calm down the village that had become a *ranabhumi* ('a blood-soaked land'). Pullalur got this reputation because of two important battles fought in the region. One was between the Chalukyas and the Pallavas.

In this battle, going by stone inscriptions of each, both the Pallavas and the Chalukyas claimed victory. We don't know which is correct, but the Chalukya inscription says that the Mahabharata war happened in 3138 BCE. The nearby village of Takkolam also saw a bloody battle between the Cholas and Rashtrakutas. The inscription also says that when farmers ploughed the soil many years after the battle, they found human bones. It is curious they choose this rather complicated way to date this battle. Perhaps they felt this battle was as important as the Mahabharata and, therefore, referenced this battle to the grand epic. (Pullalur was also the scene of a battle in which Hyder Ali and Tipu Sultan fought the British much later in 1780 and defeated the British brutally.)

A depiction of the Mahabharata war in Halebidu, a Hoysala site

KARNATAKA

We don't have detailed records of battles in Karnataka from this time. However, from the text *Manasollasa* (or *Abhilashitartha Chintamani*), an early 12th-century Sanskrit text by the Chalukya king Someshvara III, we have information on the composition of the Chalukya army, the building of their forts, and even how they captured and trained elephants and horses.

Chalukya armies had six kinds of troops: *maula* (hereditary soldiers), *bhrtya* (hired warriors), *sreni* (soldiers that were retained by merchant guilds), *mitra* (armies of an ally or friendly power), *amitra* (troops that once belonged to the enemy) and *atavika* (forest tribes). Interestingly, mention is made of elephants, infantry and cavalry but not of chariots. Perhaps because horses (being imported) were expensive, there were not many chariots in the armies that the Chalukyas fought, so they didn't think to include them.

However, Sangam poems do talk about chariots. In the Chola period, for example, the temple in Darasuram (older than the chariot-shaped Sun Temple of Konark in Odisha) near Kumbakonam, is fashioned like a chariot. Scholars believe the use of the chariot could have declined because of the hilly terrain.

For example, if the Chalukyas and Cholas had to fight each other, they would have needed to cross the Western Ghats. The mountains would have had roads for traders to cross with their caravans, but not paved roads for chariots.

Chalukya armies did have chariots, managed by an officer called a '*ratha adhikari*'. This official had to be an expert in horses, Ayurvedic treatments for horses, and repairing chariots. He also needed to know battle terrains, be physically strong, and speak and act politely as he was in close contact with the king.

The army was commanded by a *maha senathipathi*. Born to nobility, he was expected to be a brave, a good fighter, a quick thinker, and an expert in many languages and dialects so that he could speak to and inspire his troops of different origins. He was also expected to know how to administer basic first aid and perform simple surgeries.

The recruitment to the army was open to all. Soldiers were paid in currency and provisions, and had to cook their own meals. Xuanzang, the Chinese monk, traveller and translator, mentions the Chalukya army during the rule of Pulakesin II (610–42 CE).

The hero stones from Alampur, Panagal and Nalgonda in present-day Telangana, all belonging to the 12th century CE, depict arms and weapons used in battle. The foot soldiers protected their bodies with steel armour covering the arms and extending well below the knees. The infantry carried their broad sword as their main weapon. These swords were rather long, sometimes straight and sometimes slightly curved. They also carried round shields that had rings on the underside to be fixed on the forearm. In addition, they were equipped with either a spear, or a crossbow and arrows.

The horses were not only provided with a saddle but their vulnerable parts – like the neck, loins and knees – were also covered by coats of chain mail (small metal rings linked together to make a covering to protect the body). The elephants carried the *howdah*, a carriage which is positioned on the back. The military band consisted of the kettledrum (sounded when the army was on the march), battle horns and conches. The ultimate insult to a soldier was to flee from the battlefield or be wounded in the back. The noblest way to die was to be hit in the front while fighting.

All forts at that time would have been made of mud with some stonework. That sounds like they would be shaky, but in fact they were incredibly strong because of certain gums and ingredients mixed with the mud. They had complicated entrances and many secret rooms. Even today in some forts like the one at Mahadevapatnam near Thanjavur in Tamil Nadu, one can see that the entrance into the fort is through two gates that are not directly facing each other. The invading army would have to turn and could be more easily attacked while the protecting army was hidden by the wall of the inner gate. Inside the gate, they kept snakes and wild animals that could be unleashed on the enemies. Battle-related materials, such as war machines (possibly wooden structures, with a catapult that hurled stones across a long distance), building materials, ropes and fodder, among other important war supplies, were stored in forts.

Hero stones in the Tarakeshwara Temple in Hangal, Karnataka, show a fierce battle in progress. Can you make out the different animals and weapons used?

THE ANDHRA REGION

In Andhra, apart from the periods during which the Chalukyas (seventh to 12th century CE) and the Vijayanagara (14th–17th century CE) kings ruled it, the Kakatiya rulers were in control. Known to be great warriors, they conquered all of Andhra and kept it unified for 500 years. They were originally Jains, who adopted Hinduism later, and were quite aggressive in battle. A popular imagery in poems is how the Kakatiya king played with the defeated king's head like with a football. Quite gruesome!

In their time, even farmers were good soldiers and those successful in battle were rewarded with land. Being a soldier was a popular job. The soldiers had special names: the *nayaka* was a military leader; the *lenka* was a soldier-servant who fought for the king unto death and died by suicide if the king died in battle; the *sahini* were cavalrymen or elephant corps; the *rautu* was a cavalry leader; the *kamupati* was an army commander; and the *bantu* were foot soldiers of a lower rank.

The *Palanati Veerula Katha* and the *Katama Raju Katha* are two renowned epics from Kakatiya times. These war-based plays were first recited and acted in village festivals at one time; today, those heroes are worshipped. Most of the warriors meet a very brutal death. The *Palanati Veerula Katha* is often compared to the *Mahabharata* since it talks of a pointless war between relatives. Just as in Tamil Nadu, fallen heroes were honoured with a hero stone and Andhra has many that give us an indication of what their bows, arrows, swords and other weapons looked like. These hero stones would be worshipped with flowers and food.

A stone inscription describes a battle fought by the Kakatiya king Ganapati(deva). The war drums thundered a warning to the enemy to flee to the forests. The army was preceded by soldiers holding tall poles with flags, which flew vigorously in the wind, warning the enemy to run away. The sharp-hooved horses raised so much dust when they galloped that it made the sky look like night-time. Then the soldiers slashed the heads of the enemy so finely that they were thrown into the sky, and seemed like many suns during a solar eclipse.

Another inscription mentions the army of a Kakatiya commander or chieftain called Recherla Nama Reddi, who fought for King Rudradeva. It says that the horses were as swift as thoughts and winds, warriors as savage as lions and tigers, elephant troops as towering as mountains. Soldiers were sometimes honoured with the symbols of a king, like a white umbrella and a palanquin if they were exceptionally courageous. In return, the grateful warriors would build temples and gift them land in honour of the king.

The bulk of the army was made up *rautu* and *bantu* soldiers. *Bantu* were not Kakatiyas and may have been mercenaries loyal to the Kakatiya king. Among *rautus*, the cavalry men, the exceptionally good horsemen were titled *revanta*. Several qualities of commanders (*senathipathi*) are mentioned in texts: he should be from

A hero stone now housed in Nalgonda shows a brave warrior vanquishing his enemies

a noble family, native to the region, well versed in the philosophical texts so that he fights ethically; he should have endurance, be physically strong, be able to fight with weapons and understand the deeper intentions of enemies, among others.

By the 14th century CE, the Kakatiya kings began to lose their stronghold on the empire. They were not able to keep the army well trained and attacks from the Delhi Sultanate became more frequent. Within the kingdom, succession was complicated with many claimants fighting for the throne, and once a king came to power, he had to spend more time and energy in saving his position from other relatives and nobles rather than on managing the army and protecting his territory.

So, it was no surprise that in 1303 CE when the armies of Malik Kafur, the general of Alauddin Khilji of the Delhi Sultanate, began moving south, and defeated the Kakatiyas after a month-long siege. Both sides used stone-throwing machines. The inner wall of the Warangal Fort was very smooth and impossible to climb, but inside the Kakatiyas were starving. In the aftermath, the Kakatiya ruler had to give much of his wealth away and among them was the famous Kohinoor diamond that went to the Delhi Sultanate and from there to Babur who defeated the latter in the Battle of Panipat in 1761.

In Andhra, after the Kakatiyas, the next big dynasty was of the Vijayanagara kings. Although they ruled from Hampi in Karnataka, their official language was Telugu. Their greatest king Krishnadevaraya was a remarkable warrior. His ability to conquer forts by laying siege to them and starving those inside of food and water was well known. In his book titled *Amuktamalyada*, he mentions some of his views on war and armies as short verses. Some of his thoughts on battles and fighting –

> From the money the king makes, he must keep one-quarter for charity and for his enjoyment. One part he must give to his treasury and two parts to his army. He must also constantly check if his spies are keeping a watch on his enemies, his ministers and others in the government. If any of them are found to be thieves, he must kill them without hesitation.

For a defeated enemy, he had a practical solution –

> If a person is your enemy, you have to defeat him in a battle. Don't be harsh on him; show him mercy. Take his wealth, and leave him alone. Don't hurt his pride. What harm can a king cobra do after its fangs have been removed? If you are kind to your defeated enemy, he will trust you more for being kind.

During his time, many of the borders were thickly forested and inhabited by tribes who were part of the kingdom but largely left alone. Smart kings like Krishnadevaraya were able to keep these tribes loyal to him and use them as allies. Referring to this, he says –

> Krishnadevaraya also advises a king to be friends with those who live in forests rather than fight with them.

> He says the only way to be friends with them is by being honest and fair with them so that they trust you. About ambassadors from other countries, he says that they must feel respected regardless of whether that country is friendly or not. He advises kings to promptly pay the foot soldiers and give gifts to horsemen who sell or ride horses so that the army will be motivated and well equipped.

Krishnadevaraya's successors were not as focused on the welfare and training of the army. The Vijayanagara ruler Aliya Rama Raya was defeated in the fateful Battle of Talikota (now in Karnataka) in January 1565 by an alliance of the Deccan Sultanates (Ahmednagar, Bijapur, Golconda and Bidar) to the north. The capital city was destroyed systematically over more than five months.

The thick forests, many rivers and mountains of the Western Ghats allowed Kerala to be largely unaffected by the wars of the Chalukyas, Pallavas and Cholas. The kings, via the southern tip of the subcontinent, had an entry into Kerala. On occasions, they fought each other; at other times, they traded and coexisted peacefully, and sometimes even allied to fight kingdoms like Sri Lanka.

KERALA

In ancient Kerala, about 1,500 years back, many fierce kings are mentioned in the Sangam poems. One such king was Nedum Cheralatan, who defeated the Yavanas (the Greeks, or Westerners, or perhaps even the Arabs) and paraded their chief commander around his capital city with his hands tied behind his back and his head coated in ghee. The king also organized a grand display of all the treasures he had taken from them – mostly gold and precious jewellery. One of his descendants was Adu Kottu Pattu Cheralatan (or Cheral Athan), named so because of the victory dance (*adu kottu pattu* means music with dancing and drumbeats) he broke into, brandishing his sword, in the battlefield.

Since all of Kerala is coastal, all kings had powerful naval armies. This was instrumental in the success of the Kulasekhara kings, but that did not help them against Rajaraja Chola. He crossed 18 forests (according to his inscription) to his first battle at Kandalur, which he won quickly, annexing the Kerala region under the Chola Empire. Some believe this battle was a naval one.

Taking advantage of the confusion, the local landlords or *naadu vazhi*, who represented the king, wrested more power and asserted their independence. To protect themselves, they had their own army training centres or *kalari*. The tradition continues even today in Kalarippayattu from Kerala, one of the few ancient Indian martial arts that have survived, although more for fitness or as a heritage art. Even till about 300 years ago, the *kalari* schools flourished, though the methods of war have changed dramatically since.

When the Chola control of Kerala declined in the 11th century CE, the Samuthiri of Calicut, with the help of the Muslim traders called *marakkar*, fought several battles with the local *nadu vazhi*s and became the king. The Samuthiri had split his kingdom into smaller provinces. Each had a *kalari*, where all Nair community (who were hereditary warriors) boys – and girls – were trained rigorously in using the sword and shield, the bow and arrow, and the lance.

When the training was complete, the student would pay a fee to the *nadu vazhi* and receive a sword to symbolize a formal entry into the army. There were rules for whom to fight (for example, you could not fight an unarmed person) and when to fight. In northern Kerala, communities such as the Tiyya and the Ezhavas, who were also similarly trained.

This expertise in fighting meant that they could be summoned at any time by the king. Cities like Calicut had standing armies headed by the *talachennors*. The

A Kalaripayattu duel and the typical tools used for practice

Calicut Samuthiri depended on the Nair community and the Arabs to provide soldiers for his army and navy even in the 15th and 16th centuries CE. The Samuthiri had a gun-manufacturing department headed by the *tinayancheri elayath*. His cavalry force was headed by a person titled *kuthiraivattathu nair* and the navy by the *kunjali marakkar* from the Muslim community. The *marakkar*, located in the coastal regions of Kerala, Tamil Nadu and Sri Lanka, are the descendants of Arab traders who married local Hindu, Buddhist or Jain women.

In 1503 CE, however, the Raja of Kochi, helped by the Portuguese army, routed the Samuthiri's forces. The Samuthiri fled into a *sanketam* (a place of refuge) at a temple in Elamkunnapuzha, where he could not be captured according to the Kerala rules of war. The Kochi king took over the territory but spared the Samuthiri's life. He let the Portuguese build the first European fort in India. They ravaged the Samuthiri's territory, killing unarmed people, and turned the prices of pepper to their side. This was the start of their foothold in India.

However, the Samuthiri line rose again a hundred years later when 6,000 of his men besieged Kunjali Fort on the banks of the River Kottakkal. This time, he was supported by the Portuguese against his old allies, the *marakkar*. The *marakkar* leader was beheaded, his head salted and preserved (the descriptions say) and displayed as a warning to enemies. Eventually, the Portuguese and the Dutch gave way to the British, and Travancore and Kochi became the key ruling power centres in Kerala.

6

CRIME AND PUNISHMENT

RULES RULE

Older people often call you out when you do something 'wrong', don't they? Either it's something you 'should not' have done, or you have not done something you apparently 'should have' done.

Basically, you would have not followed a rule. Rules exist to make our lives safer and healthier, although they may not always be fun to follow.

In ancient history, when we were still living as hunter-gatherers in forests, there weren't that many rules to follow. Community living, as we know it today, hadn't begun and people led lives independent of each other.

Life as a hunter-gatherer was filled with fear of nature and wild animals, and it wasn't always easy to get food. Soon, humans moved from forests to cave dwellings, then to living near water, and finally to farming food and domesticating animals. The work was hard, but tools made it easier and, more importantly, early humans developed weapons for defence and offence. Owing to this, they were more assured of food.

As people began to live in closer connection with others, rules started to be established as a way for us to coexist peacefully. The basic rules of any society would centre around safeguarding ownership – you can't take what belongs to someone else. This could be land, water, farming equipment, property and so on. And, likewise, others can't take what's yours. Punishments were meted out to those who took what was not theirs.

Another set of rules would be about how people behaved with each other. Everyone wanted to be safe, so rules were formulated around causing bodily harm.

Then, as money became more common rather than bartering products, complex rules on spending it, paying it to others and giving it to the government (who in turn employed an army to keep you safe) got added on.

People who did not follow the rules were swiftly punished. This set an example for others, who would then think twice about committing the same mistakes.

South Indian history has many examples of how wrongdoers were punished. The crimes were nearly always the same – thinking, doing, or saying something that would affect community living badly in the short or long term. It could be stealing something, not paying taxes to the king and government, or hurting another person. However, the punishments of 3,000–4,000 years ago were quite different from what they are now.

TAMIL NADU

Many inscriptions on temple walls in present-day Tamil Nadu mention crimes and punishments. In those days, the temple in the village represented the king. So, any crime related to stealing temple property was taken very seriously.

Take Thirukazhukundram, a small suburb of Chennai, where there is a temple of Lord Murugan on the hill and another Shiva temple near it. The Shiva temple has many *prakara* or enclosed concentric spaces, one inside another. On the eastern wall of the third *prakara* is an inscription about a robbery in the temple, which was detected and solved 600 years ago.

In those days, villages had two main sources of income: taxes from citizens, and tolls or taxes paid by travellers who used roads that passed through the village. The payment was in gold coins or in food grains, mainly paddy or unhusked rice. These were stored in the temple. In the Shiva temple, there was a safe room made of stone for gold coins. One day, when it was opened and the gold coins were counted, 150 coins were missing. However, both the window and the door to the room had been locked, and the lock itself had been sealed with wax. Clearly, it was an inside job. An enquiry was promptly conducted, and the final decision became an inscription on the wall.

The security guard, Tirukalukundra Bhatta Mudaliar, confessed his crime and implicated a few other temple employees as well. The others had by then moved out of the village. As a punishment, his properties and those of his close relatives were confiscated. They were sold and the amount equivalent to 150 gold coins and the interest from that were deposited in the treasury. His right to sponsor a puja in the temple festival was also taken away and sold. At the end of the verdicts, we have the signatures of all the officials including the two leading examining 'judges' – Tondargalnayakan Tirukavanam and Srirudra Srimaheswarar. Such officials, called the *nadu vazhi* (chieftains), were appointed by the king.

Note the speed with which the enquiry was conducted and the severity of the punishment, extended even to his relatives. In today's case, this may not seem a severe punishment because those convicted were not jailed. However, in those days, local villages may not have had jails, and the harshest punishment was not imprisonment but banishing a person from the community. Compare this to such cases of theft today and ask yourself which system was better and why.

A committee of those who knew the laws of Dharma and the land decided cases in villages locally

In a case earlier than the one described above, in Tiruvotriyur, the punishment was similar. The committee members responsible for the collection of gold in the storeroom were found guilty of tampering with the quality of the gold. As punishment, their property was confiscated and sold, and they were banished from the town. Banishment was reserved for the worst crimes.

Thiruvottiyur has another interesting inscription when the women dancers went on strike, and it was such a crisis that the king had to travel all of 563 km from Hampi to solve it. It may even be the first case of a strike in India and tells us the enormous power women dancers or *devadasis* held 800 years ago.

Based on wall inscriptions, a few patterns emerge:

1. The higher the caste of the perpetrator, the stricter was the punishment.
2. Judges were not just rich and powerful people in the village, but had to be well-versed in the *Dharma Shastras*, the ancient texts on duties and ethics.
3. Cases were closed quickly and appeals to the king were rare.

We have many records from the time of the Maratha rule in Thanjavur in the form of paper manuscripts from about 500 years back. They show that punitive measures were governed largely by the above principles, though gradually the punishments became less harsh, or different. With the arrival of the British, punishments for speaking against the government became a more notable crime.

TOUGH DECISIONS

Crimes could be as difficult to judge then as they are now. Take the case of a murder in Olakkur, a small town. An inscription in the temple there says that in 1166 CE, Appan Sattan, who lived in Kudippalli, and his friend, Oraliudayan Perumal, went to hunt in the local forest. Perumal shot an arrow at a *pulvay* (waterbird) but instead wounded Appan Sattan, who died. A case of murder was registered. An assembly of those learned in law was convened, comprising Bhattaperumakkal, Periyanattar and Pannatur, all local dignitaries in the village. They heard all the arguments in the case and pronounced Oraliudayan Perumal guilty. However, because it was an unintentional mistake, he was only asked to sponsor a lamp for the temple.

KERALA

In the early Sangam period (c. 100 BCE to 200 CE), cases were heard and punishments handed out by the king since the population was relatively less (and so was the number of crimes, possibly). A town with 1,000 people would have been a very big one by today's standards.

We know from records that the roads were patrolled by watchmen carrying fire torches, and fines and imprisonment were the commonest punitive measures. As the population grew because of better agricultural practices and more food, the king began to delegate more power to local learned people who could resolve local disputes over land or water, and interpersonal issues, using ancient law books. These local noblemen allied themselves to temples and were called *devaswams*.

Around 1,400 years back, the *devaswams* became important landowners. They had many tenants, and those who did not fall in line were hung on the temple flagstaff (gibbeted) before the temple festival flag was raised. (All temples in south India have a tall metal mast on which a flag is hoisted during festivals.) It is possible they were not hanged till death, but such a ritual in full public view would have been be so shameful (and painful) that the tenants would not have dared to do anything wrong. Most crimes would have been dealt with locally by *devaswams*, appointed to govern large parts of the rulers' territories on their behalf.

In the Kulasekhara period, there was a penal code to deal with crimes and even the death penalty was awarded for serious crimes, such as stealing from the king or the local temple.

From the accounts of European travellers, we get information on crime and punishment in the kingdom of the Samuthiri of Calicut. He was the fountain of justice, and was assisted by officers and learned Brahmins who knew the law books. People did not have to pay for their cases to be resolved. Panchayats were temporary bodies that decided on property disputes or ownership of land, which were the commonest crimes. The second-most common crime the non-repayment of loans, and defaulters were strictly dealt with through confiscation of property or fines and imprisonment. Crimes such as

Gibbeting, hot pots of various liquids and trampling by elephant were some deterring punishments in those days treason, robbery and murder were more harshly dealt with, with even the death penalty being awarded to some. Whipping, flogging and mutilation were routine punishments and, here, unlike in Tamil Nadu, higher castes received milder sentences.

Banishment to Tamil Nadu was called *naadu kadathal.* It is not clear why this was a punishment, but in general, asking someone to leave the community was the most severe punishment.

From about 500 years ago, we get more information on crime and punishment from temple inscriptions.

There was no regular judicial system. There were many instances of *satya pariksha* or 'trial by ordeal'. The accused would have to put their hand inside a pot of boiling oil or ghee (called *kaimukku*), or snakes, or even fire, and then remove it. Based on the severity of the injury, they would be declared guilty or not guilty. There are records of *kaimukku* in the Suchindram Temple, now in the Kanyakumari district of Tamil Nadu. This practice was later banned by the king Swati Thirunal.

Punishments included the water wheel (*chakram chavittal*), a manually operated device to irrigate fields. The accused person would sit precariously on the wheel, held by only a few posts or rods, and the operator would use his feet to manually move the water paddles. If the operator did this fast, the man on top would fall and die.

The strictest punishment for a Brahmin would be the loss of caste. For severe crimes, the death penalty

THE DEATH SENTENCE

Capital punishment was awarded for counterfeiting currency, killing a cow, theft, murder, treason and harassment of women. Ibn Battuta, the Arab traveller who visited India between 1333 and 1345 CE mentioned that the Hindus in Travancore were given the death sentence for something as simple as stealing a nut. When a fruit dropped on the ground, nobody had the right to pick it up except the owner.

was frequently meted out. The method varied by caste: Brahmins were hanged with a rope, Kshatriyas were burnt alive, Vaishyas were drowned, and Shudras were poisoned, or so the texts say.

For some crimes, especially those involving the temple or the king's property, criminals would be cut into half. *Valakkal* was a unique punishment for a person unable to repay his debt. He would be made to stand in the middle of a circle and not allowed to move out of it until the debt was paid up.

The Portuguese rule brought in European laws in the 16th century CE. However, the laws favoured Christians, and punishments for everyone else were harsher. This, in addition to their corrupt administration, made the Portuguese unpopular and caused their eventual defeat at the hands of the Dutch.

As the kingdoms of Kerala came under British rule, the laws also changed.

KARNATAKA

The earliest references to law and order among the kings of Karnataka come from short mentions on crime and punishment in stone inscriptions that describe the gifts of kings. All inscriptions of the Satavahanas, the Kadamba and the Ganga kings mention the ruler as the ultimate judicial authority, who followed the ancient law books of Dharma. There are many of these and some contradict each other. They give us the sense that, in those days, there were multiple ways to view issues and they varied not only from kingdom to kingdom but within one too.

Among the many law books, the four oldest were composed in or before 200 BCE by Apastamba, Gautama, Baudhayana and Vashishtha. Local issues were dealt with by the village headmen or local landlords. However, at least in theory, all people had access to the king for a final appeal. The Kadamba kingdom had a separate chief judge called a *dharmadhyaksha.*

The usual punishment was a fine of three gold coins, a huge amount in those days of barter when most people might have never even seen a copper coin. Typical offences would be stealing cattle, taking away someone's water by blocking their canal, or leaving one's animals to graze in a field that belonged to another.

The death penalty was not in their list of punishments.

We have more information about the Vijayanagara Empire, which included much of present-day Andhra and Karnataka, from the travellers to the region. The

TRAVELLER'S TALE

Domingo Paes, the traveller from Portugal, describes a judge or judicial officer called a *danaik*. The account narrates how, when he left his forty-pillared chamber, several umbrellas were held above him, trumpets were sounded and Vedic hymns chanted. To ensure that they did not make autocratic decisions, judges and kings were assisted by a group of learned scholars.

Vijayanagara ruler Krishnadevaraya penned his thoughts on crime and punishment in his book *Amuktamalyada*. Traditional Hindu laws were followed under the king as the supreme authority. Those convicted were allowed to appeal to the king three times unless they were involved in a plot against the kingdom.

DUTY AND DETERRENCE

Officials could often be corrupt, and perhaps to prevent this, if some cases of theft were not solved by the police, then the stolen money would be deducted from the official's personal wealth and given to the victim.

Kings possibly had a law-keeping force, like the police of today, but there is not much information about it until the 17th and 18th centuries CE, especially in Tamil Nadu from the Maratha kingdom of Thanjavur. Many inscriptions, especially in the Tamil-speaking areas, mention arbitration and fines in the process of solving disputes, which were mostly over land ownership.

Not all kings seem to have been just, and some threatened their subjects with punishments such as trampling by elephants, taking away their land and thrusting the guilty with their parents into 'a hell filled with worms for 77 crore years'. If a king was too cruel or officials too corrupt, sometimes people left their village and settled elsewhere as a sign of protest.

Overall, one cannot conclusively call any kingdom 'good' or 'bad' and 'just' or 'unjust'. Sometimes, the kings were merciless, but their officers were not, or vice versa. Many punishments that sound brutal now were then intended to prevent crime, while forms of entertainment emphasized the ideal life. And, finally, the just rulers like Krishnadevaraya or Rajaraja Chola shine across history.

An ancient poem mentions a Pandya king called Abhirama. The king assembled all the learned people in his kingdom and asked them what the primary duty of a king was.

Was it to give gifts, or to protect people from crimes being committed against them and their property?

The poets unanimously said, 'O king, giving gifts to others will get you a place in heaven. But if you want to earn eternal fame and be remembered, you must protect your people from crime. All the sacred *Puranas* say this is the ruler's primary duty, and that is our opinion too.'

So, the great kings were those who worked to protect their people from crime. However, gifts were always welcome and appreciated. Who doesn't like them!

7

FAITH AND RELIGION

CONFLUENCE OF FAITHS

Religions are all around us; we see activities related to them and we read about them on a daily basis. In your own homes you may have an altar, a cupboard or even a room dedicated to praying, featuring pictures of gods, goddesses, saints and religious symbols. Similarly, there are temples, churches, mosques, gurudwaras and other religious places around you where you may go to pray by yourself or with your family. You may also go here to celebrate religious festivals.

Religion can be defined as a system of beliefs and practices that bring a set of people together. So, for instance, all Hindus may believe that after they die, they will be reborn in various forms, depending on the quality of their actions. Buddhists or Jains don't believe in a god as such, but they do believe in rebirth.

In their essence, you will see that all religions began with trying to explain basic questions people have about life. These include: How can I be happy? Why do things that cause me pain or sadness happen? Why are some people's lives better than those of others? In ancient times, religions – which offered spiritual and other answers to such questions – gave people inner peace and hope to get past difficult times. Religion also played a role in explaining natural phenomena, such as the eclipses, day and night, and life and death, before scientific explanations for these were found.

Many religions were born or developed in the Indian subcontinent: Hinduism, considered to be the world's oldest practised religion, Buddhism – one of the four most popular religions in the world, Jainism and Sikhism are religions that originated in India. In addition to this, Christianity and Islam, the two largest religions in the world, have been present in India – especially south India – from almost around the time when they were founded. Therefore, south India has a rich history of religions.

HINDUISM

Hinduism is the predominant religion of south India. Its pantheon has many gods and goddesses, and some deities are even genderless. Besides, it has several holy books and many saints.

In south Indian history, it is more useful to look at Hinduism through a time lens rather than one of beliefs. In this way, Hinduism can be classified into pre-Vedic, post-Vedic and post-Buddhist Hinduism.

We can roughly assume that pre-Vedic Hinduism survived till the Sangam age starting in 300 BCE, and from here on the lines began to blur. Vedic Hinduism can be said to have become more popular from 300 BCE till the third century CE.

Between the third and sixth centuries CE, Kerala and Tamil Nadu were under the sway of the Buddhist and Jain Kalabhra dynasty. After the sixth century, Vedic Hinduism changed due to the influence of the Buddhists. Jainism was extremely popular in Karnataka, Tamil Nadu and Kerala from the second century CE but declined by the seventh century CE. Buddhism was popular in Andhra and Tamil Nadu from the third century BCE until the seventh century CE.

It is important to remember that these 'changes' were not abrupt, but there was a lot of back and forth, give and take, and things happened gradually and fluidly. For example, even today, in parts of Tamil Nadu, you can see Tamil Jains – they are very similar to other Tamils in every way, and even their temples are very similar to Hindu temples in Tamil Nadu.

Every part of the region would have had nature and ancestor-based deities from the Palaeolithic times. Sadly, apart from what has been found at burial sites, we know nothing of these gods. Mountains, trees, rivers and other aspects of nature were probably worshipped. People were very close to nature and environment, and believed that we need to live in harmony with nature.

This ethos can be seen in how most of the ancient temples are in or close to areas of natural importance, such as mountains and rivers; the deities have animal *vahanas* or vehicles, who are also worshipped as deities – even today in Karnataka, for instance, the Panjurli and Bhuta Kola dances honour such ancient animal deities.

The other kind of deities at this time were those considered to be brave – either warriors or women who committed great sacrifices. They were honoured by hero stones. The really old ones were obelisk-shaped and placed on a pedestal made of brick and plaster. Or, they showed warriors on horses in terracotta. They usually had a figure of the sun and the crescent moon to signify how the memory of the courageous would not be forgotten for as long as the sun and moon rule the skies.

Headdress in the shape of a boar spirit deity, used for traditional dance

Even today, in parts of Tamil Nadu, especially near Pudukkottai, you can see such old shrines, open to the sky and heavily planted. In Karnataka, there are many hero stones, sometimes even with a sculpture of the hero and inscriptions on it expressing who they were and why they became famous. In Kerala, they have, as *kavu*, been incorporated into later temples. Such temples were in quiet places with many trees and the entire area was treated as a sacred space.

A hero stone now at the Government Museum, Bengaluru

Animals, such as snakes and bulls, and trees were incorporated into the broad umbrella of Vedic Hinduism.

They began to be revered owing to their association with Hindu gods and goddesses. Nandi, the bull, became the vehicle of Shiva, and snakes began to be associated with both Shiva and Vishnu. Many old temples, especially in Tamil Nadu, have a *sthala vriksha* or a sacred tree. These are small reminders of the pre-Vedic tradition of worshipping elements of nature.

Evidence of worshipping hero stones is aplenty in the Sangam texts of third century BCE to third century CE. By this time, we also hear of the Vedic gods of Hinduism – Vishnu, Indra, Varuna. Were they brought in from north India? Or were old, existing deities in the south given these names instead? We might never know.

However, by the third century BCE, we have many references to rituals based on the Vedas, the oldest and most sacred books of the Hindus. From then, until the third century CE, more and more people in south India were influenced by Vedic Hindu traditions: devotion to multiple deities, complex rituals that involved the recitation of Vedic verses in Sanskrit, and the belief in the soul's rebirth based on one's actions in this life.

Hinduism is the name given to the religion by the British in the 19th century CE. Earlier, this system of beliefs and practices was known as Sanatana Dharma. *Sanatana* means permanent; Dharma implies thought and action in a way that fulfils our needs and of those around us – people, animals and nature. The oldest Hindu text, the *Rigveda* (dated to 1500 BCE or earlier), and the three other Vedas (*Yajurveda*, *Samaveda* and *Atharvaveda*) comprise mantras – prayers to the deities, and *Brahmanas*, which are rules on how to conduct *yagnas* (interactions with the divine using fire, as you see in a home puja or a wedding). The *Aranyakas* comprise rituals for those who performed the *yagnas*.

The deepest questions of life – what is the meaning of life and how do we find happiness, among others – were codified around the second century BCE, into over a hundred Upanishads. They speak of a concept called Brahman, which is considered as a supreme cosmic spirit. Their verses or shlokas can be looked at in different ways, and all interpretations could be equally correct. There were six schools (*darshana*) to understand these. In the Hindu tradition, there isn't only one way to think.

Other important texts are the two epics, referred to as *Itihasas* – the Ramayana and the Mahabharata, which condense the core teachings of the Hindu faith into a story that is easy to follow. The *Puranas* comprise moral and religious stories.

There was also a group called the Charvakas, who did not believe in God. Yes, this is very confusing, but Hinduism is like that – different and often opposing views garnered equal importance.

THE RISE OF BUDDHISM AND JAINISM

The Upanishads needed a teacher to explain their deep wisdom and meaning. Across India, but more so in north India, there were six main ways to explain them – similar to the different kinds of school curriculums we have today, such as ICSE, CBSE, State Board, International Baccalaureate and so on. One of the schools, the Mimamsa, gave importance to rituals – they said that as long as one performs the prescribed rituals regularly, one would reach one's life goals. This excessive focus on rituals and the ever-increasing cost of conducting them made it harder for people to follow this method. Some wanted to know why they were doing this, but did not get an answer that explained it.

It was against this backdrop that Buddhism and Jainism developed around 400 BCE (they were founded in around 600 BCE). These faiths followed many things as they existed in Hinduism but not the rituals. They felt self-reflection and controlling one's own thoughts, feelings and actions were ways to lead a good life.

While Buddhism and Jainism were originally inspired by Upanishadic philosophy, their focus was on the main teachers of their religion – respectively, Gautam Buddha ('the Enlightened One') and the 24 Tirthankaras (those who have crossed over the endless cycle of births and deaths), of whom Mahavira is best-known.

During this time, many rituals very likely involved animals and both Jainism and Buddhism preached the principle of *ahimsa* or not hurting other living beings. They gained the support of traders and the teachings moved along with them to places where the traders went. Kings like Ashoka (c.304–232 BCE), the Mauryan emperor of Magadha (now west-central Bihar), also supported them and, very rapidly, they amassed a large community of followers. Both Jains and Buddhists established many centres of learning, and the remains of universities, such as Nagarjunakonda in Andhra, tell us how popular and powerful they were.

These two religions spread rapidly because they were promoted by travelling traders, who found these non-ritual-focused religions easier to follow on the go.

The Jains came to south India via the western sea coast – first to Karnataka, and then parts of north and central Tamil Nadu and upper Kerala. The Buddhists came via Odisha, Andhra and central Tamil Nadu, but stayed mostly on the coast. Both used the Brahmi script for Tamil and wrote many texts on the rules to live the 'right way'. They set up schools and hospitals, granted refuge to those persecuted for political reasons, learned the local languages, and spoke and wrote in them.

JAINISM

The word 'Jain' comes from the root word *jina* – one who has, through self-discipline and control of the five senses, been able to see that nothing in this world is permanent and is, therefore, in a state of bliss or perfect happiness.

Jains worship the 24 Tirthankaras (those who have crossed the lake of suffering and become a *jina*) of whom Mahavira, who founded Jainism in present-day Bihar, is the last. The sacred books of Jainism, together known as *Agama* or *Agama Sutras*, contain the teachings of Mahavira, compiled by his disciples.

Thirumanai Padiyar, a Jain scholar in Tamil Nadu during the third century CE, in his *Ara Neri Saram* ('book on the essence of living the right way') lists the core aspects of Jainism. These are *ahimsa* – not hurting any living being; *satya* – always speaking the truth; *asteya* – not stealing; *bramhacharya* – not marrying; and *parmita-parigraha/aparigraha* – not being interested in worldly attachments and not wanting to own anything.

The main centre for Jainism was Shravanabelagola, an important pilgrimage site even today. From this *moola sangha* (or main *sangha*), Jainism spread to Tamil Nadu, in places such as Kanchi, Madurai, Sittanavasal, Tiruchirappalli, and the areas around Vellore and Tiruvannamalai. Central Tamil Nadu was largely untouched by Jains for two reasons. One, the Buddhists were already numerous here; and, two, central Tamil Nadu is flat, unlike the areas in northern and southern Tamil Nadu, which have rocky hills and natural caves that offered the monks and nuns quiet places for meditation, or even for the *sallekhana* vow, following which a few Jain devotees, such as senior monks and nuns, would voluntarily fast unto death.

Jainism was popular in Karnataka, Kerala and Tamil Nadu till the sixth century CE because Jain monks (men and women) lived a simple life, learnt the local language, spoke in it and practised what they preached. They gave free education and medicine, and exhorted people to live a life of adherence to rules. Most of the Jain texts that survived are centred on principles to live a simple life. Even their stories, such as the *Jivaka Chintamani*, talk about how people constantly look for excitement of their senses, ultimately realizing that true happiness comes from owning nothing rather than many things.

The Bhakti movement in Tamil Nadu, Adi Shankara's movement in Kerala, and Ramanujacharya and Madhavacharya's movements in Karnataka caused a steady decline in Jainism as more and more local people began to go back to the Hindu tradition. However, Jainism did not disappear. In Karnataka and Tamil Nadu, there are many places where Jains actively practise their religion. In Tamil Nadu, the Thirupparuthikundram Temple near Kanchipuram has stunning paintings of Jain legends, and Vellore, Tiruvannamalai and Madurai have many Jain temples set in remote mountains. In Karnataka, apart from Shravanabelagola, Jain temples (*basadi*) are aplenty because Jainism in south India first came to Karnataka.

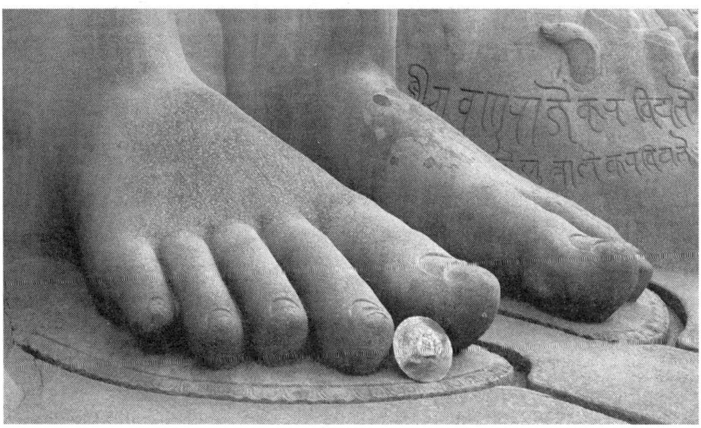

The feet of the Gommateshwara (Bahubali) statue at the Jain site of Shravanabelagola

Around the third century BCE, the Jain guru Bhadrabahu came to Karnataka with his disciple Chandragupta Maurya (Ashoka's ancestor, who gave up the throne to follow his Jain guru unto death). They settled in the Chandragiri hills where Shravanabelagola is situated. From here, Jainism spread across the south. Moodbidri and Karkala are other important Jain sites. Kallil (now a Hindu temple) in Ernakulam district, and Sultan Bathery and Puliyarmala in Wayanad district are a few of the Jain temples in Kerala. Most of the Jain sites in Kerala are in the north, closer to Karnataka.

Between the third and sixth centuries CE, Tamil Nadu – and probably Kerala – were ruled by the Kalabhra dynasty from Karnataka. They followed Jainism and this was the time the great Tamil epics, such as *Silappadikaram* (a Hindu text with many Buddhist references), *Jivaka Chintamani* and *Valayapathi* (Jain texts), and *Manimekalai* and *Kundalakesi* (Buddhist), were written.

Akkana Basadi, 'temple of the elder sister', Shravanabelagola

BUDDHISM

Buddhism developed in a manner similar to Jainism. Its main precepts were the Four Noble Truths (the truth of suffering, the truth of the cause of suffering, the truth of the end of suffering, and the truth of the path that leads to the end of suffering) and the Noble Eightfold Path: Right Understanding, Right Thought, Right Speech, Right Action, Right Livelihood, Right Effort, Right Mindfulness and Right Concentration. Buddhism was particularly popular in Andhra, with Nagarjunakonda and Amaravati being two important centres. In Tamil Nadu, they were popular in the River Kaveri delta. There was a Buddhist *vihara* in Nagapattinam, an important port built by Cudamanivarman of the Shailendra family of the Srivijaya Empire (present-day Malaysia) during the time of Rajaraja Chola. (The Government Museum in Chennai has superb idols from many *viharas* of Nagapattinam.) Kanchipuram was another important Buddhist centre.

In Tamil Nadu, the Alvar and Nayanar (or Nayanmar) saints propelled the decline of Buddhism by about the 12th or 13th centuries CE. Unlike Jainism, which is still practised and Jain temples still function, no Buddhist *viharas* or temples remain. Occasionally, stone images of the Buddha are found in different parts of Tamil Nadu. Some are worshipped by Hindus as a 'holy man', In Kerala, many statues of the Buddha have been found and the 10th century CE Paliyam copper plates mention a grant to a Buddhist temple. Neelamperoor and Kiliroor still have Buddhist temples, but here the Buddha has become a Hindu deity.

The Jain king Chandragupta Maurya's grandson Ashoka popularized and supported Buddhism. Andhra was close to present-day Bihar, and the north-south trade route that the traders of Ashoka's time took helped the spread of Buddhism extensively into Andhra and then into Tamil Nadu.

In Karnataka, Ashoka promoted Buddhism, especially in Sannati, where you can still see remains of a stupa with scenes from the Jataka tales and other sculptures carved by a sculptor from Vidarbha. The most gorgeous images of the Buddhist tradition in Karnataka are in the Shiva temple at Kadri. Scholars believe the temple was either a Buddhist temple that later became a Shiva temple, or a sacred space in the mountains worshipped by both religions. Two images here are made of an alloy of five metals in the 10th century CE: one is of a form of the Buddha called Manjushri (5 ft tall, with three faces and six hands) and the other is of Avalokitesvara (4 ft tall, with one face and four hands). It is remarkable that they were cast in such a size with such perfection.

Banavasi in Karnataka has some Buddhist remains as well, but support for Buddhism here was minimal with Jainism and Hinduism being the dominant religions because of Chandragupta Maurya moving to Karnataka, and the power and popularity of Jain monks.

Since the northern parts of Andhra were an important part of Ashoka's kingdom, it is natural that Andhra's

Buddhists were summoned for the third Buddhist council (a gathering of Buddhists) that happened in his time. At this time, there were six different schools of Buddhism in Andhra alone. After the death of Ashoka, Buddhism continued to grow with local support.

A statue of the Buddha in the ruins of Nagarjunakonda, Andhra Pradesh

Andhra has more than 100 Buddhist sites, with Nagarjunakonda, Amaravati and Bavikonda being the most famous. These places had Buddhists from Sri Lanka as well, and some of them have even built or renovated buildings here. Fourteen Buddha relic caskets have been recovered so far from the sites of Andhra, the largest number for any state in India.

Eventually, Buddhism died out in Andhra because the monks began to move closer to the Vajrayana school of Buddhism that had many rituals. Some monks and monasteries fell out of favour with the local kings. Hindus included the Buddha as an avatar of Vishnu in the *Puranas*, and encouraged Buddhists to adopt Vaishnavism (the worship of Vishnu). The more forceful Shiva worshippers, such as the Veershaiva and Kalamukha sects, also popularized their belief systems. By about the 15th century CE, Buddhism was completely extinct in Andhra.

In Tamil Nadu, Kanchipuram, the Chola region and Nagapattinam were the key centres of Buddhism. No physical structures remain in Tamil Nadu, but a lot of the prominent literature – Buddhist epics such as *Manimekalai* and the text *Pazhamozhi Nanuru* – were conceived here.

REACTION AND INTERACTION

Our information regarding how Hinduism reacted with Buddhism and Jainism comes from after the fifth century CE. They were competing for the support and attention of the same rulers and people, so there was a lot of conflict among these three religions.

Scenes of the Buddha's life, Amaravati, Telangana

Within Hinduism, there were two major changes. Adi Shankaracharya, a Vedic scholar and teacher from the eighth century CE, went back to the Upanishads and codified their teachings. Shankara was not only a good communicator – he triumphed in philosophical debates (including against Buddhists) and won popular support – but he also travelled and established monasteries, just like the Jains and Buddhists, to propagate his view of Hinduism. Several of these monasteries or *mathas* exist even today. Other saints after him, such as Ramanujacharya and Madhavacharya, also created monasteries, reformed temple administration and gave a strong institutional framework to the Hindu religion. In doing this it is very likely that they were inspired by the ways of the Buddhists and Jains.

At the same time, the insistence on the upper castes becoming exclusively vegetarian also grew in strength under the influence of the principle of *ahimsa* followed by the Buddhists and Jains.

The tradition of travelling to holy sites was something much more popular among the Buddhists and Jains. In a bid to gain popularity, this became a regular practice with the Hindus. Travel not only showed the followers the varied facets of Hinduism but also emphasized their similarities. In doing this, the goal was to build a strong sense of identity and community as the number of Hindus increased.

Famous royal painter Raja Ravi Varma's artistic impression of Adi Shankaracharya

THE DECLINE OF BUDDHISM AND JAINISM

The biggest surge in Hindu tradition, apart from Adi Shankara, was due to the

A TRIO OF SAINTS

Sri Shankara or **Adi Shankaracharya** (eighth century CE), born in Kerala, travelled across India and codified the philosophy of Advaita from the Upanishads. Simply put, he said there is no difference between us and the world outside, and it is all an illusion. The only thing real was Brahman, that which we do not have the intellect to understand or words to define. Once we know nothing is real, we are less affected by life's events while doing what we need to do. His followers are found across south India, especially in Kerala and Tamil Nadu.

Ramanujacharya (12th century CE), a Vishnu devotee, spread 'Vishishta Advaita'. His devotees reside in large numbers in Tamil Nadu and Andhra. He is best remembered for his ability to organize temple administration. His philosophy was that humans as *jiva-atma* (individual souls) are different from *brahman* (*Paramatma* or Vishnu), and there is an essence of Vishnu within all . He exhorted people to enter into *sharanagati* (complete surrender) to Vishnu. So, he too asked people to focus on their efforts and accept that Vishnu would give them the results.

Madhavacharya (13th century CE) was from Karnataka, and created the Dvaita tradition that sees humans (*jiva-atma*) and God (*Paramatma*) as being different. In this sense, his theories are the opposite of Shankara's. He too, like both the saints above, wrote commentaries on the important Upanishads and the Bhagavat Gita. He founded the temple for Krishna in Udupi, Karnataka, and the region and the state has many 'Madhavas', as his followers are known.

Bhakti movement that gained force around the fifth or sixth century CE.

Among the Vishnu-worshipping saints, the earliest three are from the fifth century CE – we don't have their names; they are known simply as *Pey* (ghost), *Bhutam* (elements) and *Poigai* (lake). Their title is 'Alvar' – one immersed in devotion to Vishnu. The Shiva-worshipping saints or Nayanars (servants of God) are 63 in all, with Karaikal Ammaiyar being the earliest. All the 12 Alvars and some of the Nayanars began to travel to different parts of south India (especially Tamil Nadu and Kerala), spreading their message through music and poetry to bring people back into the fold of Hinduism. They were able to persuade Jain or Buddhist kings and commoners to embrace Hinduism again. How, and why, were they able to do this?

Bhoothath Alvar, one of the 12 Alvars

Firstly, they used the common local language. They emphasized *bhakti* or full surrender and devotion to God, and seeing God in nature, temples and within people. They were not against Sanskrit or the Mimamsa group and their rituals – in fact, some like Peria Alvar, who sang about Vishnu, or Sambandar, who sang about Shiva, were Sanskrit-speaking Brahmins, but they went beyond language and rituals, and stressed the importance of true devotion.

Travelling the length and breadth of south India – some even went as far as Nepal in the north or Sri Lanka in the south – they sang, in simple Tamil and pleasant melodies, of natural beauty and the good qualities of the local folk. They sometimes also poked fun at the Jains and Buddhists, and urged people to return to Hinduism.

Some devotees of Shiva did not sing verses but, due to their acts of devotion, were included among saints as well by the 10th century CE in the Chola period: among Nayanars, Karaikal Ammaiyar and Amaraneedi Nayanar were traders; Enadinatha Nayanar was a *shanar* (toddy tapper); among Alvars, Tiruppan Alvar was a potter and Tirumangai Alvar was a highway thief. Cheraman Perumal, a king from Kerala, is considered a Shaivite saint while Kulasekhara Alvar, another king from Kerala, is considered a Vaishnava saint. Although the songs were in Tamil, they encouraged devotees from Kerala also to adopt Hinduism.

Besides common folk, kings such as Mahendravarman (I) Pallava began to follow Hinduism again. He excavated cave temples in Kudumiyanmalai and Mahabalipuram, among others. The Pandya queen Mangayarkkarasiyar also convinced her husband, Nindra Seer Nedumaran (or Koon Pandya) to return to the Hindu tradition.

With the decline of Buddhism and Jainism, Hindu stories began to be rewritten to project the Buddha as an avatar of Vishnu, to reassure the Buddhists who had newly adopted Hinduism. The Jains and Buddhists tried to incorporate Hindu elements as well, as seen in the Buddhist bronzes in the Chennai Museum and the Jain paintings in Thirupparuthikundram.

By the eighth century CE, Jainism became a small, almost negligible, religion, and Buddhism all but vanished in the region. Hinduism became the dominant religion once again in south India.

RELIGION AFTER THE 10TH CENTURY

There were times when the two big subgroups within Hindus – the worshippers of Shiva and the devotees of Vishnu – clashed with each other. To address this, kings such as Rajaraja Chola, tried to bring them together. He did this by installing the idols of these gods together and speaking of them as equals.

In 12th century CE, in Karnataka, arose a saint called Basava, who spoke of the equality of all faithful people. Through his poems called *vachana*, he preached that everyone, irrespective of caste or gender, had the right to be close to Shiva. He started the practice of wearing a small pendant of a Shivalinga (Ishtalingam) to constantly remind the wearer that Shiva is within their heart. Much of what we know about him is from a later Telugu text called *Basava Purana* by Palkuriki Somanatha. Basava's followers are called the Lingayats.

In the 14th century CE, south India was invaded by Alauddin Khilji's general Malik Kafur. For the first time, temples and religion were severely attacked. Temples were looted and plundered, and idols destroyed. Islam had existed in Kerala before and was known to most villages in south India because of Arab traders, but now its proponents wanted to promote Islam, not just trade.

The Vijayanagara kings rallied people around their Hindu identity to defeat the invading army and succeeded in creating a dynasty that eventually ruled all of south India. In those days, religion was one of the most imporant parts of a person's identity. In this way, they continued an old tradition of using religion to bring people together for a common cause or purpose.

ISLAM

Islam, meaning 'surrender', is one of the world's fastest growing religions and is widespread in India. The religion's followers believe in one God, Allah. The will of Allah must be obeyed strictly as codified in their holy book, the Quran.

Islam originated in the seventh century CE with their religious leader, the Prophet Muhammad, who, the followers believe, received the wisdom of Allah. The religion demands strict adherence to its tenets, which were taught to his original disciples in the Middle East, from where the religion spread to Africa and Asia.

Soon after Prophet Muhammad's death, two sects developed: the Sunnis, who believed that the Prophet had left behind no successor owing to which they went back to the Quran and the Prophet's teachings to guide them; and the Shias, also went back to these two sources, but believed that the Prophet designated his relative, Hazrat Ali, as the Caliph, or his successor.

Islam's birthplace is the Middle East. This was also the home for merchant sailors who traded with India and Europe. They brought Islam to the shores of Kerala. At that time, the primary trade route was from Kodungallur in the west, through the Palghat (Palakkad) pass into Tamil Nadu and then on to Nagapattinam and other ports in the east. They brought with them gold, horses and glass to trade and took back pepper, cardamom, nutmeg, myrobalan, cotton, pearls and ivory.

By the 10th century CE, the traders' names were changed from *yavanar* to *sonagar* or *turukkar* to describe Arabs. In inscriptions, they are also mentioned as *anjuvanar*, meaning people who pray five times. They were soon inducted into trading organizations, which included Hindus as well, and these guilds would set prices for the goods they collectively traded in.

Apart from this, the traders decided to travel together to fend off armed robbers and support each other from roadside robberies. By the 12th century CE, in Tamil Nadu, they were also given the name *roawther* and praised for their knowledge of horses. Horses were highly prized in south Indian armies and the Arab traders did brisk business owing to this. Even today, in coastal Tamil Nadu, there is a community of Muslims called *odavi*: *odam* in Tamil means boat, and this group once had expert boat builders.

The Chinna Palli Mosque in Pazhaverkadu or Pulicat, not far from Chennai, still preserves a rare document that records the fact that the *marakkar* (a group of Muslims who were maritime traders) came here in the eighth century CE because they were expelled by the governor of Baghdad, Hijaj Ibin Yusuf. According to records, the Mishkal Mosque in Calicut, Kerala, was constructed by Mishkal, a Muslim merchant and shipowner in the 1340s, whose fleet of ships traded with India, China, Yemen and Persia.

The Sunni Muslims too began to settle in certain regions. The earliest mention we find of them is in the Kollam Tharisapalli grant in the copper plates of 849 CE. The plates record a gift of land by Ayyan Adiga of Venad, the subordinate of the Chera King, Sthanu Ravi, to Theresa Palli (place for worship of Theresa) at Kollam. The grant included many rights and privileges. The signatures in the grant are in the Kufic script used by Arabs.

Even the word Malabar, that denotes northern Kerala, is said to be derived from the word 'Mabar', which in Arabic means 'a crossing place'. Arabs would stop here and then their boats continued towards China. Like the *odavi*, there are *marakkar* communities of Arab descent in Kerala. The word *maram* in Malayalam and Tamil means wood, denoting their expertise in woodcraft or shipbuilding. They even supported the Samuthiri in warfare by working in his navy and engaging in guerilla

A MARBLE MOSQUE

The Madayi Mosque in Pazhayangadi in Kannur district is built of black and white marble, and has legends that date its establishment to the seventh century CE.

However, the credit for the mosque goes to the arrival of Malik ibn Dinar and his associates, who came there armed with letters from Cheraman Perumal, a ruler of the Chera Perumal kingdom (c. 1089–1122 CE).

These missives asked the local chiefs to help the carriers of the letters in the establishment of mosques and missionary activities. The Madayi Mosque was built with the assistance of the Kolathiri Raja.

A block of white marble in the Madayi Mosque is said to have been brought from Mecca by Malik ibn Dinar

warfare. The *marakkar* are credited with creating organized defence strategies for the western sea coast.

Muslim missionaries and saints came to the east and west coast with the traders and were given freedom by local Hindu rulers to practise their religion. In one case, a Hindu king even resolved disputes pertaining to the community. In the Goripalayam Mosque in Tamil Nadu there is a record that shows that where the Nayak king ruled, based on submitted proof, a piece of contested land did belong to the mosque and not the petitioner.

Muziris (Kodungallur) is said to have the earliest mosque (believed to have been built in 643 CE) in Kerala and built in the local style, but this has since been remodelled. North Kerala has many *jarram* mosques, so called because they contain the graves of Muslim holy men. There were nine such mosques in Muziris, Kollam, Kasargod, Sreekantapuram, Baliapatam, Madayi, Dharmadom, Pantalayini and Chaliyam. Of these, Kasargod has one of the grandest mosques. Kondotty and Mambaram also have old mosques. Sadly, in the recent past, many mosques (as well as churches) have been upgraded to reflect a modern aesthetic. In doing this, they have been deprived of their architectural origins and authenticity.

The upper parts of south India – Karnataka and Andhra, were a centre for Islamic art and culture from the times of the Bahmani kingdom, established by Alauddin Hassan Bahman Shah in 1347 CE. The capital was first in Gulbarga but was moved to Bidar. By 1518 CE, the kingdom split into five smaller kingdoms: Ahmednagar, Golconda (Hyderabad), Bidar, Berar and Bijapur. These areas reflected a strong influence of Persia as, in those days, many people from Iran came here to work in the army or in the courts. This led to the creation of a unique mixture of Persian, Kannada, Telugu and Marathi. The origin of the Dakhini language, which is now (incorrectly) considered to be a dialect of Urdu, came from this rich interaction of varied cultures. Muhammad Quli Qutb Shah, who ruled Hyderabad from the tender age of 15 years, was one of the great composers in this language. He also built the Charminar in Hyderabad.

Cheraman Juma Mosque, Methala, Thrissur

Islam spread when the Deccan Sultans were conquered by Mughal ruler Aurangzeb who ruled through the Nizam in Hyderabad and the Nawab of Arcot. They eventually had to deal with the British in this region.

CHRISTIANITY

Christianity can trace its roots to modern-day Israel. It is one of the world's most widely practised religions and has had a long presence in south India. The religion is based on the life and teachings of Jesus of

Nazareth (first century CE). Christians believe Jesus to be the son of God. Christian thoughts and beliefs stem from their holy book, the Bible. It is believed that Jesus had 12 important apostles (called upon by Jesus to spread the Gospel) in his life and one of them was Thomas the Apostle. There are two major groups within Christians, the Roman Catholics and the Protestants. Roman Catholics believe in the authority of the Pope, their head based in the Vatican, while the Protestants have no single leader. They both believe in Jesus and the Bible but use different versions of the Bible. Within the Protestants a subgroup, called the Anglicans, grew in India during the British rule as this was the form of Christianity traditionally practised in England.

There are two views on how this religion came to India. One is that, after the death of Jesus, the apostle Thomas Didymus himself came from Muziris (Kodungallur) to a place called Palayur in about 52 CE, and was able to persuade many Jews and Hindus to adopt Christianity.

From there, he started establishing churches in Kodungallur, Palayur, Gokkamangalam, Niranam, Chayal (Nilakkal) and Kollam. He then travelled to Tamil Nadu and came to Mylapore, a small village in those days (now in Chennai). Here, he spent his last days preaching on the beach and on a hillock. On the beach, there is a large church named after him. Likewise, there is a hill named after him. He also spent time in a small cave called Little Mount in Chennai, a site of great significance for south Indian Christians. He was buried here, but later his remains were moved from here to Iraq, then Greece, and he was finally laid to rest in Italy. A small part of the bone of his hand is said to be still preserved in Chennai. Some even believe that a fellow disciple of Thomas, Bartholomew, was also involved in spreading Christianity in south India.

The other view is that the Christian merchants and missionaries (entrusted with spreading the Gospel and their religion) of the East Syrian or Persian Church came to Kerala and founded the church in India Either way, south India – be it Tamil Nadu or Kerala, or both – was the earliest location for Christianity in India. It was also one of the first places the religion spread to outside of its region of birth.

St. Thomas the Apostle, as painted by Flemish master painter Rubens

From the death of St. Thomas, till the arrival of Vasco Da Gama in 1498, there is no evidence of how the church was managed. It is likely that Christians at that time were a small community in parts of coastal Kerala and Tamil Nadu. The Portuguese brought with them missionaries to spread Christianity and manage the churches. They did this primarily in Kerala and coastal Karnataka. Portugal was a part of the Roman Catholic faith and they were eager to bring the Indian churches under the Pope. In 1599, a council called the 'Synod of Diamper' was convened in Udayamperur. The St. Thomas

Shrine of St. Thomas in Mylapore, as shown in an old print

Christians were reduced to a diocese of Angamaly, which was itself a part of the larger Archdiocese of Goa, administered by the Portuguese Catholics.

This forceful move led to the end of many of the traditional practices and more Latin was introduced;

this made the local Christians unhappy. In 1653, several St. Thomas Christians in Kerala came together and recorded a list of vows knows as the Kunan Kurisu Sathyam at Mattancherry. They left the Portuguese church and opposed the use of Latin. They favoured closer relationships with the practices and beliefs of the churches in West Africa, Eastern Europe and the Middle East, and came to be known as Syrian Christians.

While Kerala and Tamil Nadu have a significant population of Christians, Karnataka, especially near Mangaluru, houses a large number of Christians as well. Some of them adopted Christianity during Portuguese times; others fled from Goa in the 16th century CE because the Portuguese had made speaking their language, Konkani, a punishable offence. Poverty too was a factor due to famines. They flourished till the reign of Hyder Ali but suffered persecution in Tipu Sultan's time.

The Danish, who traded through Tarangambadi in Tamil Nadu, established the first Protestant mission in India, the Danish-Halle mission, in 1706 CE. Its two German missionaries did not receive support from the Danish governor but slowly built up local support. In 1698, they brought a printing press from Europe, which revolutionized education in south India. First, Christian religious books and then educational books began to be printed in English and Tamil, which helped in the introduction of Western education in south India.

Chennai, in Tamil Nadu, has important churches because St. Thomas is believed to have died here. The

St. Thomas Syro-Malabar Catholic Church, Palayur, where, according to the St. Thomas Christian tradition, St. Thomas performed the first baptism in India

grand San Thome Cathedral is one of the three in the world believed to be built over the tomb of an apostle of Jesus, the others being St. Peter's in Rome, Italy, and St. James in Brooklyn, USA. The first San Thome church was built in 1504 and rebuilt in 1890. At its centre is the crypt that held the tomb of St. Thomas. The statue of Mary, the mother of Jesus, was brought from Portugal in 1543, and it is possibly one of the oldest European sculptures on India's east coast. It is said that St. Thomas was killed on top of the hill now called St. Thomas's Mount or '*parangi malai*' – 'the hill of the French or foreigners'. The church has a stone cross (the 'bleeding cross' said to have the blood of St. Thomas on it).

In Kerala, the main older churches are in Thiruvananthapuram and Cochin. Those in the north Kerala or Malabar regions date from the time of the Mangalore Christian movement. St. Mary's Church in Kuravilangad, said to be built in c. 335 CE, has been renovated many times, but still has a bell featuring an undeciphered inscription, a model of a Portuguese ship and other interesting objects of Kerala's Christian history. St. Antony's in Valiathura, over 400 years old, houses a chapel for St. Francis Xavier, a Spanish missionary. St. Sebastian's Church, in Neendakara, was founded by the Portuguese more than 400 years ago. Kollam too has several Syrian Christian churches. The famous Maramon Convention, the biggest gathering of Christians in Asia, is held near the River Pamba in Mallapuzhasseri village every year. St. Andrew's Basilica (earlier Forane Church) in Arthungal remains a place of pilgrimage for people praying for good health and cures.

The Kalloorkkad Syrian Catholic Church in Champakulam, probably established in c. 427 CE, is said to have temporarily housed the Krishna idol meant for Ambalapuzha Temple. This is an example of the spirit of coexistence among the different religions of Kerala.

With the advent of the British, the activities of the church and its missionaries increased. Today, there are several Christians, representing various denominations of the religion, across south India.

JUDAISM

Judaism is one of the world's oldest monotheistic religions – meaning, a religion that focuses only on one God and His teachings as read through one important book, and the words and life of one important messenger or prophet.

Judaism has a close connection to another, more common, monotheistic religion – Christianity. Jesus was himself born a Jew before he founded Christianity. One of the Jewish holy books is also used by Christians as the Old Testament.

Jews came to India at least 5,000 years ago. They quickly blended into the local culture. In south India, many of them were on the coast of Kerala. We have read about the business links and synagogues elsewhere in this book. The number of Jews in India reduced greatly in 1948 when many decided to go to the new country of Israel that was created just for Jews. Madras (Chennai) and Nagercoil also had Jews till this time. The Kochengadi synagogue was the oldest, but it has since been destroyed.

The Jews in south India are a rapidly shrinking population, and the few synagogues and other buildings that do remain are the only reminders.

An exception to this is a small group of Jews living in a village called Kothareddypalem in Guntur district, Andhra Pradesh. They claim to be Jews who had migrated many years ago. They follow Jewish traditions and pray at the local Bene Tacob synagogue, established in 1909.

8

THE SECRETS OF TEMPLES

INSIDE THE SOUTH INDIAN TEMPLE

The power of the human brain to think of ideas is unquestionable. Such ideas, in most cases, can help human beings collaborate and function together to overcome complex challenges in efficient ways. Religion is one such idea.

In the Stone Age, early humans in India were closely connected to the environment around them. They attributed phenomena around them – night and day, birth and death – to some higher power – nature, gods, goddesses and their own ancestors. Nature was a strong force around them, which affected their lives and livelihood. To this end, they propitiated its elements.

The earliest temples were located amid nature. The *kadamba* tree, for instance, was considered sacred and associated with the Hindu god Murugan; mountains or rivers were attributed to Shiva. They would have been marked out as a special spot using some stones, and worshippers would have conducted rituals using the two most important and basic elements of life – fire and water. It is very likely animals would have been sacrificed as part of the rituals, to say thanks for a good harvest or to guard against a poor harvest.

Around the third century BCE, agriculture was supported by trade with Rome and South-East Asia. More wealth became available to rulers and the general people as well and temples, like homes, became more complex structures. An open platform that served as a temple was now built into a walled and roofed structure. They used mud, brick or wood, and roofs of thatch or wood. Some of these may have even been covered with metal sheets to protect them from rain – this style can still be seen in Kerala temples.

THE SHAPE OF THE SACRED

The hut-shaped thatched roof is the basic pattern for all temple towers, even the grandest of them. When the hut-shaped roof was separated from the square base at the neck, a taller structure could be created by stacking the same shape over it. This sequence is best seen in the five *rathas* or monument complex at Mahabalipuram. It is very possible that King Mahendravarman (I) Pallava, the patron, wanted to show travellers of the time the various forms of temples in his kingdom. So he had these monoliths carved from stone.

Although Mahabalipuram has these in a clear sequence, the styles – *kuta*, *dravida* and *shala* (rectangular *kuta*) are found in the Chalukya temples and in Andhra as well.

A rare group of temples exist in Tamil Nadu, with a ground floor, first floor and a second floor. These

THE FIVE (PANDAVA) RATHAS, MAHABALIPURAM: A SHOWCASE FOR TEMPLE BUILDING

1. The Draupadi *ratha* is the earliest hut-shaped (*kuta*) temple with an image of goddess Durga enclosed within.
2. The second ratha, the Arjuna *ratha*, has a roof or *vimana* that is a combination of many *kuta*s. Look carefully!
3. Then, the plain square of the *kuta* either became an octagon, or the angle was changed as architects improved on the basic form. They also placed the basic square *kutas* adjacent to each other, creating a longer rectangular structure or *vimana* called a *shala*. This was favoured for gateways, which had to be wider for carts to pass through. The third – the Bhima *ratha* – is of this type. The earliest entrance doorway of this style is in the Kanchipuram Kailasanathar Temple. This *shala* tower became typical of the imposing *gopuram*s or entrance

towers of many south Indian temples, especially of those built during the Vijayanagara period.

4. The development of the multiple *kuta*, one over another, is characteristic of the Dravida (or southern) style of architecture. Adjacent to the *shala* in is another, taller stacking of *kutas*. This fourth *ratha*, the Yudhishthira *ratha*, has space to walk in the first and second levels – but there are no stairs as yet.

5. Opposite these four *rathas* is one more structure, the Nakula Sahadeva *ratha*, with an elephant next to it. The elephant is there for a reason. The plan of the temple is apsidal. The *vimana* or temple tower is like the *kuta*, but the floor is neither square like the *kuta* nor Dravida (combination of many *kutas*), nor rectangular like the *shala*. This style of floor plan is *gajaprishta* – like the rear of an elephant. Curiously, this is found only in the northern part of Tamil Nadu.

temples are called *ashtanga vimana* or eight-limbed. Interestingly, they are all dedicated to Vishnu and are mostly in southern Tamil Nadu, in towns such as Cheranmahadevi, Mannarkovil and Thirukoshtiyur. The Vaikuntha Perumal Temple in Kanchipuram and the Uthiramerur Temple are others of this rare type.

The *gopuram* of the Kailasanathar Temple in Kanchipuram is made in the Dravida style

Generally, walls in temples are left plain. The *adhisthana* or the base has mouldings, which are stones cut into geometric shapes. Some, like in the Chola temples, feature a frieze, a horizontal band of sculpture, such as of animals. Then the wall is made of plain blocks of stone with *kostas* or small recesses, with pillars and a *torana* or a gateway with a statue inside.

The Hoysalas of Karnataka used the *phamsana* shape to create a new style. They focused on the temple ceilings and walls. They used a softer soapstone that was easy to carve. They took advantage of this and covered the external wall with extraordinarily detailed sculptures. Inside they showed the same detail on ceilings and in windows. Even the temple they built in Srirangam (in Tamil Nadu) for Venugopala has this style. This style did not continue after the dynasty died out.

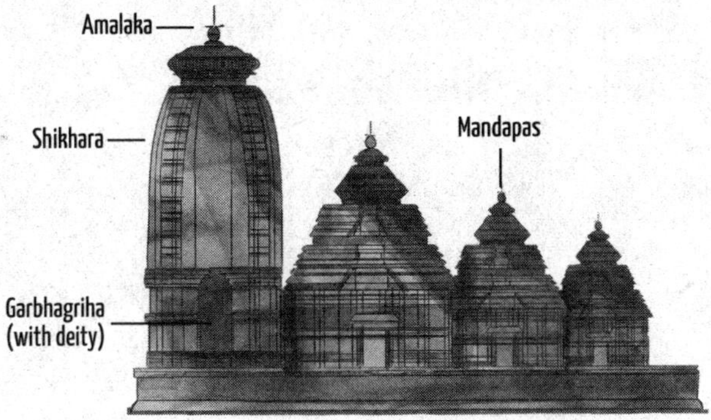

The Nagara (northern) style of temple architecture

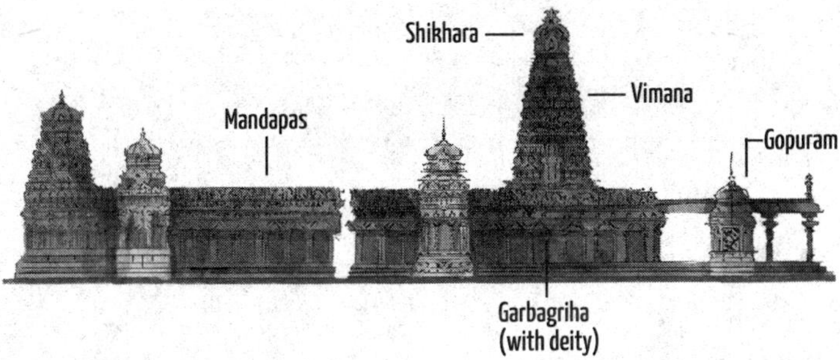

The Dravida (southern) style of temple architecture

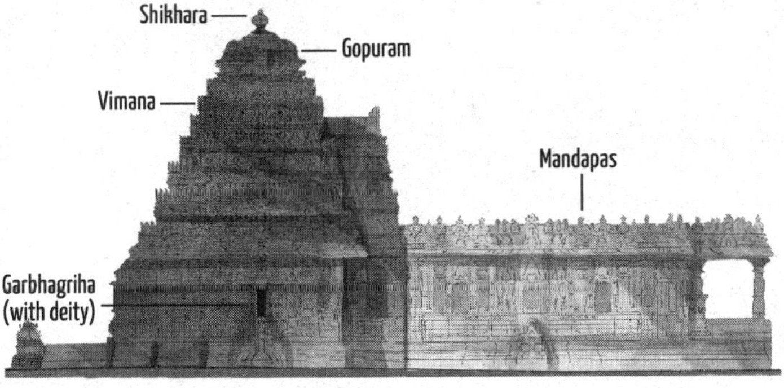

The Vesara style is a mix of the Nagara and Dravida styles of architecture

HOW THE TEMPLE GREW

This is a simple *kuta* with a square base.

When elongated into a rectangular base, the *kuta* becomes a shala.

Multiple *kutas* and *shalas* in an ascending order, smaller to bigger, make up a vimana in the Dravida style, like this one at Tirupati, plated with gold –

– or in this gopuram at Srirangam.

Kerala *gopurams* are also in the *shala* style (featured below) but with sloping tiled roofs to account for the rainy weather.

The *vimanas* are like the *kuta* but with sloping roofs for the same reason.

Kerala's rainy climate and lack of stone made wood and tiles a more practical choice. The *kuta* there was like a cone or the *phamsana* shape – a pyramid of thatched eaves, the underside of a roof.

Many temples in Andhra and Karnataka have this shape shown below.

In central India, the Guptas created a style known as the Nagara style. Here the *kuta* was taller and had a sharper curve. This *vimana* is called the *latina*. On the top, they had a finial, the ornament at the apex of a roof, not in the rounder shape of the Dravida style but in the gooseberry-shaped *amlaka*. This style rapidly spread to western India and Odisha.

Although all stone temple *vimana* styles go back to the fundamental *kuta*, the *kutas* were stacked over each other to create height in the Dravida style of the south. On the other hand, in the Nagara or north Indian style, the *latina vimana* was already tall, so these *vimanas* were stacked on the sides like hills surrounding a tall mountain. This style, known as the *shekhari*, is best seen in the main *vimana* of the Khajuraho temple complex in Madhya Pradesh. The second tallest *vimana* here is

The Khajuraho temples are typical of the Nagara style of architecture

in the *phamsana* shape. The temple in the back to the right of the image (on facing page) has the *latina* shape with a projection of the *shala* vimana that we saw earlier in Mahabalipuram.

Temple structures in the Chalukya times in Karnataka and Andhra are a little more complex because of the influences of both the Nagara and Dravida styles. Political enmity between kings did not prevent them from seeing, liking, adopting or experimenting with building styles they saw in other kingdoms.

GROWTH OF THE TEMPLE

Temples grew vertically and small, hut-shaped temples became larger, more complex, structures. This was done using stone, the most expensive material even today – and showed the willingness to spend the money needed. Larger temples meant more rooms as well.

All of this was for a reason.

There is a connection between the king, who had the money and power to build temples, and the people who primarily used the temple.

Even since the Vedic times in 4000 BCE, the chief of the clan was at the level of Indra, the king of the gods. There was a long tradition of connecting god to the king in other civilizations too, such as Egypt. By the first century CE, this had become a strong practice in south India. The temple became the representative of the king in the village.

HOW TEMPLES HELPED KINGS

What was the role of temples besides being places of worship?

They benefited the kings whom they represented. Anything people wanted the king or government to do was done by the temple for the community. Their stone walls with thick doors offered protection from external attacks. It was also a storehouse for water and food grains, in cases of an emergency.

Taxes to be paid to the king were paid to the temple and that made the temple wealthy. The kings also donated land to the temples, which in turn could be farmed, creating work opportunities, and the produce was taxed.

Sometimes, temples even encouraged people to bring new land into cultivation, which meant more money for the king, of which some part went to the temple. Temples also functioned as banks, and lent traders and others money to grow their businesses.

Temples were also places where people came together to enjoy music, dance or drama performances. The arts were incorporated into festivals and daily worship as well. These also provided jobs for actors, musicians and artistes, as well as carpenters, weavers, and others who assisted in the production.

Temples brought people together at temple festivals when different communities in the village worked together to perform rituals, and at temple processions when large wooden chariots (*rathas*) carrying metal images of deities, decorated with flowers and jewellery, were taken around the village. These occasions offered everyone, including visitors from other villages, much feasting, entertainment and merrymaking. It was like a big get-together! In this way, temples brought people together.

With so many activities at one site, the size of the temples too increased as time passed. More space was needed for the performances and storing the *vahanas* (chariots of the idols). Devotees funded the building of smaller shrines for their favourite gods. In the larger temples, there were many smaller shrines for the *parivara devata* – minor deities who were guardians of different geographical points within a temple.

As communities became wealthy, religious ceremonies too became more complicated. The earlier rituals had fire, water, food and music, but by the third century CE, temple worship rules were codified into *agamas* for each important god residing in it.

By the 10th century CE, daily worship meant 16 kinds of offerings to be made to the deity – just like at the palaces – including a seat, food, water, a ritual bath, fans, music, fly whisks and an umbrella. All of this needed storage space. Powerful ministers, relatives of the kings and even wealthy locals funded new festivals with land and even built *mandapas* or pillared rooms. Many were brightly painted, capturing scenes from various religious stories.

Festivals also needed larger and many types of metal deities, which in turn needed jewellery, clothes and flower garlands. The temples had many oil lamps to illuminate the structure at night; lamps needed oil, and people to clean them.

Rapidly, temples began to employ more and more people. Temple water tanks were not only used for festivals but also for the village, and supplied lotuses or water lilies for rituals. Some of the larger temples were pilgrimage centres, and devotees built rest houses and food centres for pilgrims. Temples also tended cows for milk and ghee (for lamps and cooking), and elephants for processions. They also had schools attached to them that imparted education on spiritual texts. Some also housed healing centres.

These many roles of the temples meant the small hut-shaped structures grew into massive complexes covering several acres, so much so that they became the central point for all activities in many villages and towns.

HOW TEMPLES WERE BUILT

In several places in south India, rulers had temples built into rocks. These amazing works of architecture and sculpture preceded stone structures and needed incredible precision. They took many years to build considering that all the work was done by hand, from the biggest to the smallest job. Immense and accurate planning was needed for these temples, some of which were carved into rock from the top downwards and others from the front to back.

A group of Hindu and Jain temples carved out of hills and rocks in Badami, Karnataka

There are many rock-cut temples in south India, some of the more well-known being the Badami cave temples in Bagalkot district of Karnataka. The most famous carving here is of Nataraja. The Pancha Rathas in Mahabalipuram in Tamil Nadu are also monolithic (made from one rock) and were made by cutting stone.

The actual process for building ancient temples is not known, but interesting secrets can be picked from *vastu vidya*, the body of knowledge related to architecture, from which came the *Vastu Shastras* – the ancient texts on architecture.

The origin story of this field of knowledge says that human beings were not able to fully understand the powers of the universe. Until the gods and goddesses tricked the *vastu purusha* – the human form of the universe – to lie face down on earth. Then, all the deities sat on top of him and created a *vastu mandala* – a grid where each deity has a square. This became the basis of temple construction, where it is the very representation of the universe on earth and each spot belongs to a deity.

Texts, such as the *Vimanarchana Kalpa* by Maharishi Marichi and different versions of the *Vastu Shastras* deal with how a temple needs to be built, and the various versions of *Shilpa Shastras* deal with rules for creating stone and metal sculptures for worship, stucco sculptures, wooden images and the paintings that decorate the walls or towers.

While there are many rules, there is a lot of freedom to innovate as well and create wonders. Some temples, such as those in Krishnapuram (Tamil Nadu) or Melkote (Karnataka), have stone sculptures or pillar decorations featuring finely carved stones. Here, holes have been drilled by hand into hard stone. In Krishnapuram, if you pass a thin wire through one ear of some of the sculptures, it will come out of the other ear or even the nose!

In Melkote in Vellore, Tamil Nadu, the pillars have complex patterns of stones carved into loops. Some temples have chains that move like metal but are carved in stone. The Nellaiappar Temple in Tirunelveli, Tamil Nadu, and the Vittala Temple in Hampi, Karnataka, have pillars made from stones with a high metal content so that sounds emanate from them when gently struck with wood. The Lepakshi Temple in Andhra has many stunning stone carvings, and the Veerabhadra Temple

Some south Indian temples have pillars, such as these in the Vittala Temple in Hampi, Karnataka, that emit musical notes when struck

even has a stone pillar that doesn't touch the floor completely but hangs from the ceiling!

Temples feature beautiful metal images and figurines too – images are often metal-plated, such as those capturing scenes from a procession. Chola temples house metal idols, while some, such as those in Srirangam and Alagar Kovil, are made of gold. Several temples, like Tirupati in Andhra and the Padmanabhaswamy Temple in Kerala, house coffers that hold gorgeous and expensive jewellery as well.

Even a small temple in a tiny village like Vazhuvur or Konerirajapuram, both near Thanjavur, Tamil Nadu, hold grand secrets. The Veerateeswarar Temple in Vazhuvur, Tamil Nadu, has a stunning human-sized bronze statue of a dancing Shiva emerging from within an elephant, holding the hide apart on both sides while doing so. It looks like he has ripped open the elephant from the inside as he steps out of it.

Shiva in the Vazhuvur Veerateeswarar Temple in Thanjavur (above) and a painting in the Jain Cave of Sittanavasal (below), both in Tamil Nadu

Konerirajapuram has a large idol of Nataraja, and another of Shiva and Parvati getting married. These were probably gifted by the sister of Rajaraja Chola, Kundavai, who built the large temple in Thanjavur. Many temples in the south, such as Ettumanoor in Kerala or the Jain cave of Sittanavasal, have paintings. Sadly, many of these are fading away owing to age, lack of maintenance and people vandalising them by writing over them, or touching them.

THE TEMPLE PLAN

There are five essential parts of a south Indian temple. All temples will have these but in different proportions. Even Jain temples in the south have the same plan. Sadly, no Buddhist temples remain, except for metal or stone images.

1. ENTRANCE THROUGH A *GOPURAM* OR ENTRANCEWAY

The door frame will be in stone. At the sides, you will see the leaf of the peepul (a tree sacred to all kings), or two women with a creeper emerging from their hands. One of them may be standing on a crocodile. These women represent the sacred rivers Ganga and Yamuna, symbolizing how water nourishes life.

Devotees will cross the step without placing their foot on it – an old tradition of respect. This is because the step demarcates the sacred space of the temple and the outside. The small physical act of raising the foot reminds us to behave more consciously inside the temple.

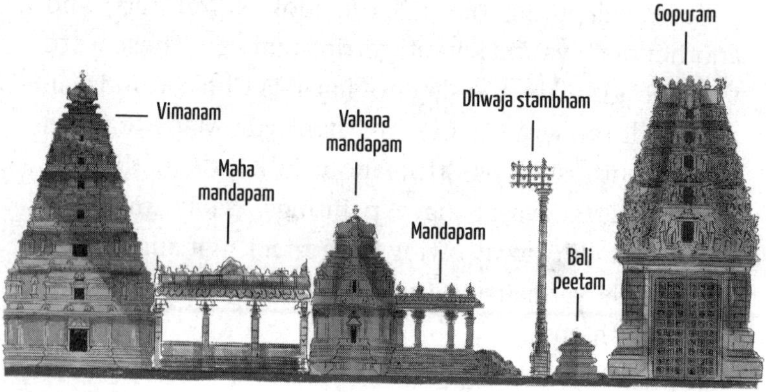

Basic parts of a south Indian temple

2. BETWEEN THE ENTRANCE AND THE MAIN SHRINE

Inside, you will find a flag post and a *bali peetam* – a raised platform with a circular top where food offerings are placed. You may, especially in Kerala temples, find many more of these *peetams* around the main sanctum where the main deity is. The flag post used to be a symbol of the king in the palace and, just as in a palace, you may see devotees praying to it. The *bali peetam* represents the various smaller gods and goddesses, most of them connected to elements of nature. For example, a *bali peetam* to the west represents Varuna or water, the one in the north-west is Vayu or wind, and the one in the south-east is Agni or fire. There are others as well.

All of them are offered food or cooked rice, before the main deity. This is a symbolic way of saying that less privileged people around us need to be looked after first. It also reminds the king or those in power that they enjoy their position only in the context of having others around.

In this space, especially in larger temples, you will find many *mandapas* on either side. Each of these pillared structures may have many sculptures. Watch out for a mythical beast – a lion with the trunk and tusks of an elephant. This is the *yali* or *vyali*, a favourite representation in south Indian sculpture.

In some cases, this area may have the temple tank. In some temples, you may find the tank outside the temple walls. This water is considered sacred, and one is usually not allowed to use soap in it or pollute it in any way. Some of the tanks may even have a *mandapam* in the middle for special prayers with the deity floating in a boat.

3. THE MAIN SHRINE

The main shrine or *garbhagriha* (meaning womb) is a small, dark space housing the main deity. The darkness probably represents the darkness at the beginning of the cosmos. Here are placed the metal deities used in processions, along with lamps, and other deities. Usually, behind the main deity is a *prabhavali* or metal arch to emphasise the form of the main deity. In Kerala, smaller metal deities will also have these – look for the delicate way in which the tongues of fire radiate from the arch.

Prabhavalis usually have two *yalis* – one on either side of the midpoint of the arch. On the top will be a

A *kirtimukha* on a pillar (left) and a *yali* (right)

kirtimukha, a lion face, sometimes with a long tongue hanging out. The legend is that the *kirtimukha* was created to defeat a *rakshasa*. Once this was done, it asked Shiva what to do next and Shiva playfully said, 'Eat yourself up!' The *kirtimukha* did precisely that and so because of its unquestioning belief in the god's words, the *kirtimukha* found a place closest to the gods in temples.

This is where the main pujas or prayers take place. Here, you will find something beautiful to see (the deity, flowers and decorations); something to touch (flowers, utensils, sandalwood paste); something to hear (bells, chants and songs); something to smell (fragrances, incense) and something to taste (the yummy *prasad*!).

You will also find that all circumambulation (*parikrama*), the act of moving around a sacred object, is done in a clockwise direction. These will include sacred plants or trees, a temple pond, and the deity/deities and the temple itself. Even the ceremonies are conducted in a clockwise direction because the earth moves that way and, thus, we are constantly reminded to follow the rhythms of nature.

In the olden days, and in some cultures even today, people would do a 360-degree turn while standing on the same spot followed by the *parikrama* around the deities, to remind themselves that God is as much within themselves as outside.

THREE IMPORTANT RULES OF ART

Temples feature multiple forms of art. You can look out for sculptures in stone and wood; or sculptures on the *gopuram* (entrance tower) and the *vimana* (tower above a shrine) in stucco – a mixture of lime, sand and an adhesive, such as jaggery, which can withstand the sun and rains; you can see creations in metal, such as idols of the deities but also lamps, vessels and other small items used for prayers. The *vahanas* and *rathas* are beautifully carved in wood and sometimes plated with brass, which is embossed and features beautiful designs. Then there are textiles – over 100-years-old samples from temples – now housed in museums. Some temples, such as the Srirangam Temple, have museums displaying many of these old artefacts.

Most towns and cities will likely have a museum showcasing artwork once connected to a temple. But how does one make sense of it and form connections? That's what we will look at now.

Generally, in India, the artist who created something usually never signed it with their name. The belief was that the creation was for the benefit or joy of the person who would use it rather than for the creator's own ego and pride.

South Indian sculptures are based on ancient texts called the *Shilpa Shastras*, which laid down the basic rules of beauty. Whether it was grand sculptures or small metal pots and lamps that the poorest of the poor used, there were some key principles to be followed:

1. ***Bhoghadhyam***: The object should be perfectly suited for the use it has been created for. For example, a sculptural panel should accurately tell the story of what happened accurately and must not make any mistakes in terms of who was there or what weapons they held. Or, if it was an oil lamp, the angle of the wick must be perfect so that the oil wouldn't drip outside the lamp and the wick would burn evenly without leaving soot on the lamp.
2. ***Sukha Darsham***: It must be pleasing to the eye. Symmetry and connection to nature were considered pleasing to the eye, such as in the symmetrical arrangements of pillars or sculptures in temples, and motifs inspired by or directly connected to nature, like a trailing creeper or the lotus flower. Nature and our environment were believed to *embody* divinity and were symbolic of coexistence.

3. ***Ramya*:** It must cause inner delight and/or make us think and reflect on whether we are following Dharma. The person looking at the sculpture of a goddess subduing a demon should be encouraged to examine if they have any evil qualities of the *asura* within themselves, and how to get rid of them; or what the qualities were that helped the goddess triumph over evil, and how they could develop those within themselves.

UNDERSTANDING A SCULPTURE

Sculptures and even paintings either depict individual deities, or a story.

According to the *Shilpa Shastras*, there are complex rules about how each deity should be depicted – how many arms, which weapons, whether they must be seated or standing, what jewellery they must wear and so on. These rules are listed even for the representation of celestial beings, such as *devas* and *rakshasas*.

The measurement of each deity was described with usually the length of the nose as the unit. The measurements of other body parts were in proportion to this.

When you see an image, it is likely to have a deeper meaning for how we need to think or behave. For example, a lotus blooms in dirty water and rises towards the sun. Every time we see a lotus in an object of art, the artist wants us to remember not to be guided by harmful thoughts and instead do things that give positive energy to people around us. To this end, you must ask the following questions when you see a sculpture:

- What am I seeing?
- What is the story I think the artist may be telling?
- Why have they shown it the way they have?

At the start, you may not find it easy to get an answer online or in books. Slowly, by observation and comparisons, you will start understanding how old the artwork is, of which dynasty, and from which state.

FOR INDIVIDUAL SCULPTURES

When looking at a sculptured image in a temple, you might have noticed that they always look straight back at you, especially if they are the main or an important deity. This deity will seem to look straight back at you with the same emotion with which you look at it – that's how the artisans meant it to be.

Note the weapons or objects they hold in their hands, as all of them have deeper significance. For example, a deer signifies a constantly jumping mind. In Shiva sculptures, you will see the deer he holds looking at him, telling us to focus on Shiva instead of being distracted. The image of a *hamsa* (a mythical swan-like bird said to be able to separate milk from water) reminds us to imbibe only good qualities, or focus on good lessons from difficult situations. A peacock symbolizes beauty; a cow, docility and generosity; a snake, fertility; an elephant represents grace and majesty; lion, courage; and a rat (Ganesha's vehicle), the ability to survive.

Here is an image (*right*) of a god seated in the '*lalita asana*' pose. His matted hair is designed into a crown. We know it is Shiva because of the long hair, the crescent moon and a lady's face (River Ganga) on his head. In one hand, he holds a *parashu* or battle-axe, in the other, a deer. One lower hand is in the *abhaya mudra*, offering protection; the other one holds the *dhatura* flower associated with him. He is seated on a *padma pita*, a base resembling a *padma* or lotus.

Some individual sculptures, like this one (*left*) currently in the Government Museum in Chennai, tell a story. This statue was originally in a temple in Udayagiri in present-day Odisha. When Vijayanagara king Krishnadevaraya conquered Udayagiri, he brought the sculpture from there and had a temple built for this deity where it still stands in Hampi. In the plunder following the fall of Hampi, conquerors removed it

BE A SCULPTURE DETECTIVE

No.	Aspect	Pallava 600–850 CE	Early Chola 850–1100 CE
1	Face and torso	Oval face, natural in pose and moulding; flat torso without much flexion, and flat nose	Somewhat circular face and sharp nose; torso moulded in front
2	Limbs and arms	Rounder and more slender, upper arms shoot off from the elbows	Start from shoulders, limbs shown slightly stiff
3	Headdress	Cylindrical	Tends to be conical
4	Emblems/ Attributes	Plain, held naturally in the hands, Vishnu's Chakra in *prayoga* fashion, as if it is going to be thrown to the front	Continues to be mode with the *prayoga chakra* in the conventional way

Here are clues to help you date the sculptures you see.

Late Chola **1100–1350 CE**	**Hoysala** **1026–1343 CE**	**Vijayanagara** **1350–1600 CE**
Tendency continues here: circular face, somewhat sharp nose	Oval and rigid in appearance, generally straight	Somewhat expressionless, prominently sharp nose, double chin, torso has traces of folds above the navel. *Tirumana* symbol appears on Vishnu's forehead
Slightly prominent; stress on anatomy	Start from shoulders, limbs shown a bit stiff	More prominently shown
Slightly tapering towards top	Conical, very heavily ornamented, sometimes very similar to the *latina vimana* style	Full; tapering with a bulb-like projection at the top; heavy decoration
Held in between the raised first and second fingers; thin flames added to Vishnu's emblems	Very highly ornamented with a long, downward projection also heavily carved with swags of bead type of ornamentation	Conch and discus decorated with festoons and flames, separately shown

No.	Aspect	Pallava 600–850 CE	Early Chola 850–1100 CE
		The deer and axe are shown towards the face of Shiva.	Still closer to the face
5	Sacred thread	Falling over the right arms in most cases; double clasp	
6	Shoulder tassels	Not seen in Pallava times on both sides	
7	Necklace	Single and simple	

Late Chola 1100–1350 CE	Hoysala 1026–1343 CE	Vijayanagara 1350–1600 CE
They are away from the image		Distinctly away from the image
Naturally shown in the usual position from left shoulder across the waist to the right side	Naturally shown in the usual position from left shoulder across waist to the right side of the hip	More detailed and wraps around the chest prominently
Slowly appear on the left side and then on the right side	On both sides till the armpits; very heavily ornamented, sometimes in three loops as well	Appear on both sides with decoration
Sometimes two are shown	Usually three: one close to the neck, unornamented; the next, till the chest; and the third, longer till the belly button. All very heavily ornamented	Ornamented with a visible mango pendant

from the temple and broke it. During the British times, it was moved to the museum. If only it could speak!

Buddhist and Jain images may look similar – both showing a seated human in meditation, sometimes with an attendant on either side. However, if you look closely, there are differences. The Jain Tirthankaras will be shown with an animal carved into their seat. Each Tirthankara is associated with one animal; for example, Rishabhanatha with a bull, and Mahavira with a lion. Some of the Buddhist metal deities may look like Hindu deities, but if you look closely at their crown, there will be a small image of the seated Buddha in the centre.

Here are images (*above*) of a Pallava Vishnu (*left*) and a Hoysala Vishnu (*right*) – check the differences based on the table on the previous pages.

Images from 1,300 years and before have relatively less ornamentation, but the human body is shown more naturally and realistically. Later, especially 800 years ago, during Hoysala rule in Karnataka, and Vijayanagara rule over south India, the body of the sculpture became stiff and great attention was paid to details like nails, veins in the wrist and feet, jewellery and even textile patterns. Early sculptures tend to have less detail but more lifelike figures. Later, there are more details but the natural form of the body is reduced; figures are posed, stiff and a little dramatic.

Can you make this out from the two images below? The first one is the earliest known Nataraja sculpture, from the Pallava period. Details are relatively fewer but notice the movement. Compare that with this later Vijayanagara image from the Madurai Nayak dynasty in

the temple of Thirukkurungudi – a lot of detail (check out the sandals) but the figure is rigid and stiff.

SECRETS OF SCULPTURES AND PAINTINGS

Sometimes it's obvious that a sculpture or a panel of sculptures is communicating an event or a sequence of events or the story of a person. Here are some simple guidelines to help you understand sculptures better, because most times there will be no captions near the image and, even if there are, it will be a few basic details, such as dates, the names of those featured and an event title.

PANELS TELL A STORY

Larger panels of paintings or sculptures tell longer stories. Here are a few basic tips and tricks to help you figure out what they are saying:

1. The movement of the story: The story moves from your left to the right as you face the image.
2. The central figure is important: Usually the most important person is depicted in the middle.
   If the centre is empty, then your eyes involuntarily start turning left and right, which is exactly what the artist wants you to do.
3. Size matters, clearly: The taller and bigger the person in the panel compared with the other figures shown, the more important they are likely to be. Notice the hands of the images; they will usually be pointing towards the main event.

The depiction of vertical clouds close to Bhima in this sculpture communicates that he is REALLY BIG compared to Hanuman, whose tail he is holding

In Thirukkurungudi in Tamil Nadu, a creative sculpture (*left*) shows Bhima (from the Mahabharata) unable to move the tail of the old monkey (actually, Hanuman). The clouds are used to show how tall Bhima has become!

Let us look at a popular example in Mahabalipuram, from the Pallava period, around 1,600 years ago. It is a massive sculpture, open to the sky, carved on the face of a 90x30-foot boulder located in the centre of the town. It is popularly known as the *Descent of the Ganges* or *Arjuna's Penance*.

Scholars differ on which story from the Mahabharata this represents: the penance of Bhagiratha, after which Shiva brought Ganga down to earth; or Shiva giving the *pashupata astra* (or weapon) to Arjuna after he meditated on a riverbank. Some believe it could be both. The key theme of the story is that Shiva gives something to a person (Arjuna, or Bhagiratha, or both) on the banks of a river.

READING A SCULPTURE

In the centre, Ganga is descending and almost in the centre, the tallest figure is Shiva with his palm facing front, fingers pointing down (the *varada mudra*, or the boon-granting pose). Notice the movement of all the others towards the centre – clearly the river is the focus. (We do not know why the sculpture is incomplete on the left.)

The central figure is important – at the centre, the cleft has been used to indicate a deep river and there are many *nagas*

(half snake, half human, living underground). This means that the river is important. Among the figures, Shiva is the largest, followed in size by the meditating sage standing on one foot. The ascetic is in deep penance. His hands are in the *mudra* of seeing the sun during mid-morning prayers. So, the size and the *mudras* of the figures tell us that Shiva gave something to the sage at mid-morning.

This Buddhist frieze (*left*) tells the story of King Suddhodana calling three soothsayers to interpret the dream of Queen Maya (the central figure), mother of Lord Buddha. A scribe records the interpretation.

The Jain temple in Thirupparuthikundram has 16th-century paintings on the ceilings and walls, with captions like in modern comic books. See the one below: on the top are royal figures praying to a Tirthankara to stay; you can then see that he leaves and stands alone.

These are only basic rules. The best way to become a good art detective is by observing sculptures and paintings, and learning about the stories narrated and events described in the related texts.

9

GRAND CITIES AND PORTS

A RICH AND PROSPEROUS REGION

During ancient times, people lived by themselves or, at best, as a few families together. From about the second century BCE, families began to cluster and these grew into villages. Some of these further grew into towns and even into bigger cities.

The difference between towns and villages is that towns had a stronger form of governance – a group of people who managed common issues, such as disputes, sharing of resources like water and collecting taxes. Cities were much larger and would even have armed forces to protect them. Mahabalipuram in Tamil Nadu or Muziris in Kerala had multiple communities of people staying together and these being ports meant that many sea vessels came here. Therefore, there was a need for a strong government presence to regulate these operations.

Places such as Kanchipuram, Badami and Warangal were certainly cities – they were large in size, they were the capital cities of kingdoms, and the literature of the time mentions them as being spread over large areas with fairly substantial populations.

Across south India's history, there have been many others towns and cities too. Some, such as Kodungallur (Muziris), have shrunk. Others, such as Hampi have completely collapsed, and present-day metropolises, such as Chennai, Hyderabad, Thiruvananthapuram and Bengaluru, have been created by merging many smaller villages, some of which have existed since ancient times.

BEING URBAN

There are many reasons why a village turns into a town or a city, a process known as urbanization. To start with, more land getting farmed, and improved ways of irrigating crops and storing the grain harvested are essential features. More food being made available means that more people can live in the area. This is why towns and cities are often found next to waterbodies.

Artisans creating items for sale and traders buying them to sell elsewhere is another reason for a village to urbanize. In Keeladi or Karur, the discovery of many beads indicates that there were many workshops making these to sell to traders, who in turn sold them in other places in India or even abroad.

Yet another reason was the presence of an important temple to which many people came, and offered gifts in the form of land or money. So, towns like Srirangam and Udupi owe their growth largely to the temples they flourished around. The Chidambaram Temple was the venue for the coronation of the Chola kings and it is very likely that it was already a city during their time.

The opposite of urbanization is deurbanization, the process by which cities become reduced to a smaller town or village. This could be because of changes in the water source – for example, Muziris lost its port, it is believed, when the River Periyar changed course; or it could be because of political changes, such as when Thanjavur was reduced to a village from a grand capital city when Rajendra Chola shifted the capital. Hampi was a large city by international standards, but became a small village after it was invaded and occupied. Kodumbalur is now a small village in Tamil Nadu – it was once a powerful city because of agriculture and

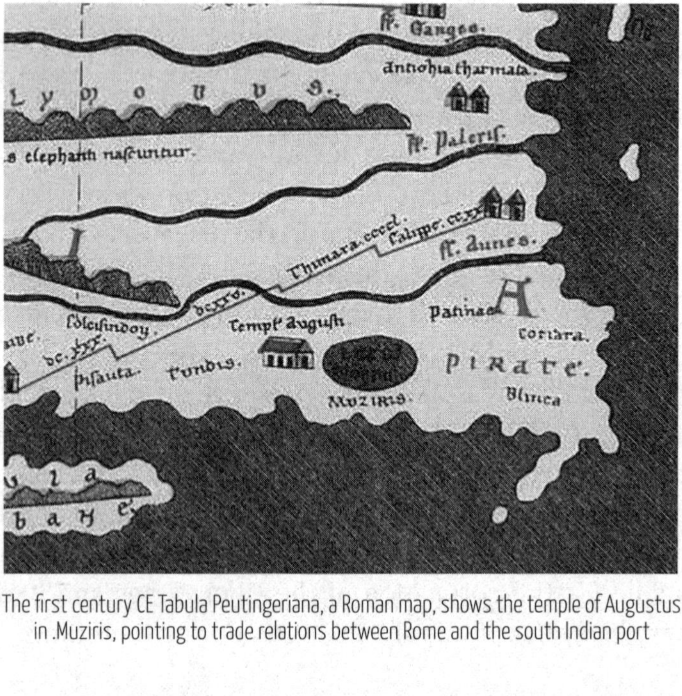

The first century CE Tabula Peutingeriana, a Roman map, shows the temple of Augustus in .Muziris, pointing to trade relations between Rome and the south Indian port

trade, but when the Chola Empire died out, Kodumbalur vanished except for a few huts and temples. History has many such stories of fall from glory.

Not much research has been done on ancient urbanization in south India. Tamil Nadu has early records in Sangam literature, which lends information to the archaeological excavations of sites in the state and other places in south India as well. Andhra is a fascinating area to research since, from the third century BCE till the third century CE, it was on the trade route between north and south India, and many travellers, such as Buddhist monks from India and abroad, visited it.

In Tamil Nadu and Kerala, juxtaposing the archaeological evidence and the Sangam poems, there were many important towns and cities, more because of the flourishing trade with Rome than because of agriculture. However, there were no formal trade organizations, only individual traders loosely organized to form guilds.

As mentioned earlier, the region was divided based on the *thinai* (or environment). The five ecological zones were connected by trade. Kurinji, the mountains, had aromatic wood and honey to offer. Mullai, the forests, were the areas through which traders passed from Tamil Nadu to Kerala and traded ivory, then an important export to Rome. Marudam was the land comprising rice fields and cattle farms.

The rulers were anxious to protect the area known as *vendan*, the part of the towns and cities focused on manufacturing. Kings fought each other to conquer ports on the coast. They also tried to hold sway over river routes, which were essential to operating trading ships and the wares they brought. The Neithal regions – sea coast or plains near water sources – housed the main ports, all of which would have been towns or cities.

There are many descriptions of what rapidly growing cities of south India looked like. All of these are from the literature of that time. Since they are in Tamil, they speak only of places in present-day Kerala and Tamil Nadu. However, foreign travellers like Xuanzang visited the south and their descriptions give us an idea of villages and cities in Karnataka and Andhra.

Based on these descriptions in verse and the many inscriptions from around 2,000 years ago, we can reconstruct a picture of what a town looked like and how it functioned at the time.

LIFE OF THE PEOPLE

A population of about 1,000 people in the past would have made a big city. Data on how long people lived is difficult to find. The number of children dying at birth was very high. If one crossed one's 15th birthday, there was a strong chance one could live till 50. Ancient medical texts, such as the *Charaka Samhita*, talk about 100 as the lifespan for a human. The detailed procedures for celebrating 60th and 80th birthdays as momentous occasions recorded in religious texts means that it was uncommon for people to live that long back then.

People identified much more with their family, their caste (occupation) and their town rather than the kingdom they were part of. Since all the issues of the town were resolved locally, they did not have much connection with the king except for paying taxes.

One-sixth of the food grain produced was owed to the king. This would usually be stored in the temple

VILLAGE TO CITY

Villages tended to be largely self-sufficient, using the barter system, and when that became complicated, everything began to be equated to one commodity. Initially, it was rice and salt (in the olden days, one measure of rice was equal to two measures of salt). This did not mean that coins didn't exist – many of the excavated sites have revealed a bounty of ancient Roman coins.

The Sangam texts don't mention complex systems of taxes, so experts think that most of the places would have been self-governed, with kings having very little control. By the third century CE, the Marudam and Neithal regions had grown wealthier. This was because the food sources here were more plentiful than in the forest and hilly regions. The rule of kings and the presence of traders meant more kinds of jobs were available – metalwork and weaving being two important trades. The Marudam region's villages were able to grow faster into towns and cities, and become relatively wealthier; they were able to purchase whatever they lacked from the forest and hilly regions (where the settlements were still small).

granary and used as payments to local officials and temple staff. The exchange of currency was possibly kept to the bare minimum.

Communities of people connected by their occupation tended to stay together. Even today, if you take a map of old cities, such as Chennai or Thiruvananthapuram, you will find many streets named after tradesmen, such as weavers or oil sellers. For example, there is still a street for coral merchants and an area of washermen. Some streets had an elaborate gate to mark as an entrance, and most towns may have had a protective 10-foot mud wall, with doorways.

Although we have information only from Tamil Nadu, we can make intelligent assumptions about shared commonalities between it and nearby regions. Towns tended to be located on the banks of rivers or around large tanks of water. Cities, such as Madurai, were continuously inhabited in various locations along the banks of the River Vaigai. And this was for more than 4,000 years!

The farming community lived together in an area called *ur*. The traders lived in an area called *nagaram*. The Brahmins lived in an area called *agrahara* near temples. Homes typically shared walls with each other and had back gardens for vegetables, fruit trees and greens. It was the usual practice to cultivate one's own vegetables. Wealthier people would have owned cows. Slavery and keeping of servants was quite widespread.

Houses with mud walls and thatched roofs would have been the most common – the mud baked in the sun would have been strong but would have needed to be repaired routinely. Wealthy people would have had homes built with brick and terracotta tiles, and very wealthy ones would have even had two-storeyed houses.

Foreigners were collectively called *yavanar* (from the root word Ionia, derived from Izmir in present-day Anatolia in Turkey, even though all the *yavanar* did not come from here). There were many *yavanar*s, some just visiting to trade, others settling in south India, where they had dwellings in the city. They lived together in one part of a city and this area had broad roads that were well lit even at night with oil lamps, according to the literature of that time.

On the roads across villages travelled the *nanadesi* or *desai ainuruvar*, who were merchants making their way, along with their caravans, over land from the east to the west coast. Highway robbers were a constant threat, so traders were well equipped with weapons and knew how to use them. Textiles were an important item of export as was pepper, which was carried in oval baskets slung over donkeys. Pearls, beryl and other semi-precious stones as well as expensive items, such as ivory, were sent in large quantities to Rome to make artefacts – in fact, Roman writer Pliny complained in his book, *Natural History*, that India was bleeding Rome of its wealth. India did not want Roman artefacts much, and preferred to get gold and silver instead.

WHAT'S IN A NAME?

Towns have changed over the centuries, but based on names, we can understand how closely people felt connected with the geographic location or the original purpose of the village. *Pakkam* were towns that were near the sea, *paadi* was the cantonment for armies, and *kurichi* a place near the mountains. *Puram*, *cheri* and *pettai* all indicated a large town. *Kulam* (for example, Ernakulam in Kerala) and *samudram* are indicative of a large waterbody close by. In Kerala, *puzha* and *nadi* mean rivers, and villages, such as Thodupuzha or Alapuzha are towns situated on the banks of rivers. Again, in Kerala, *kal* and *vai* could also be towns near the sea, the estuary or the backwaters. Many towns in Kerala end with the word *kadu* – those were places next to forests. *Thurai* or *azhi* means a harbour; Mahabalipuram, for example, was called *'neer peyal thurai'*.

Places were often called by names based on their geographical location or highlight, such as the harbour of Mahabalipuram (with its famous Shore Temple)

CITIES IN TAMIL NADU AND KERALA

The most detailed descriptions of cities come from the Sangam texts, such as the *Silappadikaram* and *Manimekalai*. It is very likely that they can apply not only to cities in Tamil Nadu but also to a port town such as Kodungallur (Muziris) in Kerala. We have lengthy descriptions of Madurai that even mention thieves who were scared of the night police.

Another text talks of a lighthouse in Mahabalipuram, where ships from Greece and Rome anchored, and which was a port of the Pallavas. An elaborate account of Mahabalipuram can be found in a song called the '*Perumba Naatru-padai*' from an anthology called the *Pathu Pattu* ('Ten Songs'). In this, the poet Uruthiran Kannanar sings of King Tondaiman Ilantirayan:

> *The crowds are like warriors who swarm the port;*
> *The port is beside the sea where women lose their* makara *fish-shaped earrings to the sea;*
> *The birds mistake these for the* sikkili *fish and pounce on them and take them to the shore;*
> *In the rocks they discover that these are not fish and cast them away.*
> *Near the sacrificial fires of the Brahmins*
> *The heaps of these earrings are like the lanterns of the Greeks in their ships,*
> *And they shine like the stars in the sky –*
> *Such is the town of Neer Peyal Thurai!*
> *On the outskirts of the town, horses that are the colour*

A 16-century CE wide-angle painting of Calicut (now Kozhikode in Kerala) shows different kinds of boats and ships, boat repair work, net fishing, a fort-like structure, houses and even an elephant!

of milk, with white manes, are among the many treasures in the ships from northern lands;

Beside these are the double-storeyed houses of fisherfolk, and those of other trades, and a large building that serve as the treasury;

Each house is prosperous, with many cattle, goats and sheep;

The women of the houses wear twisted anklets on their pretty feet;

Their necks are festooned with green beads, their heads with stalks of the konrai *blossoms.*

They sleep peacefully at night and wake up

As gracefully as the peacocks dancing in the hills in monsoon;

They walk slowly to the sound of their anklets among the fine houses that kiss the sky, and play with balls on the terrace to the sound of their bangles;

The game continues on the pearly white seashore.

If you are bored of watching this spectacle, entertain yourself in one of the many hotels,

Each one strewn with flowers with red petals, and entrance arches with fine carvings;

The drinks are made by pretty women;

The shops around have the slush of the washed vessels where pigs drink the liquor and rice flour with relish;

The male pig savours this in his family's company, and you too will savour it.

Towering above the city is the lighthouse, like a prop that holds the sky from falling;

No man can climb it; no ladder can match its height;

At its top is a balcony on which a lamp is lit to welcome ships from foreign lands –

Such is the great city of Mamallapuram.

Coastal towns seemed to have been very prosperous because of the flourishing trade. The poet Kapilar, from more than 2,000 years ago, mentions the fleet of ships that made the Chera king prosperous. In Kerala, at this time, as gleaned from Sangam poems, the caste system was not as rigid as one expects it to be.

In Kerala, villages had a *manram* (referred to in the present-day as *mannam*, and *ambalam* in Tamil Nadu) that served as a meeting place. Music, dance and theatre were popular pastimes. Performances included several string, wind and percussion instruments and *panars* (singing bards) performed here.

Today, this is re-enacted when we see artistes perform the *villupattu*, in which they hold a stick and beat a stationary bow with bells to a rhythm, making the bells jingle. While seeing performances using such instruments, one can't help but be transported to a time in the past: cool evenings warmed by bonfires, the soft glow of oil lamps illuminating the venue, the wind carrying the aroma of cooked food, and people chatting in between sips of drinks made from palm fruit.

Of course, everything did not remain uniformly prosperous. Between 410 to 470 CE, Rome was attacked by the Visigoths from northern Europe. In 470 CE, Rome was finally conquered and trade with India was severely affected. In the fifth century CE, the towns and cities across south India that relied on trade with Rome must have been impacted. Many would have become deserted ghost towns overnight.

Trade with Europe, through the Arabs, and trade with South-East Asia did continue, but, looking at the literature and inscriptions of that time, domestic trade seems to have become more important. From then on, villages, towns and cities continued to benefit from local traders. Even if these tradesmen did not make as much money as before, they did have enough business to pay taxes in the towns they passed through. They even constructed temples or repaired temples on the way.

Between 1,300 and 1,500 years ago, much of Kerala was occupied by the Chalukyas. Jainism and Buddhism were the more popular religions of that time. However, after these religions declined in popularity, we don't have much information about this period. Just after Kerala was conquered by Rajaraja Chola, the Kulasekhara rule ushered in a level of prosperity because of extensive trade. We read of traders becoming very wealthy and powerful by following a very honest way of doing business. Chinese traders purchased pepper, cinnamon, teak wood, ivory, pearls and cotton fabric, while they sold fishing nets, silk and porcelain ware in south India.

There were schools in both Kerala and Tamil Nadu. For the Brahmins, since their main role lay in interpreting law and assisting the king in the administration of the villages, schools were close to their temples. Their lessons started very early in the morning. This included not just the study of religious texts but also law books and practical maths. They also took lessons in astronomy to communicate matters relating to time and the seasons to the community.

Other communities, especially craftspeople, probably did not have formal schools like the Brahmins. Their learning was more practical. They learnt the skill of their parents by keen observation and practice.

Proverbs, stories and songs were all educational in nature and directed towards how to live in a community and learn to accept change. The *Tirukkural* written by Thiruvalluvar and the verses of poetess Avvaiyar are some examples that emphasize living harmoniously. In Kerala, particularly, there were schools teaching the traditional martial art *kalari* and special training was offered to be a *chaver*. *Chavers* made up suicide squads to protect the king or important trade warehouses.

From travellers, we have a description of the Kulasekhara king's capital, Mahodayapuram. It had different localities, like the *senamugham* where the army lived, and another called *kottakakkam*, where the king had his palace. One area had an observatory as well. From inscriptions of the Kulasekhara period, we have lists of taxes that people had to pay on the produce after harvest or on professions, or even on ladders used to climb up trees to get coconuts!

The capital of Venad, Kollam, reflected the wealth of the cities because of international trade that took place here around 1,100 years ago. It was a docking point

THE MERCHANT GUILDS

Both in Tamil Nadu and Kerala, there were strong merchant guilds. These were groups of merchants who cooperated and collaborated to protect their rights and safeguard their interests. They were also very generous. They made several donations or improvements to local temples not just because of their faith but because contributing to a temple meant giving to the community and providing employment.

The Tharisapalli copper plates in Kollam, Kerala, record a royal grant by Ayyan Adikal, the chieftain of Kollam, to a Syrian Christian merchant called Mar Sapir Iso. From this, we learn that merchants even took care of the defences of Kollam town.

A similar inscription in Tirukoilur in Tamil Nadu mentions how a village supported a group of traders. In return for the villagers'

hospitality, traders brought from them essentials, such as salt for their homes, and also paid tolls and taxes that increased the village income. Such close and harmonious connections existed also with traders who were Christian or Jewish.

The Quilon copper plates (above); a coin of Roman emperor Augustus found in Pudukkottai, Tamil Nadu

for Chinese junks (ships) returning from Arabia. The travellers praise the king's officials who immediately visited a ship that entered the port. They noted down the details of the ship and its cargo, and reported back to the king. The ruler offered them a great sense of security. So much so that they could even enter open fields without worrying for their own safety or their ship's. The markets and streets were lit at night and much of the business happened at that time to avoid the heat of the day.

The Samuthiri, the prosperous ruler of Calicut, was described as wearing pearls and other jewellery by travellers to Calicut (Kozhikode), as seen in this painting of Vasco da Gama meeting the ruler

Pepper, cinnamon and ginger are listed as the most important trading goods of Kollam.

Besides the chronicles of travellers, the many songs composed by the Alvars in praise of Vishnu and by the Nayanars in praise of Shiva mention several temples in south India. Many of these comprise long descriptions of towns and talk about beautiful trees, wide streets and wonderful houses. But most frequently, they speak of the people: honest, helpful and pious.

Later descriptions of Kerala are hard to come by, but there are references to Karnataka and Andhra from the Vijayanagara times, and Tamil Nadu was likely to have been similar as it was part of the same empire. Here, as in Karnataka and Andhra, the temple was the centre of life in the town. People would go there at least twice a day, and the temple or a place close to it in the centre of the town had an *ambalam*, a place for public meetings. Members of the town or village met here and took decisions about important matters. Cases of corruption

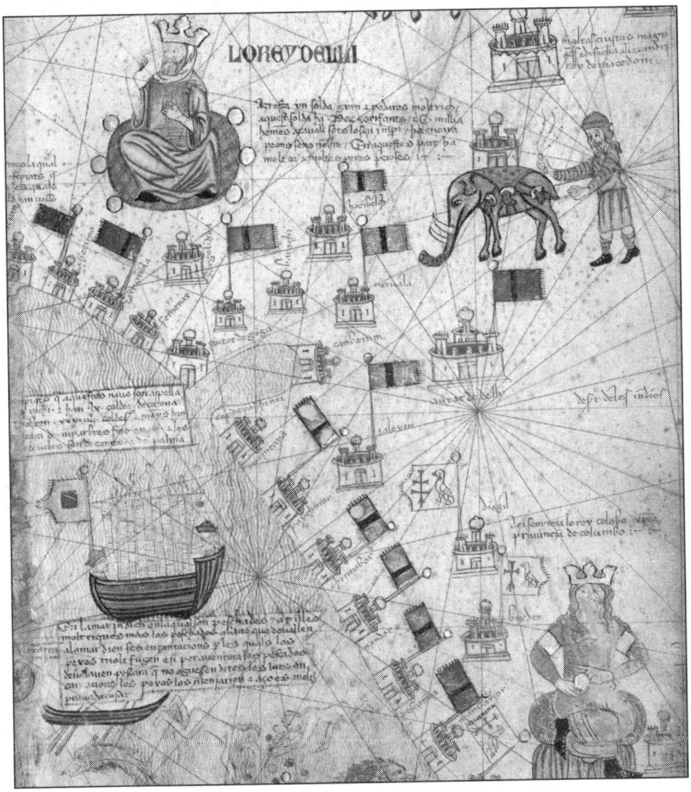

A section of the Catalan Atlas of 1375 CE shows the Sultan of Delhi on the top right and the king of Vijayanagara at the bottom. What else does this tell you?

and stealing would be judged here. This space was also used for entertainment. The most popular forms were dramas with music and dance. These were usually re-enactments of the epics and actors – only men – through music and dance, gave people hope or helped them think about deeper issues in life, such as good and evil. This group of entertainers was usually paid by the village from the common income collected in taxes.

MARCO'S MEMOIRS

Marco Polo (1254–1324 CE) was a merchant from Venice, Italy, who travelled to Asia. Many others did too, but he wrote about it and it made him famous. His book is one of the most well-known travelogues in history. He started his travels when he was just 17–18 years old and lived in China for 17 years. He was a favourite of the Chinese emperor Kublai Khan. When the emperor was in his eighties, he reluctantly allowed Marco Polo to go back. It was on this journey by ship that Marco Polo is said to have skirted the east and west coasts of India.

He himself admits that some of his accounts describe not what he saw but rather what he heard from other travellers. There are also many versions of his manuscript. However, his work is important because it offers a flavour of life in India at the time and it inspired others in Europe to set sail to India for its spices.

While writing about Kerala, he complained of the intense heat. In fact, he wrote that the water in the rivers was so hot that if an egg was dropped into the river, it would get boiled!

He was shocked that people wore very little clothing and all of it unstitched, just wrapped around; but who needed clothes when rich people wore so much jewellery! The king had a necklace of rubies, emeralds and sapphires; he was covered from his neck to his waist with strands of pearls. He says the king wore bracelets of gold and gems on his limbs, and all his jewellery was equal to the riches of a whole city. Most of his descriptions are of traded goods. He mentions indigo – cloth made using this dye was highly prized in Europe. (Indigo is the pigment later used to give denim jeans their typical blue colour, but now they are dyed synthetically.) Marco Polo describes the entire dyeing process.

He concluded that 'everything they have' is better than 'what we have'.

Marco Polo travels to the East

KARNATAKA AND ANDHRA

The overall pattern of towns and villages here more than 900 years ago would not have been dissimilar to Tamil Nadu and Kerala. We get some information on Karnataka from the *Manasollasa* (or *Abhilashitartha Chintamani*), the 12th-century CE Sanskrit text composed by the Kalyani Chalukya king Someshvara III. However, the more detailed accounts for this region, both before and during the Vijayanagara rule, are from the accounts of the many foreign travellers who visited this region.

From inscriptions, we know that the Chalukya merchants came together to form guilds to fix prices, lent money to one another and travelled together for the sake of safety. Kalyana, Managorut (Mangaluru) and Malé were important ports.

We also have information on the weights and measures of the products they traded in: a *mana* was equivalent to 11.2 kg and a *peru* to about 17.28 kg. *Rajamana* was a standard weight. During the Rashtrakuta period, we get to know about copper mines in present-day Bellary and diamond mines in Golconda. Textiles from the region were also sold to the Arabs in return for gold coins.

Traders came to south India's ports from China, Malaysia and Sri Lanka. They bought spices and cotton textiles, and sold their silk. South India also had traders from Persia and Arabia, who mostly sold dates and traded horses. South India offered nearly 50 different types of silk, according to the *Basava Puranam*, a 13th-century CE Telugu epic poem by Palkuriki Somanatha.

The coastal cities had many traders; as money and expensive goods were exchanged here, they were often protected by fortifications. Konangi, Motupalli and Masulipatnam were a few of the larger ports with forts. Ports levied taxes called *oora rooka* and *ulvari* on traders.

From inscriptions in Andhra from the 12th to 15th century CE, we know of groups or 'castes', called *samayas*. Villages had very few of them, but a town or a city would have had all 18 *samayas*. If new professions came up, one of these would break off into a smaller sub-caste or subgroup. These 18 castes were:

Mahajanulu: Brahmin
Sri Vaishnavulu: Priests of Vishnu temples
Komatlu: Traders
Kampulu: Protectors and cultivators of land
Telikivevuru: Oil mongers, who made and sold oil
Salevaru: Weavers
Gollavaru: Shepherds
Akkasalavaru: Metal workers
Sanivaru: Women employed by temples
Vadrangulu: Carpenters
Kummarulu: Potters
Vastrachchedakulu: Tailors
Charmakarulu: Shoemakers
Rajakulu: Washermen
Kshurakarulu: Barbers
Balinja-setti kandru: Toddy tappers
Boyalu: Hunters/watchmen
Kammarulu: Blacksmiths

MORE TRAVELLER'S TALES

An early description of Andhra comes from the accounts of Chinese pilgrim Xuanzang, who travelled across many parts of India 1,500 years ago. Since he was a Buddhist scholar, he primarily recorded the lives and times of Buddhists.

While in Andhra, he first travelled across Vengi – the land between the rivers Godavari and Krishna. Pedavegi is a small town today, but in those days, it was a big city, the capital of the Vengi line of Chalukyas. Xuanzang mentioned many Buddhists there as well as Hindus and Jains. He described the weather as hot and the people as warrior-like.

Describing a Buddhist monastery in the region, he spoke of how it had many storeys, with beautifully painted towers and balconies. He then moved on to Dharanikota and Amaravati. The remains of the Amaravati stupa can be viewed in the Government Museum in Chennai. Some of the panels have detailed carvings of the Jataka stories from Buddhist literature. He said the people here were fierce and impulsive. He also mentioned that the temples in Nagarjunakonda received many travellers.

From there, Xuanzang travelled further to Kanchi and then on to western India through Karnataka. He entered what is present-day Maharashtra, then partly ruled by the Chalukyas of Karnataka. He said that the soil was fertile, the climate was hot, and the people simple and honest. They were extremely helpful and, at the same time, did not hesitate to take revenge on those who had done them harm. We are not sure which city in this Chalukya kingdom he visited, but he does mention a Buddhist centre of learning with more than 5,000 priests. This was an enormous number of priests to be housed in a shrine those days. He also praises the high level of education in the area. He also visited the Ajanta Caves and mentioned the fabulous cave paintings! From there, he moved to Bharuch in Gujarat.

An eighth-century CE cave mural in China depicts Xuanzang's return from India

Each of these groups had their own associations or guilds, elected leaders and strict rules, which, if ever flouted, would mean eviction from the group and even the village/town. They participated in administrative issues, ensured that the quality of their work was good and resolved any disputes people had over their level of service. *Samayas* also owned communal land and collected their own taxes from their members. They even acted as the king's representative, weighed the harvests, and ensured that the share of the harvest due to the king was paid. Some of them were also part of the *ayagar*, a set of 12 hereditary officers.

The *ayagar* was appointed by the king in each village or town, and was responsible for checking that the gift deeds made by kings and others in the past were properly executed. They were paid for this service through fees (*mirasi*) or with tax-free lands. Some of them were called *reddi*, *karnam*, *talari* or *niru kattu*.

Kingdoms earned a lot of wealth from trade and agriculture. Land tax was imposed. Gold and silver coins were in circulation. In the villages, taxes such as the *pullari* and *angati mudhra* were collected; these were mostly levied on agricultural produce or professions, such as metal working or wood carving.

The kings of Orugallu (now Warangal in Telangana) established hospitals, baby-birthing centres, and higher education centres to teach Sanskrit and the Vedas. Any disputes on taxes were usually resolved locally.

The *Pandithardhya Charitra*, written by Palkuriki Somanatha, gives us information about present-day Warangal and the main towns of the Kakatiya kings. He mentions that people in the villages were slowly adopting Hinduism, especially Veera Shaiva or a hyper-focused form of worshipping Shiva. This meant that many Buddhist and Jain temples were being turned into Shiva temples or simply abandoned.

With the rise of the Vijayanagara kings in 1336 CE, Hampi, on the banks of the River Tungabhadra, became the most important city in the south. It was so beautiful and rich that people from across the world came to marvel at it. We have an enchanting description by Abd-Al-Razzaq, the Persian ambassador to Kozhikode:

> The city was surrounded by seven thick stone walls with several acres of space within each wall. The final few acres of land were within the city itself. All the gates were made of thick wood and were manned by soldiers who inspected everything passing through it carefully and collected the taxes due.
>
> Inside, the bazaars near the king's palace sold pearls, rubies, emeralds and diamonds. Kings tried to attract merchants from other far-off lands to come and settle here. They lived in houses with flat roofs. There were also many streams that ran in canals made of chiselled and polished stone. The palace had several rooms including many that stored big bars of gold. The elephant stables had roofs made of strong wood. The mint was close to the governor's home and was guarded by a large army of 12,000 soldiers.

Al-Razzaq travelled to these regions in 1440 CE. While in Hampi, he mentions a grand three-day festival, which the king viewed from atop a nine-storey tower (probably the pyramidal '*dibba*' in Hampi). It featured elephants in full armour, and dancers wearing stunning jewellery and dancing behind a screen. The writer was bedazzled by the golden throne and a square cushion sewn with three rows of pearls on which the king sat.

The extant monuments and ruins of Hampi in Karnataka give a sense of how vast and prosperous the area must have been under the Vijayanagara kings

In between all the descriptions of wealth and the good life, we also find some peculiar notes, for instance, a description of footwear! Domingo Paes, who visited Hampi during the reign of Krishnadevaraya, says:

> ...no one ever steps into a room being visited by the king, unless he is barefoot. The shoes worn by rich people had pointed ends in the ancient manner, and there are other shoes that have nothing but soles, but on top are some straps that help to keep them on the feet. They are made like those which the old Romans wore.

There are other descriptions of important cities in the Vijayanagara times and all of them speak of how wealthy the cities were and how they were filled with traders selling different goods and visited by many people from the world over. The cities were surrounded by fertile land and farms that grew rice and other food crops.

With the arrival of the British, trade became even more important not only for wealth generation but also for political power, and new cities, such as Madras, came to be. However, the critical change was not only that wealth slowly moved to British cities, but more of it went out than came in. India continued to be an important country for trade, but now it supplied raw materials for British factories. India stopped being a producer of luxury goods that had commanded high prices, and became a producer of raw materials and consumer of British goods, which made the British wealthy.

10

LANGUAGE AND LITERATURE

A TREASURY OF LANGUAGES

Imagine not being able to talk about your day with your friends or family! Language is an important part of our identity as it is the primary way in which we can socialize with others. Our ability to verbally communicate with others is vital to the human experience of living.

Literature, which is a product of the written form of language, gives us an insight into our and others' lives and thoughts. How we live, what we think and what we do, recorded in literature, act as a portal into the past. It shows us how a culture or a region has changed and developed over centuries.

The four main languages of south India – Tamil, Telugu, Kannada and Malayalam – and Sanskrit have several thousand volumes of writing, including stories, poetry, plays and grammar. Over centuries, languages have also frequently borrowed and learnt from one another. Today, language has become a political tool for some people and there are bitter exchanges over which is the 'older' and, therefore, more 'superior' language. It's more important to understand instead how language can unite people, and how its various expressions in literature, from which people can learn important things, can move people to do phenomenal things now and in the future. It can also offer us hope in difficult times and express thoughts in an evocative way. A conversation around how the languages of south India grew and added richness to the lives of people is a more valuable discussion to have.

There were kings and kingdoms that favoured one language over another. Likewise, there were just as many kings and kingdoms that supported many languages at the same time. As these south Indian languages developed, there was a simultaneous contribution to and growth of Sanskrit as well in each of the four main south Indian languages. Most kings and poets of the region would have been conversant in more than one language and some, such as Shahaji of Thanjavur, could even do incredibly complex things like compose a Telugu poem using the rules of Sanskrit grammar.

Some unique works are peerless treasures, such as the Sanskrit works by the linguistic genius Chidambarakavi of Thanjavur. Read from left to right, his *Shabdartha Chintamani* narrates the story of the Ramayana, and read from right to left, it tells the story of Krishna! The *Kathatrayi* does the same with the Ramayana and the *Bhagavatam*.

KANNADA

The oldest evidence we have of the script of Kannada, the language spoken in Karnataka, is from about 1,600 years ago from Halmidi village in Hassan district. An inscription from the time of the Kadamba king Kakustha records a royal gift in the form of a poem. From this, we can conclude that even then the language was developed enough to have a tradition of poetry rather than be used as simple text, and that it was commonly understood. The inscription on a stone slab was originally found buried and was erected by some villagers in the temple. Sadly, children had used it for stone target practice till its importance was realized in the 1930s and it was moved to the Mysuru office of the archaeology department.

The script is cursive and does not yet have the box-shaped cap on top of each letter of the alphabet that is called *tallekattu* (the mark denoting the vowel sound – like the *matra* in Hindi – to the consonant in Indian

Old Kannada inscription at Akkana Basadi in Shravanabelagola, Karnataka (1182 CE)

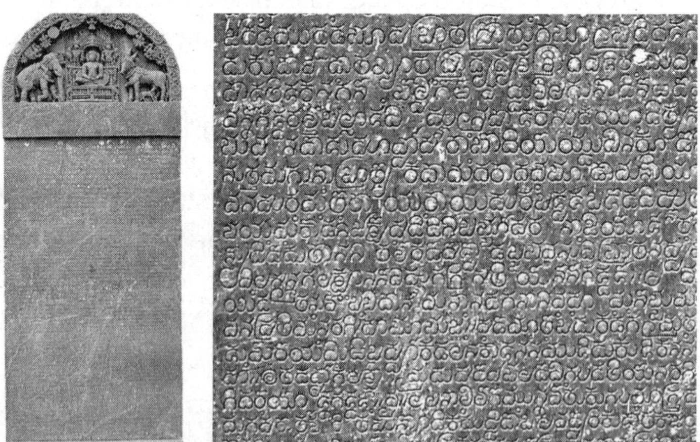

and South Asian scripts). The absence of the line on top allows the script to be written in artistic ways and many later Kannada stone inscriptions from the Hoysala times, in places like Akkana Basadi at Shravanabelagola, are works of art because of their calligraphic style.

Some believe that much before the time of the Halmidi inscription, both Tamil and Kannada were dialects of the same language and they developed differently. Kannada, then, would have been spoken by the common people, and a mixture of Kannada and Prakrit spoken in the royal courts. Prakrit, a language older than Sanskrit, was spoken across most parts of India by the common folk. Looking at sculptures and paintings, it seems that the villages and towns would have reverberated with songs and poems to which they even performed dances.

Very few of these remain today. The move from villages to cities for employment and the popularity of other forms of media and entertaintment, such as films, have caused many art forms in the villages to either die out or lose patronage.

Inscriptions from around 1,000 years ago abound in Shravanabelagola. The hill is famous for Jain shrines and, just as in Tamil Nadu of that time, Kannada and Tamil were extensively used by Jain monks. It is possible that Jains and Buddhists preferred to use local languages, such as Kannada and Tamil, to reach out to people to follow their religion. Most of the Kannada inscriptions are records of gifts to Jain *basadi*s or temples, and many are in verse, spelling errors included!

The ancient texts in Kannada range from poems to prose, and from philosophy to retellings.

Rashtrakuta king Amoghavarsha I's *Kavirajamarga* (sometimes thought to be written by the theorist Sri Vijaya), a work on how to write skilful poems, is a famous text, which gives us information on the life and culture of the people, including the fact that ordinary folk understood and used the rules of poetry.

A favourite form of writing was the *champu*, a mix of poetry and prose. We have many of them on Jain philosophy or on the lives of the Jain teachers or Tirthankaras, such as the *Adi Purana* and *Parsvabhudaya* by Jinasena, a Jain monk.

Vikramarjuna Vijaya by Pampa, who lived around 940 CE, is considered one of the greatest works of its time. Interestingly, it is a condensed version of the Mahabharata but with the inclusion of Jain ideas, and equates his patron, King Arikesari II (930–55 CE) of the Rashtrakuta dynasty, to Pandava prince Arjuna.

The Hoysalas were also generous patrons of the language. The many texts composed during their rule are quietly waiting in many libraries in Karnataka, to be translated into other languages. *Girija Kalyana*, describing the marriage of Shiva and Parvati, by Hariharadeva, is one such example.

During this time, works like Kesiraja's *Shabdamanidarpana*, a book on Kannada grammar, helped the development of the language. The *Govidya* by poet Kirtivarma is considered to be the earliest

Kannada work on medicine. This was also the time of the *vachana*, literally meaning 'dialogue', written by those deeply devoted to Shiva. One of the composers, Palkuriki Somanatha, was proficient in Telugu as well. Basava or Basavanna was among the most famous writers of *vachanas*.

Kumaravyasa (pen name of Viranaranappa of Gadag), who wrote the *Karnata Bharata Kathamanjari*, a poetic rendition of the Mahabharata, and the work of the Haridasas, devotees of Lord Vishnu, are important texts of the period. The Haridasas were wandering saints and singers who propagated the teachings of Madhavacharya Some, like Kanakadasa and Purandaradasa, composed and sang many songs to comfort and give hope to the poor. They were in Kannada and had the same ideas as the poems of the kings and nobles in Sanskrit: of devotion to God, being kind to others, and seeing God in everyone and everything. For example, in one verse, Purandaradasa talks to his own tongue. He asks it not to be petty and to not blame others without thinking about what mistakes it could have made. He then requests his tongue to not backbite. He wished it helped him instead, in chanting the names of Rama, the ruler of the world.

During the Vijayanagara period, while Telugu achieved more prominence, Kannada poets, such as Kumara Vyasa, wrote the Mahabharata in Kannada. The script during this time, especially on stone inscriptions, became larger and less artistically written.

RICE VERSUS RAGI: A DEBATE

Kanakadasa's work *Ramadhanya Charithe,* written about 500 years ago, criticized the growing differences between the rich and the poor. He did this by comparing wealthy folks to the rice they ate, and the poorer ones to the ragi they consumed. In his work, rice and ragi are two characters debating which is the best. Rice says it is superior because it is found in the feasts of kings, in rituals (used as *akshate*), in the daily food offerings to God as *naivedya*, and as the first solid food to infants; also, it is found in Brahmin homes.

Ragi replies and reminds rice to raise its eyes and see the poor people and not just follow those with money. It reminds rice that it is ragi that gives nourishment to pregnant mothers, people who are ill, and when there is a famine or any calamity, it sustains all animals and people, since rice may not be available readily.

Conversations dealing with social issues are very often found in *champu* poems. The deeper meaning is to remind everyone of the core belief of an agrarian society – that everyone in the community is equally needed by others. The rice versus ragi verse would have also generated much laughter, but in the humour is a subtle and powerful lesson for us.

An artist's impression of Kanakadasa

TELUGU

The name of the language spoken in present-day Andhra and Telangana is probably derived from *ten* or honey (meaning as sweet as honey). Scholars say that it is composed primarily of words of Sanskrit and Prakrit roots, but old inscriptions in Prakrit contain Telugu words when mentioning land boundaries, so there must have been an old language that incorporated Sanskrit or Prakrit words to create new hybrid words in Telugu. By the seventh century CE, it had become a sophisticated language, with more rules of grammar, and important works of literature began to be produced exclusively in Telugu. It was spoken in Andhra – the coastal region and the area where the rivers Godavari and Krishna flow; Telangana – the dry central region of fierce warriors; and Rayalaseema, which is below Telangana and between Karnataka and Andhra.

Telugu has more independent letters than any other Dravidian language. It has 53 unique and fundamental letters; Tamil has 30 of them. They represent fine shades of difference. Some sounds, such as *JH* are not found in Sanskrit; others, such as *SH* and *KSH* are not found in Tamil. Owing to this, it became the favoured language for music and, even today, the south Indian school of music, known as Carnatic music, is dominated by Telugu compositions. Most Telugu words end with a vowel; therefore, when singing, you can hold the note for longer. This not only offers more scope to the artiste but also sounds more beautiful.

Early Telugu literature was influenced by the Buddhists. We don't have texts from that period, but the golden age began with Nannayya Bhattaraka and his 11th-century retelling of the Mahabharata. Though incomplete, it is the first great work in Telugu. Within 200 years, the script also got standardized into the elegant style it is written in today.

The shining period of Telugu language was during the Kakatiya rule. King Prataparudra wrote a book on law called *Saraswati Vilasam*, Palkuriki Somanatha wrote many outstanding works, including a 'tongue-twister' poem, titled '*Shiva Gadhyam*'. The powerful words of the poem sound as if Shiva is dancing vigorously to the meter of the poem.

The Reddi kings who came to power after the Kakatiyas were also notable patrons of the language. Poets wrote *slesha kavyas*, or poems which could, using the same words, tell different stories when read in different ways – sometimes as many as three stories!

Writing wasn't treated like a full-time job. Kings and sometimes other wealthy patrons, such as court nobles or rich merchants, would pay the writers in advance in gold, food and silks so that they could work in comfort. Honour and praise were the motivators for poets.

There were women poets too. In one story, a poet called Pinnaviranna had to recite his Mahabharata in court the next day but had not written a word until his lady friend helped him. Another poet Potana searched desperately for a phrase and, finally, it was his daughter who came to his rescue. These two stories show that male poets, when confronted with a writer's block, were helped by the ladies in their house who were as good as they were in poetry, if not better! Atukuri or Kummara Molla, a female potter, wrote a version of the Ramayana, which is read widely even today.

Atukuri Molla, a woman potter and poet, featured on an Indian stamp

The golden age of Telugu was in the time of the Vijayanagara kings. They ruled from Karnataka and Telugu flourished in Karnataka, Andhra and Tamil Nadu. Krishnadevaraya was a great composer himself and his court boasted eight famous poets: Allasani Peddana, Nandi Thimmana, Madayyagari Mallana, Dhurjati, Ayyalaraju Ramabhadrudu, Pingali Surana, Ramarajabhushanudu and Tenali Ramakrishna. We know of Tenali Ramakrishna's funny stories, but he was a serious poet as well.

After that came Kshetrayya, a poet who mainly wrote love songs and used words onomatopoeically, to make them sound like their meaning (for example, in English, such words would be clap, zap, pitter-patter and gargle). In the case of the poem, to simulate the flowing of water, Kshetrayya would use words with the sounds of *la*, *pra*, *ra*, which mimicked the rhythm of flowing water.

Several verses are thus very pleasing to the ear and can be recited effortlessly, such as those by Bhadrachala

TENALI RAMAKRISHNA: WIT AND WISDOM

In ancient days, across India, the king was considered divine. How, then, could the system ensure that the king did not let this absolute power go to his head? The law books advised kings to rule in consultation with ministers. The other group of people who kept the king's ego in check were poets. Ministers and poets, using carefully chosen words and proverbs and other figures of speech, tactfully gave advice to the king and prevented him from making decisions that were hasty or not thought through.

Apart from this, there was another group, the jesters or the *vidushakas*, who used comedy and satire to get their message across. Intelligent kings listened to such people. We have the names of poets in many courts but rarely jesters. Mahendravarman (I) Pallava was good at poking fun at himself, but the most famous jester was Tenali Ramakrishna (also called Tenali Raman or Ramalinga) in the court of Krishnadevaraya. There are many oral traditions about how he was born in poverty and moved to his mother's town of Tenali in Andhra Pradesh and then to the court of King Krishnadevaraya. However, we don't have any contemporary records that mention him in the court. Many of these stories are similar to those of King Bhoja and Kalidasa, or even the much later Akbar and Birbal. Some scholars believe that though these people existed, they were not connected in the way we know them.

Tenali Raman is also credited with writing the *Panduranga Mahatmyam* in 1530–42 CE, just after Krishnadevaraya's death. This humorous work speaks of how Nigama Sharma is a naughty child, and his parents, unable to control his mischief, ask his elder sister to move in and look after him. She does so, but one day he runs away. After his many adventures, he finally reaches Pandarpur and becomes a 'good' guy. Among the many humorous passages, there is one in which his eldest sister discovers his absence, and instead of crying over his disappearance, she cries about losing her nose-ring (one of the smallest and least expensive ornaments for people in those days).

Artist's impression of Tenali Ramakrishna

However, regardless of whether Tenali Ramakrishna actually lived or not, his stories are witty and creative in their way of dealing with problems. Their enduring popularity could also be because he always has the last word even if it is against people like the king or the priests who are superior to him in stature. Even today, he is famously known as a *vikatakavi* – a Sanskrit/Hindi word meaning a poet who is also a jester.

Ramadasa. In his time, about 500 years ago, great works of Telugu literature were composed in Tamil Nadu under the Nayak rulers. They ruled parts of Tamil Nadu like Madurai and Thanjavur, and extended the use of Telugu to these parts. Many Telugu-speaking people migrated to Tamil Nadu in these times, mainly in the 16th and 17th centuries CE.

Much later came poets like Tirupati Venkata Kavulu. He composed a humorous imaginary conversation between the goddesses Lakshmi and Parvati when they met in a gathering of divine beings. Here's an excerpt:

> LAKSHMI: So, your husband is the one who carries that Ganga?
> PARVATI: And yours an actor who keeps switching roles...
> LAKSHMI: Isn't your husband the one who mounts a bull?
> PARVATI: And your husband is the one using an eagle for a vehicle? (*A bull moves according to the wishes of the rider, while an eagle can't be controlled that easily!*)
> LAKSHMI: Your poor husband wears snakes for ornaments.
> PARVATI: And yours has verily a snake for a bed!
> LAKSHMI: Your husband resides in the cremation ground.
> PARVATI: And your spouse is but in the middle of the ocean.

The audience would have loved the humour of this in those days, but there is a deeper meaning – that daily life is full of differences and conflict, but we need to keep finding ways of dealing with that while working on our relationships, and there is no 'ideal' world.

MALAYALAM

The word Malayalam is a palindrome – a word that reads the same from left to right and right to left. Spoken in Kerala, it is an ancient language. Some believe that there was a common language from which Tamil and Malayalam emerged, while others believe that Tamil itself was of two types, *chen* Tamil or 'pure' Tamil, and *kodun* Tamil, which was more colloquial.

Around 2,000 years ago, when Kerala was ruled by the Chera kings, they spoke Tamil too and some of the most beautiful verses in Tamil literature are from the Chera times. Ilango Adigal, the Chera prince, wrote the *Silappadikaram*, an epic that tells the story of Kannagi: Kovalan, her husband, was killed in haste by the Pandya king, who was so distraught when his injustice was pointed out to him, that he died from shock, and so did his queen. Kannagi's anger still did not abate; it transformed into a fire that destroyed much of Madurai.

Till about 1,000 years ago, the Tamil script in southern Tamil Nadu was *vatteluttu* or round letters, and they look very similar to the Malayalam script of today. When the Cholas defeated the Pandyas and occupied southern Tamil Nadu, they changed the script. The Cholas occupied Kerala only briefly, so the Malayalam script has remained intact.

Evolution of *vatteluttu*

Between 1,500 to 2,000 years ago, Sanskrit also influenced Malayalam and many of the words in today's Malayalam are from Sanskrit and Tamil. Tulu, a language spoken in coastal Karnataka, close to north Kerala, is currently written in the Kannada script. The language is slowly disappearing since native speakers from the younger generation are moving on to other languages. The language has a very powerful oral tradition of songs sung or recited at festivals, especially one called *paddana*, which is like an autobiography of the Bhuta or spirit of the forest. Other *paddana*s are songs sung during farming activities, and one of them is about a brave and courageous woman called Siri and her equally courageous daughter. *Paddanas* are precious because they tell us of the life of ordinary folk whose history is seldom recorded in the grand poems or inscriptions of the past.

From 600 years ago, the golden age of Malayalam began with kings and courts patronizing the genre of poetry-storytelling called *champu*. Kathakali dancers and other dances also needed stories and plots for music and drama performances, and *aattakatha*s ('dance stories') came into being.

Kathakali dances were sophisticated formal dances performed in the temple as an offering to the deity. One *aattakatha* is on Vali Vijayam, or the defeat of Bali, an important story from the Ramayana: Sage Narada goads Ravana to catch Vali. The *vanara*, without turning around, wraps his tail around Ravana's 20 hands. Soon. Ravana is tightly wrapped up into a knot in Vali's tail. When Vali jumps across the seven seas for his morning prayers, he senses a heaviness in his tail and only then sees it all knotted up with Ravana entangled in it. Finally, he releases Ravana, who returns home a humbler man.

This entire Kathakali dance would have gone on for about two hours in the temple precincts in the warm glow of oil lamps. The audience would have been much entertained and finally left with the reassurance that even the mighty will fall if they are too proud.

Across India, essential social values were transmitted through performances, like the one described above. In Kerala, ideas, such as the need for patience, taking action against wrongdoing, not stealing, and so on, were communicated through *thullal* performances that encouraged the creation of many songs in simple Malayalam, showcasing stories of valour and love, and offering hope, courage and entertainment to the audience.

The creator of the *thullal* was a witty poet called Kunjan Nambiar. As the story goes, the Samuthiri of Kozhikode had built a tall *deepastambha* or lighthouse. He invited every poet to sing its praises, and they composed long and very appreciative poems. When Kunjan Nambiar's turn came, he wasn't very impressed with what he saw but had to obey the king. His verse was short –

Deepasthambham maha ascharyam
Enikkum kittanum panam!
(Loosely translated:
The Deepastambha is awesome,
But I also need money!)

The Samuthiri, impressed with the terse honesty of Kunjan Nambiar, gave him a gift. There are many stories of how, using such satirical wit, poets across ancient times kept the ego of rulers in check without hurting their self-esteem. In Nambiar's work called *Karthaveeryarjunavijayam*, we have a list of what people ate in those times and what food products were taxed: pepper, coconut, areca nut, mango, jackfruit, low-quality maize, cucumbers, tubers and broken rice are mentioned, with the last four referred to as staples for poorer people.

TAMIL

The oldest among south Indian languages, Tamil is spoken not only in Tamil Nadu but is also an official language in Sri Lanka, Malaysia and Singapore. It is one of the world's oldest, continuously spoken languages and has sophisticated literature from at least 2,000 years before. However, the language itself is much older. Complete studies of the excavations in Keeladi and Adichanallur may date it back by another 1,000 to 2,000 years.

The earliest set of Tamil works is from the Sangam period, roughly 2,000 years ago. The word Sangam means a 'gathering'. In today's Tamil Nadu and Kerala, there was a great gathering of poets and the most important of their poems were collated. It must have been the World Cup of Tamil poetry! There were three such gatherings, known as *muchchangam*. The poems from the first and second Sangams have been lost. From the third Sangam, over 2,400 poems were compiled into

18 books, thanks to the efforts of U. Ve. Swaminatha Iyer (1855–1942) who went from village to village, found them, edited them and published them. The Sangams were hosted by the Pandya kings, but the poems are about the Chola, Chera and Pandya kings. Many kings were poets too and many poems are by women, who were very well educated in those days. The poems tells us about the daily life of the time and serve as an excellent resource for information about the region. Sangam poems are broadly divided into *akam* or poems connected to the feelings of human beings; and *puram* or poems of glory and heroism.

Akam poems reveal that the region (which included Tamil Nadu and Kerala) was divided into four zones and each had its own communities, musical instruments, gods and goddesses, food and occupations. Sangam poets – both men and women – were deeply observant of nature. They were even able to note the time at which a flower changes colour from green to red. They compared this change to spoken words: tender (green) words being twisted into hateful, angry (red) words. Avvaiyar was a great poetess of this time and her short verses answering questions are particularly interesting. Here is an example of what is the greatest thing in the world:

> *...But Brahma who created the world is even bigger*
> *Brahma himself was born inside the navel of Vishnu, who is therefore bigger*

THE DISCOVERY OF SANGAM

U. Ve. Swaminatha Iyer

About 150 years ago, a young man called U. Ve. Swaminatha Iyer, who was born near Thanjavur, made it his life's mission to search the entire Tamil region and bring back all the old Sangam-era texts written on palm-leaf manuscripts and preserve them in book form. He faced many difficulties but did not give up. It was only because of him that Tamil is today recognized as a classical language, and we can write about Tamil history in the Sangam period in books like this one.

For his efforts, he is affectionately known as the 'grandfather' of Tamil. Fortunately, he also wrote about his own life and from that we get a sense of how schools functioned in his childhood. Students had to be up at 5 a.m., go to the river to wash up and bring fine river sand that they would spread to practise writing the alphabet in it using their fingers. Almost all learning was through memory, and they learnt language, mathematics and the sciences through practical applications. Weekends were not holidays, but new moon and full moon days were.

Vishnu reclines in the milky ocean, so the ocean is bigger
The entire ocean was sipped from one palm by Agastya
Agastya was born in a pot of mud, so a fistful of mud is greater than all the above
The mud comes from the world, which is therefore the biggest but...
The world rests on one head of a many-headed cobra
That is only the size of Parvati's little finger
She resides in one half of Shiva, who is therefore greater than all the above
And Shiva resides in the heart of the devotee, which is the greatest of them all...

Buddhism and Jainism were important religions in these times and many texts come from their followers. The *Pazhamozhi Nanooru*, for example, is a text of 400 poems on how to lead a good life. One of them describes the difference between wise people and fools. The wise ask three questions before they do anything. Unless they get a positive answer to these, they will not start.

The questions are:

How will this help me?

Who else can help me?

And how will this help others (living and non-living things) around me?

The *Silappadikaram*, *Manimekalai* and *Jivaka Chintamani* are what survive of the five great Tamil epics. The others – *Valayapathi* (Jain text, author unknown) and *Kundalakesi* (Buddhist text by Nathakuthanaar) – are sadly lost. They are all serious works, but also offer delightful pieces of information on how, for example, women were very good at a version of volleyball in those days.

About 1,000 years ago, the Alvars and the Nayanars composed several devotional works in Tamil, set to music, in praise of Shiva and Vishnu respectively. These give us valuable descriptions of villages in the region, and about how the *panar*s and *pandarathar*s continued to sing songs of love and heroism during festivals. Some verses even connect how having many trees is a reliable way for getting more rains, and therefore water. From them we also know that villages continued to have the *panar*s and *pandarathar*s, who sang songs of love and heroism during festivals.

From then on, gradually, the scope of Tamil literature turned to religion and devotion. Not all of it was serious philosophy, though. There were poets like Kalamegha Pulavar who wrote witty verses. He used homonyms to compare the oddest things. For example, by a clever play of words, he says, that as the inside of the coconut and the dog's mouth is whitish, and its outside brown – a coconut and a dog are the same. In another verse, he proves that a mirror and a lotus are the same. Can you think of how?

Today, Tamil continues to be taught in many countries as a secondary language owing to its rich linguistic legacy and presence as an avidly spoken language.

Now that you know so much about these four hero languages, perhaps you will want to explore them more.

11

SCIENCE AND TECHNOLOGY

SCHOLARS, SCIENTISTS AND KNOWLEDGE EXPERTS

In India, while formal education in *gurukuls* or temples was reserved for the higher castes, such as Brahmins, nearly everyone learnt maths and some science with a practical purpose since all jobs – and indeed life itself – needs some knowledge of these subjects. Most people probably knew the basics of division, multiplication, addition and subtraction. Some scholars went beyond practical application and looked at deeper theory. We will get to know about them in this chapter.

The numerals and place value system used today originated in India. Letters were also used to denote numbers. In fact, in Tamil books published as recently as 90 years ago, 1 is written as 'க' or 'Ka' and 2 is 'உ' or 'Uu'. Although in textbooks today we learn about science and maths more as Western concepts, most of those existed in India either earlier or simultaneously.

MATHEMATICS

Mathematics was important to daily life in many ways. Buying and selling or bartering of goods, calculating the area of land for buying or selling it, calculating how much water a field needed and how to build canals all needed elements of division, multiplication, addition, subtraction, and knowledge of formulas and geometry.

THE MEASUREMENT OF TIME

The more complex calculations in maths related to the need to measure time, for example, to know when the cooking would be done or how long a lesson had to go on for. The more complex time calculations were in farming and other livelihood-related activities, for instance, when the monsoon season would start or when the tides would rise and ebb. Farmers would usually plant on a full moon because the full moon's capillary effect is said to affect how seeds absorb water and sprout.

The ancients sky-gazed a lot. The *Yajur Vedanga Jyotisha*, the oldest surviving Indian book on astronomy, calls it the 'science of determining time' – *kaala vidhaana shastram*. This was written by a rishi called Lagadha, probably around the 14th century BCE.

There are three kinds of days in the Indian calendar. A solar day (*divasam* or *dinam*) is from sunrise to sunrise, and is divided into sixty *naadis* or *ghatis*. The word *ghati* or *ghatam* in Sanskrit means water pot. Time was measured by how long it took a full pot of water (of a certain size) to drain completely. Smaller units of time were measured using smaller vessels, called *udhaka* or *drona*.

The lunar day is from moon rise to moon rise. The *nakshatras* (or star fields) are the spaces or 'mansions' in which the moon is placed on a said day. The moon appears adjacent to 27 different *nakshatras* in the course of its orbit so the *nakshatra* cycle is a 27-day cycle.

The lunar month follows a 30-day cycle because it is counted from a full moon to the next full moon. The months are named after the *nakshatra*, ending on the day the full moon is next to it. This worked in the beginning. By the second century CE, we also have solar calculations. How did this come about?

As the initial calendar was focused only on the moon over a period of time, they found that 12 lunar months did not add up to a solar year. They wanted this to match the solar year because they also calculated the equinoxes, and the way they affected the seasons and, therefore, the crop and plant growth.

To understand the solar year, one needs to understand equinoxes and solstices. The equinoxes occur twice a year, when the sun is directly above the equator, in March (beginning of spring) and in September (beginning of autumn). The two solstices respectively fall usually on 22 June (the summer solstice or the start of *dakshinayana*, when the sun travels southwards), and 22 December (the winter solstice, also called the start of *uttarayana*, when the sun travels northwards). They mark the seasons, which were important for farmers.

However, celestial bodies like the sun, moon and earth are moving at varying speeds. The variation maybe very small in a year, but it adds up over several centuries, so astronomical calculations need to be revised every so often depending on the movement of the celestial bodies.

Based on these calculations over a period of time, the lunar month was not just 30 days but actually 29.5 days. The solar days came to 365 or 366 days, but 29.5x12 is 354 days. This means there is a gap of 11 days per year. In five years, this would become a difference of 55 days. This means in five years our calendars would be wrong by an entire season.

To remedy this gap between the lunar year and solar year, astronomers created the *adhika masa* (extra month) calculation. The 11 days were added up every five years and 55 days were split into two extra months once every five years. At the end of the fifth year, the solar year and lunar year start on the same day. The five-year period when they are aligned together is called *yuga*. (This is different from the *Yuga* in the *Puranas*.)

Somewhere around the first or second century CE, some astronomers believed it was easier and more accurate to work out the calendar based on the movement of the sun, which was fixed at 365 or 366 days, rather than the constantly changing lunar months. So, south India landed up with multiple calendars. In the lunar calendar alone, some would count a month from new moon to new moon, others from full moon to full moon. This means that the festival days would change by almost half a month. Others used the solar calendar. And there were those who used the solar calendar but retained the months from the lunar calendar.

PANCHANGA: THE INDIAN CALENDARS

Elders in your family will be familiar with the Indian calendar (especially to look up festival days), a booklet called the *panchanga*, published every year. This is far more complex than the Gregorian calendar we follow today and will not only give you the date but the astronomical movements and details of planets, stars and minute measurements of time. The *panchanga* literally means 'five parts': *tithi* (lunar day), *nakshatra* (the 'mansion of stars' the moon is aligned with), *karana* (half-day), *yoga* (a particular angle of the sun and moon) and *vara* or *vasara* (solar weekday). Used mostly by astrologers today, in the olden days this was the reference book for farmers to time their agrarian activities and for people to set time.

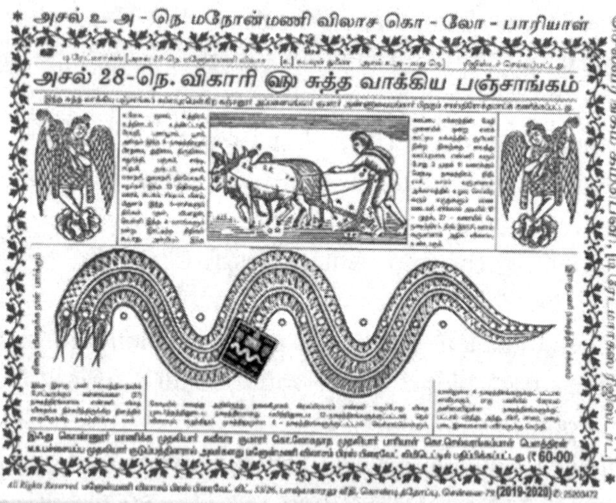

A *panchanga* in Tamil

The *panchanga* will give you the positions of the sun, moon and other planets in the latitude and longitude coordinates for a fixed place on earth and details on actual times of sunrise, sunset and the phases of the moon. The original calculations were made based on formulas in Sanskrit astronomy books, such as the *Suryasiddhanta* and *Grahalaghava*. Because of astronomical changes, and the different practices across the country, it became difficult to even set the date for important festivals. Therefore, in 1955, astrophysicist Meghnad Saha was asked to combine all versions and create a national *panchanga*. This calendar came into effect in 1956.

ASTRONOMY AND ASTROLOGY

In ancient times, astrology was a popular science aligned with astronomy. *Jyotisha* or astrology texts come in many varieties: *siddhantas* described grand concepts and theories, and established mathematical and astronomical concepts; *karanas* were written to serve as simpler, smaller versions of *siddhantas* and accommodated local variations – they served as guides to make *panchangas*, the yearly calendar that everybody in the village could understand.

Even till the 1940s, in many villages across south India, the wealthiest family in the village would convene a meeting in the new year when the local 'wise man' would read out the *panchanga* for the whole year.

Almost all the texts were usually written in the form of poetic verses, mostly in Sanskrit. They would have been taught as a rhythmic chant (for easy memorization and recall) rather than a lecture.

Today, the formula for calculating the circumference of a circle is $2\pi r$ (π – pi). Pi as a ratio between the diameter and circumference was well known in the fifth century CE. However, it was not called anything at that time in India or Greece (where the concept was also known). The Greek letter Pi (π) began to be used for this ratio only in the 18th century CE.

Around 800 years ago (in the 14th century CE), a famous astrologer-mathematician called Madhavacharya from the village of Sangamagrama in Kudalur (different from the saint Madhavacharya), defined an infinite number series whose sum was pi. This was revolutionary since it meant a number could be represented by an infinite series and this concept led to the birth of calculus, which is taught even today. This series was later independently discovered by European mathematicians James Gregory and Gottfried Wilhelm Leibniz in the 1670s. It used to be called the Gregory-Leibniz series but is now more correctly called the Madhava-Gregory series.

Madhava converted the series to a *shloka*. However, to rhyme words with numbers (a difficult task in a *shloka*), he used a technique called *bhutasankhya*, where objects represent words. Almost everyone then would have known that there are seven *swaras* in music. So, when he wanted to use the number 7, he used the word *swara*. The number 9 was *graha* (there were understood to be 9 planets then). Likewise, 4 would be *vedas*, 5 would be *shara* or the 5 arrows of Manmatha, the god of love, and so on.

Another famous astronomer and mathematician in Kerala was Parameshwara Nambudiri. He noticed through careful observation that Aryabhata's formula (written in 499 CE) for predicting eclipses did not work in Kerala (in 1430 CE, when Parameshwara was studying

THE MADHAVA SERIES

Madhavacharya was a skilled maker of astronomical instruments. He was part of the Kerala school of astronomy and mathematics. His most famous contribution is sums of infinite series. To calculate the circumference (*paridhi*) of a circle, Madhava said:

व्यासे वारिधिनिहते रूपहृते व्याससागरभिहते ।
त्रिशरादिविषमसङ्ख्याभक्तमृणं स्वं पृथक् क्रमात् कुर्यात् ॥

vyaase vaaridhi-nihate rupa-hrte vyaasa-saagarabhihite |
tri-sharaadi-vishama-sankhyaa-bhaktam-rNam svam prthak kramaat kuryaat ||

Which means that to calculate the circumference (*paridhi*), we must multiply the diameter (*vyaasa*) by four times one minus *tri-sharaa-aadi-vishama-sankhyaa-bhaktam-rNam-svam-prtak.* This phrase in italics is complex and yet compactly expressed. It implies a sequence of odd-number (*vishama sankhyaa*) denominators (*bhaktam*) starting (*aadi*) with three (*tri*) and five (*sharaa*), negative (*rNam*) *svam* (positive) alternately (*prtak*). Tri means 3. The word *sharaa* is a *bhutasankhya* word for the number 5 and *saagara* (ocean) is a *bhutasankhya* word for the number 4; *abhihite* means multiply; *rupa-hrte* means to subtract from one, and *kramaa* means series. That expression, therefore, captures the concept that there is a series of odd numbers as reciprocals (one divided by the number),

paridhi = 4 x *vyaasa* x (1 - 1/3 + 1/5 - 1/7 + 1/9...)

The sum of the series in the brackets adds up to π/4, and this became a breakthrough mathematical series.

this), and, therefore, he adjusted the calculations based on his studies. Based on this, he wrote a book titled *Drk Ganitham*, meaning 'calculation by observation'. Among his other *shlokas* connected with maths, the most important ones are about area calculations.

Madhava's disciple Kellalur Nilakantha Somayaji (1443–1555 CE) was an ingenious astronomer and mathematician, and in his book *Tantra Sangraha*, he came up with a quasi-heliocentric theory, where he propounded the theory that the planets Mercury and Venus revolve around the sun.

Significantly, this was nearly two centuries before Polish mathematician and astronomer Nicolaus Copernicus proposed that all planets revolve around the sun.

In Karnataka, around 1,300 years ago, a Jain mathematician called Mahavira, who was at the court of the Rashtrakuta king Amoghavarsha Nripatunga, authored the *Ganitha Sara Sangraha* in Sanskrit. This is possibly India's first known text exclusively on mathematics. In it, he mentions how the knowledge of maths is important in every sphere of our life. You might call it an 'Anthem for Mathematics'. He says (as translated by R. Gopu, a co-founder of the Varahamihira Science Forum, and part of the Tamil Heritage Trust):

In worldly life, in Vedic learning, in religious practice,
In business, in everything, mathematics is useful.

In romance, economics, in music, dance and drama,
In cooking, medicine and in architecture,

In prosody, poetry, logic and grammar,
In all the arts, mathematics reigns supreme.

Tamil texts, such as *Kanakkadhigaram* and *Asthana Kolahalam*, and Telugu texts such as *Pavuluri Ganitam*, also deal with maths. *Pavuluri Ganitam* is named after Pavuluri Mallanna, who translated Mahavira's *Ganitasarasangraha* from Sanskrit to Telugu in the 11th century CE.

Mathematical devices were used by the spiritual teacher Vedanta Desika, who wrote mainly in Sanskrit. He wrote verses arranged in ways so that one could read them like a chariot wheel or even a chessboard!

Doesn't all this sound so incredibly ahead of the times?

PHYSICS AND ARCHITECTURE

Practical applications of physics were evident in the use of pulleys and levers. All stagnant waterbodies, such as ponds, lakes and wells, had these to draw water out. They were vital for the irrigation of fields.

Water management was essential across south India, especially in Karnataka, Andhra and Tamil Nadu where rivers were either fewer or seasonal. Dams were known in ancient times; the Cholas, for example, had a check dam that was, most probably, made with mud and stones. In Hampi, even today, you can see an aqueduct from Vijayanagara times.

The study of *vastu shastra* has been appropriated by astrologers. Originally, it was knowledge connected with all the aspects of physics, maths and other sciences that architects and builders needed to know. For example, they used light and shadow to plot the directions.

When any building had to be constructed, it was essential to know the directions it would align with and the inclination of the land. These have a bearing on how the building would be impacted by wind, light (heat) and water.

When a plot of land was cleared, water would be poured to check where it spread evenly (flat land) and where it stagnated (lower-level land). To check for the quality of soil, a large pit would be dug, and the soil removed would be put back in. If the removed soils went back in with just a few handfuls to spare, it meant that the soil was well compacted and stable, and therefore fit for construction. If on the other hand, there was a lot of space for new soil to be added, then it was concluded that the soil was loose and not suitable for building on.

When the soil was loose, the Kakatiyas had a solution. They would lay out the plan of the building on the land and then identify where the load-bearing pillars would be. These spots would be excavated, the holes filled with a mixture of sand, lime, palm jaggery (for binding) and *karakkaya* (the black myrobalan fruit), to form a firm foundation for the pillars. This would make such buildings even earthquake-proof.

The British learnt this technique from Indian builders and used it when they constructed large buildings in present-day Chennai, which is on the coast and has loose sandy soil.

The method for determining the directions (east, west, north and south) on a plot of land was through light and shadow. Temples, the only buildings made of stone and therefore permanent, were oriented towards the east–west or north–south axis.

After the land was cleared, a *shanku* (gnomon) was erected in the centre. This was a tall wooden pole with a nail on top, ending in a sharp tip. Using shadows, the circle around this pole would be calculated.

The *Shulba Sutras*, texts which are part of the *Vedangas*, describe how to find the true east, regardless of the latitude, to set the east–west line for a temple, palace or town. The method below from the *Katyayana Shulba Sutra*, describes how to find the true east using simple devices like a stick, rope and pegs, and is very typical of Indian astronomy.

> *Plant a* shanku *on level ground*
> *Draw a circle with rope measured by the* shanku
> *Where shadows fall on circle, fix a stick (morning, evening)*
> *That line is the* praachi *(line connecting the two sticks), the east–west line.*

All the great temples of south India were built by excavating stone, cutting it into precise blocks and then placing them with perfectly aligned joints. There was no error, and the angles were straight.

All of this was done with just a hammer and chisel, and complete focus and precision. The earliest cave temples needed more perfection, because even one mistake could cause the entire project to be abandoned. In these cave temples, all the sculptures are also made from the same rock, and they are perfectly aligned to the doorways and pillars.

CHEMISTRY

The study of chemistry was incorporated into two areas – metal casting and paints. Metal casting was for farm implements, cooking vessels, idols and cloth, and for dyeing cloth as well. All these techniques evolved over many generations of careful observation and adapting to local conditions, and were passed down orally.

METALLURGY

The use of metal defined the passage of history. In the last 2,000 years, from the humble cooking vessels to the world-famous Chola idols, the lost-wax technique was used across south India.

The idols are particularly noteworthy since they are made of five metals, each of which has different melting points. It takes great skill and concentration to combine the molten metals together to cast the idol.

Even small vessels used as toys were made by this complex method. Casting such small items with fine details require enormous patience.

While the Chola idols from Tamil Nadu are famous, Kerala metalworks from medieval times usually consist of idols of deities. Many times, these can be seen set within arches or *prabhavalis* with 'tongues of fire'. Such images are now found only in old temples and in museums. In some old Kerala temples and palaces, the ends of the wooden rafters in the roofs had a metal covering to protect the wood. Even these were worked in metal using this technique. Fortunately, this fine technique survives even today.

Metalwork of Kerala

THE LOST-WAX TECHNIQUE OF CASTING

There are two methods of casting images in metal. In Sanskrit, the words *ghana* and *sushira* are used, respectively, for solid casting and hollow casting (a way of pouring liquid clay into an empty plaster mould for producing a shell of a particular shape). Want to know how they made solid images by the lost-wax technique popular in south India? This is how it is described in old texts:

The lost-wax technique has not changed since it began. The beeswax and dammar gum *(kungilium)* must be correctly mixed with a little oil. This thick substance is made into the required image by the *sthapathi* (creator of images). Great care is taken since this will be the template for the final metal image. The *sthapathi* has to be an expert in proportions, ornaments and weapons since all of this will be added into this image.

A Chola bronze sculpture of Krishna

Next, comes the making of the mould. The wax model is given several coatings, with fine clay secured from an anthill and mixed with a combustible material, like paddy husk and cow dung, to make a thick mass.

The clay mould is then carefully dried in mild sunlight or in the shade. Care should be taken to see that no cracks appear and the wax model does not melt. After a few days, the clay mould is ready for casting. The wax is then melted out of a hole.

While the wax model is prepared and gets ready for the preparation of the clay mould, the metal alloy is prepared. Five metals called *panchaloha* are used in the auspicious alloy. These five metals are copper (usually in the largest proportion). silver, gold, brass and zinc (sometimes tin or lead). They are said to represent earth, water, fire, air and ether (*pancha bhutas*) denoting how the divine embodies all these principal elements. Master craftsmen would then remove the clay cover and add finer details like eyes and intricate textile designs with a small, sharp chisel and hammer. The weight of the metal for the image is determined by the weight of the wax in the mould. Normally, the metal is to be eight times the weight of the wax. The metal is poured through the hole into the clay mould to form the image.

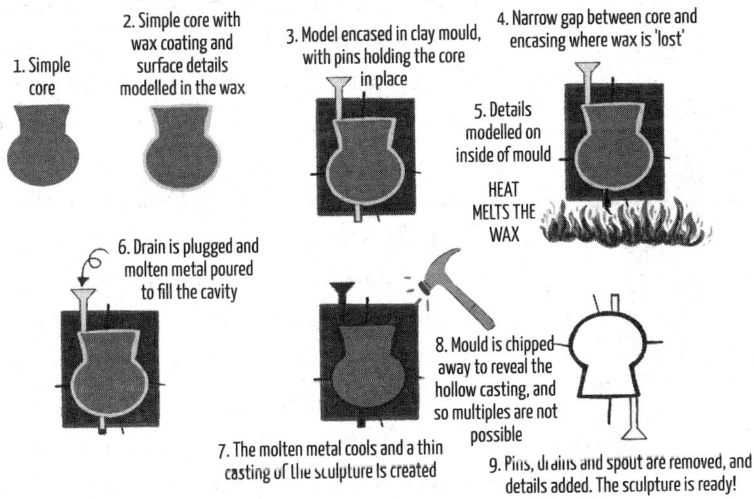

Stages of the lost-wax method of metal casting

However, the Wootz steel method, which was famously used in the production of swords, is lost forever. Steel is an alloy of iron and carbon. In the old days, even 3,000 years ago, villages used to have small crucibles or stone pots where iron would be heated until it became liquid, and then mixed with coal and wood (providing carbon for a rust-free product) to make tools for farming and weapons like arrowheads, spearheads and swords.

A rare dagger with a gilded copper, ruby-eyed bird-shaped hilt and a knuckle guard ending in a dragon's head from Bijapur or Golconda (circa late 16th century CE), Alugaily Collection – London

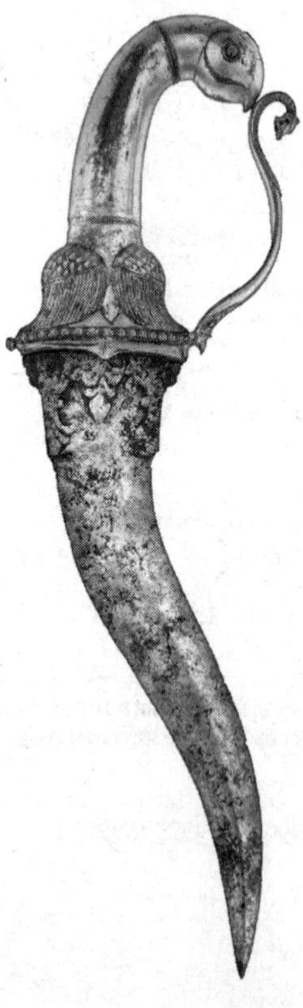

The demand for it was so high that much of it was exported to Turkey and nearby regions for weapons. Sadly, with the industrial revolution in Britain and the gradual decline of the Indian armies in favour of the English East India Company, the technique was forgotten.

Somewhat like the Iron Pillar that has never rusted (now in the Qutub Minar complex in Delhi), in Thanjavur, on a mound near the southern gateway of a place called Beerangi Medu, stands the world's largest forge-wielded cannon, the Rajagopala Beerangi, which too has never rusted. The secret of the non-rusting iron, just as in the Iron Pillar, remains a secret here as well.

The Rajagopala Beerangi in Thanjavur, Tamil Nadu

Old books like the *Anandakandam* of the 18th century, housed in the Sarasvati Mahal Library in Thanjavur, mention how a lab for melting metal must be built near a good water source and the patron god for them was Rasabhairava, who had to face east towards the rising sun, which relates to the light and heat of molten metal.

Kerala has preserved the *aranamula* technique of polishing metal to such an extent that it shines like a mirror. Legend has it that this method came from Tamil Nadu. The mirror is made from an alloy that contains copper and tin. The proportions are a secret, but we know that it requires complex polishing techniques applied over months to make the metal as reflective as a mirror. Kerala bronze vessels or *varpu* are also famous. Some are even six feet long and cast from one mould.

Another unique metal tradition exists in south Maharashtra/north Karnataka. The Bahmani sultans came from Persia and ruled the Deccan, while being constantly at war with the Vijayanagara kingdom. Ruling from the 14th to 16th centuries CE, they had brought with them the Persian technique of inlaying, where one metal wire would be hammered into another metal as a design. They used a blackened alloy of zinc and copper and inlaid it with silver and, sometimes, copper too. The black base became a contrasting colour for silver and copper. This technique spread to Hyderabad as well and the city became a hub for it. It is called *bidri* because of the region it became originally famous in – Bidar in Karnataka.

A large silver-and-brass inlaid zinc alloy (*bidri*) hookah base from Bidar (circa 17th century), Alugaily Collection – London.

PIGMENTS AND COLOURS

In painting, the study of pigments displays a deep knowledge of chemistry. Paints were used for textiles, walls and wood. Paintings in Tamil Nadu from the Chola, Pandya and Pallava times have survived as fragments in the Brihadisvara Temple of Thanjavur, the Talagirisvara Temple in Panamalai and the Kailasanathar Temple in Kanchipuram, respectively.

Kerala has a few from that period as well. The oldest in the Kerala style is in the Thirunandikkara Cave Temple, now in Tamil Nadu's Kanyakumari district.

The style was the wet fresco method, where the paint was applied while the plaster was still wet. The painter

Mural of the Chola period on the walls of the Brihadisvara Temple, Thanjavur, Tamil Nadu

had to know the chemical reactions that the pigment could undergo. Paints themselves were procured from many different sources. Gold, silver, copper and lead were also ground to powder to extract paint pigments. Stones such as lapiz lazuli gave the colour blue; turmeric and indigo plants also lent their colour to pigments. Pigments, in the form of a powder or paste, had to be mixed with thinning or bonding agents to make them suitable to be applied to a surface.

Paintings were made not only on walls and wood but on cloth as well. The painted cloth was hung either on the wall or ceiling, or pasted to a wooden board. Such examples of painted cloth from south India are now mostly found in museums abroad like the Metropolitan Museum in New York, USA, and the Victoria and Albert Museum in London, UK. They are mostly panels that were hung on walls or tents. A fragment of Tipu Sultan's tent now in Powis Castle, in the UK, is an example of how colourful and intricate these textiles were.

A Thanjavur painting: a continuing art heritage

The Thanjavur paintings are painted on fabric stuck to wooden boards. This style of painting, still popular today, was created by the Maratha ruler Serfoji (Sarabhoji) II Bhonsle (1777–1832 CE) in the post-medieval period. He is credited with combining the older cloth-on-board style with using gold leaf in an embossing technique: a 3D effect that was created by applying thin layers of powdered sawdust or very fine clay made into a paste (gesso) with tamarind seed glue. Pieces of mirror and coloured glass were stuck into this paste and the area coated with gold foil to give an impression of real jewellery.

The National Museum in Delhi and the Chhatrapati Shivaji Maharaj Vastu Sangrahalaya in Mumbai both house fine collections of these paintings. Mysore paintings are similar but painted on paper with no gesso or mirrors; they have more rounded figures as well.

While painted fabrics were used for walls and tents, the main purpose of these was to wear them. Painted textiles were used in coastal Andhra, for example, even till the British times; and Europeans sought such painted cloth called chintz or calico.

BIOLOGY

YOGA AND AYURVEDA

The practical application of biology was in farming, and human and animal health. Emphasis was placed on not just physical wellness but the mental and emotional aspects as well.

The connection was seen in this way: our body, like the world, is made up of various elements – fire, water, air, space, earth. Our five senses connect the inner body to the world around us. In the traditional Ayurveda ('wisdom to live a long life') school of medicine, the essential premise is that when there is an imbalance of one of these constituents, illness appears. Curing illnesses was not just about taking medicines but adopting a lifestyle of maintaining flexibility through yoga, healthy eating, and mental calmness through meditation and other methods.

Today, Kerala is well known for Ayurveda, but in the olden days, not only did all villages have traditional physicians, but the women of all families knew simple remedies using roots and plants to treat common illnesses. The Sangam poems too have several references to traditional medicine.

Hospitals were attached to temples and one of them was near the Vishnu Temple of Thirumukkudal, close to Chennai. From a long inscription that covers almost the entire outer wall of the temple, we know that in 1068 CE, a grant was made to the hospital, pharmacy and college in the village. There were 35 students and inmates in the college-hospital and they all had mats to sleep on and got oil and warm water for their Saturday baths. There were nurses, surgeons and a physician named Savarnan Kodandaraman Ashvathama Bhattan. There was a 'barber' to assist patients and students, and patients were served meals. The list of medicines in the pharmacy will be familiar to those who follow Ayurveda.

Even until about 150–200 years ago, most of the health issues in the village were taken care of by a member of the barber community known as a *savarnan*. They had deep knowledge of medicines recorded on palm-leaf manuscripts and in their own memory. They would have been able to perform some types of surgeries too. Later, King Serfoji (Sarabhoji) II of Thanjavur was deeply interested in combining the best of Indian and Western medicine. He even had a skeleton made of wood and was an expert eye surgeon. His detailed eye surgery notes with hand-painted illustrations of the eyes before and after treatment can be seen in the Thanjavur Palace library.

In Kerala, healthy living was seen as involving food, sleep, physical fitness and medicine. Health and hygiene were connected with each other, and elaborate rules of personal cleanliness were laid out for normal folks to follow. Kalari, the martial art, was originally created to maintain physical fitness. In addition to native practices, the knowledge systems of the Muslim community from Arabia also influenced the practice of medicine. The Unani system practised even today comes from their infusion into the existing Indian framework.

MEDICINE

Fragrance was considered an important medicine and saffron, cinnamon, jasmine, a special ginger called *hely* (cultivated in Cannanore, present-day Kannur in Kerala), camphor and many other sweet-smelling herbal objects were used as preventive medicine.

Although Buddhism's popularity had waned by the ninth century CE, their medical knowledge was adopted into curative practices. All streams of medicine, including Ayurveda, Islamic healing traditions and folk medicines, were used by people, and they remained as open choices in the pluralistic society of Malabar. Nevertheless, Ayurveda, based on classic Sanskrit texts, was handled predominantly by a particular professional practitioner, the *ashtangavidhyas*, the term derived for their mastery of all eight branches of the Vagbhatananda tradition, such as *kaaya* (general medicine), *baala* (paediatrics), *graha* (astrological), *urdhwanga* (above neck), *shalya* (surgery), *dhamshtra* (toxicology), *jara* (longevity), and *vrusha* (infertility).

In Kannada, ancient texts mention many plants and trees of medicinal value. The *Manasollasa* has many details of not just human medicine but also veterinary (for cows, horses, elephants) medicine, and beverages for each disease. Ancient texts describe many antidotes for snakebites (which continue to be a killer in India) and scorpion bites.

In the 16th century CE, Vaidya Narasimha Soori wrote the *Vaidya Sara Sangraha* ('the ocean of knowledge about medicine'). He quotes from many previous texts that have since been lost. In the examination of the patient, he says that the pulse, the urine and the tongue need to be checked before a diagnosis. Treatments for hiccups, fever (he classifies them into 13 kinds) and other diseases are prescribed. There is a separate chapter for the treatment of diseases in children. The formulas to make these medicines is also given.

Another text titled *Panaje Pandithara Ajje Madhdhu* ('grandmother's medicines') was compiled by Panaje Vaidya Shankaranarayana Bhattar. Its first part is for the health of the facial area, skin and heart. The second part is about preparing medicines, including available herbs and lists of diets that need to be followed.

Dhanvantari, physician of the *devas*: note the leech in his lower right hand

Telugu also has many key texts on medicine, written in consonance with Sanskrit ones. The patron deity here is an avatar of the god Vishnu, called Dhanvantari. He was represented with a leech in one hand (it was used for bloodletting, the practice of removing toxins by letting leeches suck out blood) and a pot of *aushadha* (medicine) in another hand. Ayurveda and Unani medical systems were important, with the latter being more popular in the Hyderabad region.

Nannayya's *Andhra Mahabharatam*, Telugu's oldest known text, has many references to medicine. It mentions that a king must have experts who are well versed in the eight steps of Ayurveda. In another reference, doctors are expected to cure the mental and physical illnesses of their patients in a proper manner. Srinatha's *Kasi Kandam* is about the hill temple of Srisailam. Among other benefits of going there, he mentions easily accessible herbs that *sidhars* or doctors of those days would give to patients, the magic recipe of alchemy, and how to pluck and process herbs for medicines. Mahendra Giri Hill in Srikakulam in Andhra was said to have many rare herbs.

In Krishnadevaraya's court, a poet called Peddana and the king himself (in the *Amuktamalyada*) mention the use of metals as medicines. The *Yogi Vemanna Pathiyam* lists sandal and coal as helpful for good teeth. Yogi Vemanna advises against looking at the sun or an eclipse with the naked eye. The best way to stay healthy, he says, is to keep hunger, worldly needs and anger in control, and not speak or act thoughtlessly.

At the time, *vaidyas* or doctors were equated to God by the community, according to Telugu texts. Among many texts, the *Vastuguna Deepika* by Erra Venkataswamy is a lexicon of Ayurveda, listing medicines and how to use them. It even mentions mantras to recite as you take the medicine! There are texts connected to the eye as

FOOD WARNINGS

Vedanta Desika was a remarkable genius of the 12th century CE in Tamil Nadu. He was proficient in many languages and was not only a philosopher but also a creative linguist. One of his works, the *Ahara Niyamam*, has an interesting list of foods to be eaten, and to be avoided (in those times). Here are a few:

- Calcium that is extracted from seashells;
- Food that is not offered to God first;
- Food that is reheated;
- Mushrooms;
- Water that is old or collected from dirty sources;
- Food that has been touched by cloth, smelled by someone or partially eaten by someone;
- And he says, we must not eat alone but with others.

well by Dhurjati, a Telugu poet and an *ashtadiggaja* in Krishnadevaraya's court. *Dhanvantari Vaidya Lahiri* by Granti Venkata Subbarayulu, dedicated to the Shiva temple of Bezwada, focuses on medication for children. Diagnoses by checking the pulse (using the left wrist for women and the right wrist for men), and examining the mouth, tongue and eyes are also mentioned. The book also has many Telugu proverbs connected with medicine.

Regardless of whether you choose Western or traditional methods of medicine, or a combination, it is worth remembering that south India has had an ancient and practical approach to ease living since way back in the past.

12

MUSIC, DANCE AND DRAMA

NOTES, BEATS AND DRAMATIC FEATS

As human beings, we have more than just our senses, we have imagination as well. Using it, our basic needs for communication, play and leisure, and connection with others have been expressed in many ways across ages.

Cave paintings across south India show people standing together and sometimes doing what looks like dancing. Musical instruments of that period were predominantly flutes made of wood or bone. A rare lithophone, or a rock that naturally has musical qualities, was adapted into a musical instrument in Palaeolithic times in Tenkasi, Tamil Nadu. These are basically rock gongs, stones that emit a metallic sound when struck with a wooden stick. Many of these were arranged together to form a series of notes. It is fascinating that these stones are probably from about 10,000 BCE, but even as late as the 15th century CE, in the same region, people could carve such stones into pillars that emit musical notes when struck. Two of these are in the same region in Tamil Nadu – one in the Nellaiappar Temple in Tirunelveli and the other in Madurai's Meenakshi Temple. There are others in the 15th-century Vittala Temple in Hampi, Karnataka, and the Darasuram Temple steps in Tamil Nadu are also lithophones.

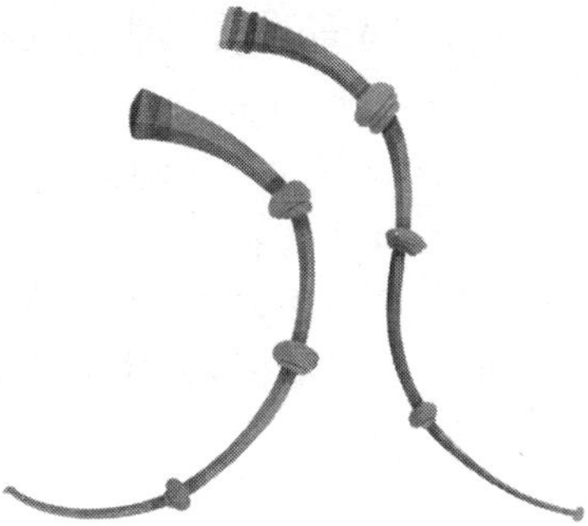

Kombu horn instruments

Other instruments were whistling through the mouth, animal horns and shells; you could create a lot of noise! Even today in temple rituals, the conch and the C- or S-shaped horn instrument, the *kombu*, are used. Those who play them are probably not aware that they are continuing a tradition from over 30,000 years ago!

In Kupgal in Bellary district of Karnataka, there is a series of small rocky hills with paintings from the Neolithic and Megalithic periods. Most are connected to cattle and some depict people as if in a group dance. Some of the rocks nearby can make metallic sounds, so archaeologists believe that music and dance formed an important part of rituals to either capture more cattle or to give thanks for a successful cattle raid.

Music and dance are as old as humans themselves. Parents sang to soothe their children to sleep. Marriage, birth and similar events were occasions for people to get together, connect and be entertained by music and dancing. Drama in India has always had a close connection to music and dance, and overlapped with them. Musicians made basic hand gestures when they sang, dialogues in plays were sung to music, and actors did some rhythmic footwork (*nritta*).

Till the third century CE, whatever we know of music, dance and drama is only for Tamil Nadu and Kerala, based on Sangam literature. For later periods, we have more information about these arts in Karnataka and Andhra as well.

Music and dance, like other aspects of life, were different in each region as described by the Sangam texts. *Thaalaattu* were lullabies; *nadavu* comprised songs to accompany the planting of rice; *eesal* were humorous songs that made fun of another side in a gentle way and that party responded with a similar *eesal* song; *kummi* were songs sung alongside the *kummi* dance; and *oppari* was sung to condole a grief-stricken, bereaved person.

Animals mesmerized by music – the sound of Krishna's flute

This ancient system of music gradually developed as Carnatic music in south India; it is different from Hindustani music that is prevalent in Maharashtra and, above it, in north India. Both Carnatic and Hindustani music are based on seven notes, but the forms that they are sung in and the accompanying instruments differ. For instance, forms of Hindustani music are *dhrupad*, *khayal*, *tarana*, *thumri* and *dadra*, and the instruments used are *tabla* and *tanpura*, while forms of Carnatic music include *alapana*, *niravala* and *kalphaswaram*, and instruments include the *veena* and *mridangam*.

A musician playing the *kinnari veena*, one of the many types of *veenas*

TAMIL NADU

In the Sangam times, musical notes had Tamil names – *kumal*, *tuttam*, *kaikilai*, *uzhai*, *illi*, *vilari* and *taram*. Each region had many ragas or *panns* (melody) and some were unique to the region, such as the Kurinji *pann*. *Valaipattu* were songs sung by women as they pounded grains into flour with a long pole. Many songs were composed in honour of the deity of the region – Muruga or Karthikeya. During battles, women sang the *vilari pann* to keep greedy foxes from attacking wounded soldiers. Other songs were sung to cheer up or even heal injured warriors.

In the Mullai or forest region, people danced the *acchiyar kuravai* with accompanying songs. The music and dance were so pleasant that, the texts say, flowers blossomed, elephants became tame, robbers forgot to steal and ghosts vanished – what an imagination!

There were special singers too. The *panars* were travelling composers and singers, accompanied by

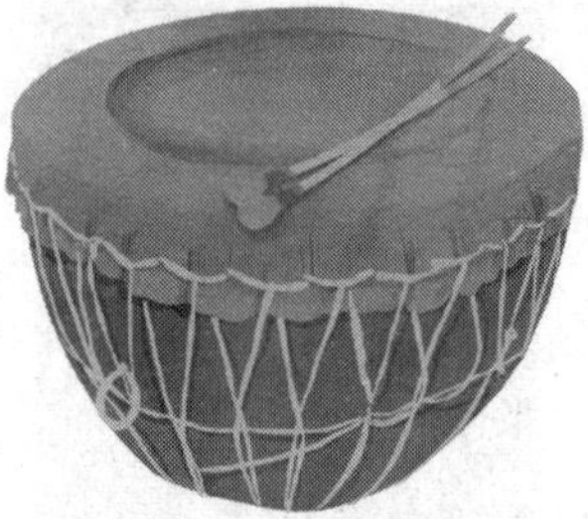
Murasu drum

women singers called *patiniyar*. It is from their detailed descriptions in songs that we learn so much about the daily life of ordinary people of the time. Another group of professional singers and expert dancers were the *viraliyar*, who possibly did not travel much.

In the Marudam fields and river valleys, the many kings had *porunar* or poets who accompanied the armies to motivate them with songs of heroism and praise for the soldiers' bravery. The king's palace had a large *murasu* or drum that was considered as sacred as the king. It was kept on a raised platform and decorated, and would be beaten when a battle began. Seizing the *murasu* of a king was a sign of victory in war.

Texts like the *Silappadikaram* and *Jivaka Chintamani* offer us information about dancers and musicians. They mention the presence of many books on the rules and procedures of music and dance – a sign that these were popular and were subjects of study. They describe the way a stage should be set up and illuminated, and reveal that both men and women were good dancers.

Dancing and performing would have encouraged other arts such as jewellery making, embroidery and textiles, stage design and make-up, but not much is known about these ancillary arts of the ancient period.

From the seventh century CE, we have a king such as Mahendravarman (I) Pallava who wrote two witty, satirical plays in which he pokes fun at himself and the monks of that time. The two plays were lost in Tamil Nadu but continued to be acted in Kerala as dances in temples by Kathakali artistes. The *Mattavilasa Prahasana* and the *Bhagavadajjukkam Prahasana* are valuable texts that not only tell us about daily life in Kanchi but even give us a list of trees found in the king's palace at the time!

Inscriptions of the Pandyas and Cholas till the 13th century CE give us the names of dancers. Women dancers were devoted to the temple (*devadas*is) as were the players of musical instruments like the *kombu* and *maddalam*, among others. At a time when women who lived in families could not own and sell their property, *devadas*is were allowed to do so and were highly respected for their public service. They funded *puja*s in temples, irrigation projects and even festivals. The ultimate honour for a dancer was, in the Chola period, to receive the title of 'Thalaikolli'. This meant she was an expert dancer and had a person in front of her hold a long, gold-plated wooden pole encrusted with precious stones on top.

Rajaraja Chola, when he built the Brihadisvara Temple in Thanjavur, endowed it with more than 300 *devadas*is and instituted complex rules on how they would be replaced, and about the houses and land given to them. Very often dancers, musicians and dramatists were paid by the village.

In this time, Shiva temples had incorporated the songs of the 63 Nayanars or saints into their daily rituals. The verses were sung by a community called the Oduvars, who still continue the tradition. Vishnu temples incorporated the 4,000 songs of the 12 Alvar saints into their daily ritual, with devotees reciting them. The tradition of singing, dancing to and explaining the songs was with a community called the Arayar, and this is done in a few temples in Tamil Nadu even today. At the Srirangam Temple, for example, they even perform these while holding the *veena* vertically in the old style.

In the 15th century CE, music, dance and drama had a revival not just in the courts and palaces, especially in Thanjavur, but in the villages as well. *Karakattam* and *poi kaal kudhirai* (where men and women get into a horse-shaped doll and dance) were important dances. The *villu paatu*, a bow-shaped instrument whose strings are gently tapped to make the attached bells jingle, accompanied by the *kodam*, a large earthen pot, was popular in villages.

Panchamukha vadyam

During summer, when the fields were fallow, villagers got together to perform plays with sung dialogues, some basic *nritta* (footwork) and *abhinaya* (gestures and expressions). These traditions continue even now but are much rarer. In temples, music and dance were funded by the temples. Temples in Tiruvarur and Srirangam had almost 20 different instruments, and very detailed procedures for when and where each would feature, which raga would be played and which dance would be performed. The *panchamukha vadyam*, a five-faced drum, was played even till a few decades back but is now extinct.

From 1532 to 1855 CE, in Tamil Nadu, the finest music, dance and drama flourished in the Thanjavur region, supported by the Telugu-speaking Nayaks (who were ruling on behalf of the Vijayanagara kings) and the Marathas. Kings like Vijaya Raghava Nayaka, who ruled from 1634 CE to 1673 CE, improved the *veena* by making the frets fixed rather than movable. He invented new *talas* and ragas. Kings like Shahaji adapted episodes from the older epics into full-length dramas. Sanskrit, Telugu, Tamil, Marathi and, sometimes, even Kannada were the preferred languages and some dramas had combinations of these.

The *Natya Shastra Sangraham*, compiled and adapted from the *Natya Shastra* in this time, has many interesting chapters that deal with stage set-up, elocution advice, colour combinations, development of storylines, and preventive measures for a fail-safe performance. Music recitals were popular and singers would sing just one raga for several hours without repeating a set of *swaras*. There are many stories of arrogant musicians humbled in debates and competitions.

As Maratha rule ended in 1855 and the British occupied Tamil Nadu, the patronage of music and dance

A Bharatanatyam dancer

moved to the traders. Drama continued as a village activity. While many music and dance traditions survive, much was lost when the *devadasi* system was banned by law.

The traditional dance of the *devadasi* women in temples was also known as Sadir. By the 19th century, this community was no longer as respected as before. In the 1930s, experts and lovers of this dance, such as Rukmini Devi and E. Krishna Iyer, felt the need to revive the dance for younger students and give it the status it deserved. They modified the dance by altering some of the *abhinaya* (gestures) and called it Bharatanatyam.

There are many theories on why they chose this name: perhaps it was because the dance followed the rules set out in Bharata's *Natya Shastra*. Or it could mean the dance of Bharat, or even because, *Bha* is for *bhava* (feelings and emotions), *Ra* is for raga (melody of the songs to which the dancer dances) and *Ta* is for *talam* (the beat). The dance is now popular across the country and the world.

Today, there are many *bani* or styles of Bharatanatyam, each with its own nuances, but the overall way of performance and the postures are the same. The Thanjavur quartet – four brothers called Chinnayya, Ponnayya, Sivanandam and Vadivelu, who lived in the 19th century, codified the dance into the form it is today. A typical performance is accompanied by musicians, a string and percussion instrument, and a *nattuvanar* who keeps the beat.

Today, these arts continue to be learnt and performed by many, but several arts, such as travelling musical dramas, have barely survived in these times of television, OTT services and movies.

KERALA

Kerala's classical arts tradition had a common connection with Tamil Nadu until the fourth century CE and then branched off, though the music followed the south Indian system of ragas and *swaras*, and the dances and dramas were based on the *Natya Shastra*. Costumes and local variations were very strong, with northern Kerala traditions being similar to southern Karnataka ones. The deeper influence of Muslims and Christians due to the ancient trade connections has also created unique art forms.

From the fourth century to the 11th century CE, some Kerala temples, such as the Thrikodithanam Temple in Kottayam district and the Trivikramangalam Temple in Thiruvananthapuram, have sculptures of dancers. One has dancers with a *kodai* (umbrella) and another with a *kodam* (pot), showing the popularity of the dances called *kodai koothu* and *kodam koothu* (*koothu* means dance in Tamil). Another sculpture from these temples shows a dancer with musicians as well. Musical instruments of these times included the *veena* and *kuzhal* (flute). By this time, temple dance and music performances were in the hands of a trained group of men called the Chakkaiyars, who performed to the music of another community, the Nambiars. Music was connected closely to the temples. Some kings, like Ravivarman Kulasekhara of Venatu (1299–1314 CE) were well versed in music.

Koodiyattam or Kutiyattam

A unique aspect of classical arts in Kerala was the distinctive drama style from as early as the eighth century CE. Shaktibhadran wrote the *Ashcharya Chudamani*, a full-fledged drama based on the Ramayana. During the reign of the Kulasekhara kings in the 10th century CE, plays about kings became popular. The poet Tolan composed passages and speeches for the art form Koodiyattam, which combines ancient Sanskrit theatre with *koothu*, a performing art from Sangam times. Koodiyattam was performed based on the texts, *Attaprakaram* and *Kramadeepika*, both dealing with rules and recommendations for actors and stage skills.

While in other south Indian regions, drama focused more or equally on music and dance, in Kerala they were more focused on the acting and dialogue delivery, and not on dance at all. Many ancient plays authored by Sanskrit playwright Bhasa and others are performed even today.

Theatre became an essential part of temple ritual practised in the larger and more popular temples having a *koothambalam* or a covered stage, built according to the rules in the *Natya Shastra*. They were excellent examples of Kerala craftsmanship in wood: large, yet excellent acoustically. Complex joints ensured a minimum number of pillars for the audience to view the stage. The use of wooden slats made the lighting discreet and kept the theatre cool.

Kerala has had a strong tradition of martial arts through *kalari* schools in each village. In these schools evolved the martial arts dance of *parisakali* by the Mappila Muslim community of north Kerala. It is a mock fight between boys holding short sticks in one hand and a red straw shield in the other hand. *Valeru* and *kunteru* are two other dance-like performances where the dancer/warrior throws a javelin or sword many a time and catches it by the shaft or hilt.

Kathakali and Mohiniattam are the two historical dances Kerala is famous for. In the 12th century CE, Jayadeva's *Ashtapadis*, comprising hymns to Krishna, were introduced in Kerala and became popular because of their richness of language and music. It inspired devotion to Krishna and in the 17th century CE, Manaveda, the Samuthiri of Calicut, composed the *Krishna Giti* on the life of Krishna for a performance in the most popular temple for Krishna in the state – Guruvayur. Thus was created Krishnattam, a series of eight plays that became a temple art. In north Kerala, in a spirit of creative rivalry, the raja of Kattarakara created the Ramanattam or the story of Rama in dance. A popular tradition was created of the *aattakatha* – eight stories performed over eight nights, developing into the classical dance-drama, Kathakali.

In the 17th century CE, the raja of Vettatnad introduced a series of important changes in Kathakali: dancers did not have to sing; the masks for the *rakshasa*s were replaced with special headgear; two drums, the *chenda* and the *maddalam*, were introduced; the *chutti* (mask/make-up) along with the white mask protruding under the chin, and colour schemes for make-up were systematized – green was for those with good moral values; the colour red, weapons and fiery moustaches were all for the negative characters, with red, white or black beards also for the evil ones; those with spiritual and gentle qualities wore simple costumes and ornaments without the bulging skirts, overcoats and headgear associated with the other characters. To the light of tall metal lamps, characters would enter from behind a screen held by two supporting performers.

A Kathakali dancer

The evil characters would grab and throw away the screen, while the good ones would allow the supporting performers to gently fold the screen!

Usually presented in a mixture of Sanskrit and Malayalam, there can often be humour in a Kathakali performance. For example, Ravana, while trying to refute Sita's argument that a relationship between her and Ravana will be unequal, rattles off examples of how unsuited people often get married!

The many *nadu vazhis* or smaller kingdoms of Kerala encouraged Kathakali in the 17th and 18th centuries CE by funding schools to teach the drama, train musicians and create new plays. Fortunately, Kathakali remains popular even today and continues to innovate with new stories and themes.

Another classical dance from Kerala is the Mohiniattam, literally meaning 'the dance of Mohini', which evolved from the dances of the *devadasis*. This dance form was highly encouraged by the great king-composer Swati Thirunal (1813–46 CE), who has more than 400 classical compositions in both Carnatic and Hindustani style to his name.

Kathakali inspired a dance tradition in churches called Chavittu ('to stamp down with the leg') Natakam (drama/dance), a kind of dramatic opera, in which the actors would sing and stamp their foot hard on the wooden floor to create a beat. The stories would be Christian and the actors would be trained in *kalari*. The costumes and the plays were modelled on European plays. Gothuruthu Island, where this is said to have originated, houses an academy teaching this art form.

Another syncretic dance is the Margamkali, which is traditionally performed in a subgroup of the St. Thomas Christian community. The song it is danced to is in Malayalam. It tells the story of the life and work of St. Thomas. Historians have linked it to Jewish song and dance traditions and Indian ones.

Margamkali dancers dance around a traditional brass lamp

The folk music and dances of Kerala, like other parts of south India, have a very old history. *Vanchi pattu* were songs that boatmen would sing as they ferried passengers and goods along the many backwaters of Kerala. Agricultural labourers had their own songs. *Vadakkan pattu* were ballads of heroism. *Pallipaadal* were Christian songs in Malayalam with a mixture of Syriac, Latin and Tamil words. There were songs for weddings, such as *mailanchi pattu* and *charthu pattu*, and for ceremonies in the church. The *pattukal* sung by Mappila Muslims have a strong Arabic flavour.

The earliest dances in Kerala were developed by tribes and communities, to the accompaniment of their music for their deities in hills and forests. As in other places, these deities over many centuries began to be identified with mainstream Hindu deities like Shiva and Vishnu. Yatrakali and Sanghakali are such dances, with the former using swords in a kind of war dance, while the latter is a group free-for-all dance.

Theyyam or Theyyattam is one of the oldest folk dances still performed as a form of worship of the Mother Goddess, a prehistoric tradition blended with the worship of Devi/Bhagavati or Parvati. The dancers wear impressive costumes and make-up; the steps are very vigorous. Long drums and cymbals, among other instruments, lead the dancer to a frenzy or trance. Sometimes, the dancers carry flaming torches. The Theyyattam is performed as an offering in 17-day festivals. Hill tribes also perform it in their temples.

Vellattam is a similar dance performed as a daily offering. Pana and Kalaiyar Kali are other dances performed in temples around a tall lamp. The *pambu thullal* is a dance mimicking the movements of a snake, a symbol of fertility, in front of a *kolam* (a floor design like a *rangoli*) designed like a snake to represent a deity. *Pulluvakudam* is the percussion instrument used.

Kerala's performing arts history till the colonial period is a fascinating mix of prehistoric, Hindu, Christian and Muslim cultures, blending into unique classical traditions. From the colonial period, especially post-Independence, in Kerala and other parts of south India, the classical traditions have received support in urban areas, but folk traditions suffer a gradual decline due to poor financial returns and changing tastes.

KARNATAKA

The music, dance and drama traditions of Karnataka can be divided into two parts: the classical traditions, influenced by Bharata's *Natya Shastra*, performed in temples and palaces; and the local traditions based on regional legacies of the land.

Classical music, dance and drama were closely connected, especially for entertainment. The style of music was called Carnatic from somewhere between the 11th and 14th centuries. Theatre would have had dialogues set to music, and actors performed basic *abhinaya* (gestures) and *nritta* (footwork). We know of classical traditions only from the reign of the Chalukyas. After that, in the Vijayanagara period, they are similar to that of Andhra. After the decline of Vijayanagara, the best performers moved to Thanjavur. In the 1850s, when Thanjavur too declined, many came back to the new kingdom of Mysuru, which became a great seat for music and dance even after the British conquered the region.

The Chalukya-period text *Manasollasa* mentions the significance of music, dance and drama in the life of the people. Many instruments and books are mentioned, and the *veena* is given high importance. Sculptures in many temples in Badami and elsewhere give us an idea of how dancers would have looked. A few names and details of dancers from Chalukya inscriptions give us an idea of how famous, popular and wealthy they were. The Vijayeswara Temple mentions Challabbe, a great female dancer in the eighth century CE, and Achalan, an actor and dancer who was an expert in the *Natya Shastra*. In the Mahadeva Temple in Itagi, a grant was made for dancers to live on the main road near the south gate. Priya Ketala Devi, the queen of Vikramaditya, was a great dancer. Sule, Patra, Poti, Boddi, Deva Ganika, Devadasi, Vilasini and Sani are a few of the titles given to dancers and perhaps they referred to different types of dancers who specialized in particular styles.

A Jain text called the *Shanti Purana* by Ponna (10th century CE), mentions an event when 32 dancers danced like a pearl necklace, and created colour images by moving the flower petals on the stage with their feet.

There are many sculptures of dancers in the temples of the Hoysala period. The Hoysala queen Shantala was an expert dancer. She was called 'Natya Sarasvati' and 'Vichitra Nartana Sutradhare', indicating she was a creative and innovative dancer. A verse from a poem of this time mentions actors dancing energetically to the story of Shiva's slaying of Andhakasura.

Haridasas, such as Basava (12th century CE), sang in easy-to-understand Kannada about personal experiences, the problems of life, and how faith in God was important to tide over difficult days. A Shiva devotee, he also sang extensively on the oneness of human beings. Instruments of this time include the *valaga* and a wind instrument known as the *nagaswaram* (not *nadaswaram*) in Tamil Nadu. The *jalataranga*, a set of porcelain bowls filled with water and struck with a wooden stick, was also commonly used at this time.

During the Vijayanagara times, the sage Vidyaranya, who was the guru of the first two kings of the dynasty, composed a text on music, titled *Sangeeta Sara* ('the essence of music'). The greatest musician of the period was Purandaradasa, a diamond merchant who gave up his wealthy life to become a Haridasa. It is his system of teaching music – both the raga and the notes – that is used even today for Carnatic music.

A stamp honouring Purandaradasa

By this time, there were two kinds of dances. In the Margam tradition, very popular even today, through the music, lyrics and *abhinaya*, the dancer emotionally becomes the person in the song (for example, Rama pining for Sita) and in that union (*margam*) she is able to elevate the feelings of the audience to feel the same connection themselves. The other tradition, called Desi, is dance for entertainment. Both were popular in the Vijayanagara court, but we hear more of the Desi style.

In one popular dance in Hampi, as described in a text, many dancers formed a circle while playing the *kolattam*, using a short stick to make rhythmic sounds as the dancers lightly tap each other's sticks and move in patterns. Dancers would enter the stage in pairs, using objects like fly-whisks, spears or swords for complex dances. According to texts, dancers were expected to move as gracefully 'as a snake in shimmering sunlight'! Acrobatics was also a part of dance performances. The palace had a *nartana shala* or a school to train drama, dance and music artistes.

Although, after the Vijayanagara kingdom collapsed, many performers went to Thanjavur and other courts, the Bahamani sultanates had their own music and dance

LIFE LESSONS FROM DANCE

Jain texts from the Chalukya times give us information about dancers and dance. In Pampa's *Adi Purana* (eighth century CE), the hero, Vrishabhadeva, is watching a dance by 'Nilanjana' in his palace. She enters from behind a curtain held up by two other dancers (this practice is seen in plays even today). The text mentions how the stage was lighted, that there were many string and percussion instruments, and how she danced at three different speeds with all nine emotions (*navarasas*).

She dances for a long time, with excellent footwork, *abhinaya* and very complex movements, and no one wants her to stop. Suddenly, she falls and dies due to exhaustion. But Indra, the king of the *devas*, quickly creates a new Nilanjana who continues the dance.

Only Vrishabhadeva can spot this replacement.

He realizes the temporary nature of the human body and even the joy of seeing something beautiful or hearing something sweet. He gives up his royal life and and becomes a Jain monk, seeking what will give him permanent happiness.

Dancers and musicians, a sculpture in the Airavatesvara Temple complex, Darasuram, Tamil Nadu

Sculptures of dancers on the wall of the Mahanavmi Dibba, Hampi

traditions inspired by Persia. Some of these blended with local music, such as the Jhavna, an Arabic style of love songs, in the court of Tipu. This is said to have inspired the short Carnatic musical genre called Javalis. The *kanjira*, a common instrument in Carnatic music concerts, also came to India through Arab traders at this time. The entry of the violin into Carnatic music may have happened in Tipu's time or through British influence, depending on which historian one believes. Later, when the British helped replace Tipu with the Wodeyars in Mysuru, there was a great revival of classical music, dance and drama in Karnataka, especially in Mysuru.

The period of origin of the folk traditions of Karnataka is uncertain. The dances of rural Karnataka could be of two or three types. Dances and music for rituals and worship of deities included Nandi Dhwaja, Karaga, Gorava, Bhuta Kola, Veeragase, Veerabhadra and Soma. Nandi Dhwaja is a dance where one or two performers dance while carrying very tall flags featuring the image of a Nandi and adorned with strings of bells. Soma is a dance for the guardian deities of the village. Kancharaya, a lamb (later, a representative of Vishnu), and yellow-donning Bhuta Raya (later, a representative of Shiva) dancers wear large, painted masks that have fearsome expressions where the wearer can see only through the nostrils of the mask. They also wear many bells, anklets and wristbands. Villagers offer grated coconut mixed with banana, jaggery, honey and cardamom to the dancers who take the form of the deities. The Bhuta Kola is a dance where the dancers either paint their face or wear heavy and beautifully cast bronze masks. Popular deities are Panjurli and Pilichandi, to whom the dancers give thanks and pray for a good monsoon, bountiful harvests, and prevention of attacks by wild animals.

Sculptures record different kinds of musicians in the Chennakeshava Temple in Belur, Karnataka

Dances for entertainment, fun and bringing people together included Koda, Kolatta, Pugadi, Dollu, Dudi, Suggi, Halage, Hoovina Makkalu, Hutri and many others.

Dances for artistic expression, sheer joy and a nod to religion included many of the animal dances, where the many dancers would wear elaborate make-up and mimic animals. Such dances include Anjaneya (monkey), Simha (lion), Karadi (bear), Kudire (horse), Kombaat (deer), Preta (ghost), Sudugadu Siddha (a holy man of the graveyard) and others like Bhuta Kola. It is likely that these dances are as ancient as the classical traditions that date from before the Chalukya kings.

ANDHRA

Similar to other south Indian regions, classical dances and music were enjoyed in courts and temples as well as in villages and tribal communities. Andhra dances are classified as *aradhana nrityalu* – for the temples as *puja*, *shastreeya nrityalu* based on the *Natya Shastra* texts, *prachara nrityalu* – dance for entertainment especially in villages, and *atavika nrityalu* – dance of the ancient tribal communities that may be prehistoric.

We have little information on music and dance before the Kakatiyas. Bharata in the *Natya Shastra* mentions Aandhri raga and the Kaisika Vritti as the special melody and dance of the Andhra region. The Amaravati stupa (third century BCE to the fourth century CE) shows the *yazh*, a stringed instrument popular in Tamil Nadu, being played here in a sculpture. The *yazh* was replaced

Sculpture of a dancer in Ramappa temple, Warangal, Telangana – note the high-heeled footwear!

by the *veena* by about the 10th century CE.

The high status of dancers in the Kakatiya times can be gleaned from the many inscriptions about them. The Panagal Temple inscription of Mailamba tells us she was a dancer, well versed in music, *nritta* and playing musical instruments. In the Dharmavaram Temple, mention is made of Reccarla Nani Reddy who led the local temple's musicians and dancers. Machala Devi, a dancer during the reign of Prataparudra, was such a living legend in her lifetime that she had her own *natya shala* (theatre school) and had a drama enacted about her own life! These performers were obviously wealthy enough to donate significantly to the temple and important enough to be recorded in an inscription.

Some idea of how they looked is seen in the many temples in Warangal, especially the Ramappa and Swayambhu Lingeswara Temples. During the rule of Ganapati, his elephant troop commander Jaya Senapati (1253–54 CE) wrote a book on music and dance, called *Nritta Ratnavali*. Srisailam had a special dance on Maha

YAKSHAGANA: A SPECTACLE OF STORIES

Yakshagana, a grand tradition of music, dance and drama is common to both Karnataka and Andhra. In Tamil Nadu this tradition is called *theru koothu*. In Karnataka, it is performed in the coastal areas and near Mysuru. The stories are from the Ramayana and Mahabharata. All roles are played by men, the dialogues are slightly musical, there are elaborate gestures and a little bit of dancing using the limbs, especially footwork.

The grandest part of the Yakshagana is the costumes: elaborate crowns, shoulder ornaments, swords made of a grass called pith covered with either bits of mirror or gold paper and sometimes brightly painted. The costumes used to be embroidered in the past. The musical instruments vary across different states. In Karnataka, *jagate* (a metal disc struck with a wooden stick), *shruti* (somewhat like a harmonium, working on the system of bellows), *maddale* (a percussion instrument) and *chande* (a drum) are common. A group of singers on the side sing important dialogues as a refrain. Many Yakshagana practices conform to the *Natya Shastra*. Performances start in the evening, when there is no farming work going on, and go on until next morning. Yakshagana troupes struggle to survive these days.

Yakshagana,
a storytelling tradition

Shivaratri for which kings gifted land for funds. The Kakatiyas were said to have brought Vishnu-related ideas and dancers from Odisha to Srikakulam Temple.

Somanatha, the great poet of the Kakatiya times, wrote in his poems that musicians knew 108 *talas* (beat structures) to keep time to ragas or songs. Plays were popular and were performed on large stages with many curtains. Dances were performed by both single and group performers. The dance teacher was allowed to carry a long, crooked stick to show his position as a guru. Dancers kept fit by doing many exercises.

After the fall of the Kakatiyas, the best dancers and singers were concentrated in the Vijayanagara capital in Hampi, or in temples, especially famous ones like Tirupati and those in Kanchipuram.

Yakshagana was also very popular at this time in Andhra. Many Brahmins began enacting plays with music (but less dance) while following the *Natya Shastra* rules, called Bhagavata Mela. These continue to be performed across Karnataka, Andhra and Tamil Nadu.

Stunning sculptures of dancers and musicians in the Ramappa Temple in Warangal – they really look like they are moving!

When the Qutb Shahi dynasty ruled Andhra, especially Hyderabad, music imbibed a strong Arabic and Persian influence. The *shehnai* and the *naubat* (drum) are considered auspicious instruments even today. *Marfa*, a type of drum, a kind of music and also a type of dance using daggers, came from East Africa to Hyderabad along with many of the Nizam's soldiers.

Two ancient classical dances of Andhra are the Kuchipudi and the Vilasini Natyam, both having seen a revival in the last few decades. Kuchipudi is a village near Vijayawada and the dance is said to have developed here in the 17th century CE from earlier origins. First performed by only men and mostly with songs on Vishnu, today its scope is broader. Vilasini Natyam is a style of dance performed in temples by *devadasis*, and uses special songs called *choornikas*.

A Kuchipudi dancer performing Kuchipudi Tarangam, balancing on a plate with a pot of water on her head

In inscriptions in Tamil Nadu, Karnataka and Andhra from the 10th to 17th centuries CE, we see a a dance called Perani. The dancers are men, with a clean-shaven head except for a small tuft, their bodies fully smeared with holy ash. They wear many bells, hold fly whisks and dance

A graceful pose by a dancer in a sculpture in Ramappa Temple

in honour of Shiva, with complex footwork, both very energetic (*tandava*) and graceful (*lasya*). A dance by the same name is popular in Andhra and Karnataka, but it's not clear if they are related.

Andhra's village folk and tribal communities have several dances, many of them dating back to ancient, even prehistoric, times. One such is the storytelling-based Bainda Kathalu by the Bainda people who worship Kolupu, a mother goddess now identified with Parvati. Another such tradition is the Bonalu, also an offering to an ancient mother goddess now identified with Ujjaini Mahakali. Her Telugu names include Mysamma, Pochamma and Katta Mysamma. To receive her blessings, a procession is taken out with the *potha raju* or village protector. Women carry a *bonalu*, a pot with flames, and dance. The Chindu Madigas also have their dance-dramas, as do communities such as the Dhimsa, Lambada, Chenchu and Savarna. Unfortunately, these traditions are fast disappearing.

CHRONOLOGY OF THE MAIN DYNASTIES

WHO CAME AFTER WHOM

Here are the main ancient and medieval dynasties (and their rulers) of south India for those interested in the details of names and dates. As you will see, we do not know the names of all the rulers and sometimes the period of their reign with certainty. The references to the early Pandyas, Cholas and Cheras come only from the Sangam poems, and these lists are partial. Names are spelt in many different ways. Here is a resource if you want to know more: https://sangamtranslationsbyvaidehi.com/historical-references/

THE THREE CROWNED KINGS

PANDYA

The name probably comes from *pandu* or very old.

- **Symbols:** A pair of fish; the neem flower.
- **Start time:** At least 100 BCE, may be earlier.
- **End time:** 18th century, due to attack by Alauddin Khilji of the Delhi Sultanate.
- **Territory:** Southern Tamil Nadu, and parts of Kerala and Sri Lanka.
- **Capital:** Madurai; Tenkasi.
- **Famous for:** Selling pearls and other goods especially to Rome; super famous for promoting Tamil. Texts like

Madurai Kanchi, poems of Arivudai Nambi (a Pandya king) are texts to learn not only about the life of those times but also how we can live our lives today. Pandya queens were also great poets.

- **Unforgettable:** Kadungon's deeds have been described in detail in the poem *Maduraikkanchi* and his name is also mentioned in the *Silappadikaram*. Nedunjeliyan II conquered most of the Tamil region. Maravarman Sundara Pandyan conquered the Cholas but let them rule their land. Srimara Srivallabha built many tanks, canals and water reservoirs, such as Sri Vallabha Pereri.
- **Succeeded by:** Tenkasi Pandyas, Madurai Nayaks, Vijayanagara Empire, Delhi Sultanate, Jaffna kingdom.
- **Must visit:** The temples on the banks of the River Tambraparni, Madurai; their old port Korkai. Their cave temple in Kalugumalai is carved from one huge rock!

EARLY PANDYAS

Rulers: Nedunjeliyan I ▸ Pudappandiyan ▸ Mudukudumi Paruvaludhi ▸ Nedunjeliyan II ▸ Nan Maran ▸ Nedunjeliyan III ▸ Maran Valudi ▸ Musiri Mutriya Cheliyan ▸ Ukkirap Peruvaluthi

MIDDLE PANDYAS

Rulers: Kadungon (590–620 CE) ▸ Maravarman Avani Culamani (c. 620 45 CE) ▸ Jayantavarman (c. 645–70 CE) ▸ Arikesari Maravarman Nindra Seer Nedumaran [identified with Koon Pandya] (c. 670–710 CE) ▸ Kochadaiyan Ranadhiran (710–35 CE) ▸ Arikesari Parankusa Maravarman Rajasimha I (735–65 CE) ▸ Parantaka Nedunjeliyan (765–815 CE)

▸ Rasasingan II (790–800) ▸ Varagunan I (800–30) ▸ Srimara Srivallabha (815–62 CE) ▸ Varagunavarman II (862–80 CE) ▸ Parantaka Viranarayana (880–900 CE) ▸ Maravarman Rajasimha II (900–20 CE)

PANDYAS UNDER THE CHOLA EMPIRE

Rulers: Sundara Pandyan I ▸ Vira Pandyan I ▸ Vira Pandyan II ▸ Amarabhujanga Tivrakopa ▸ Jatavarman Sundara Pandyan ▸ Maravarman Vikrama Pandyan ▸ Maravarman Parakrama Pandyan ▸ Jatavarman Pandyan ▸ Srivallabha Manakulachala (1101–24 CE) ▸ Maravarman Srivallabha (1132–61 CE) ▸ Parakrama Pandyan I (1161–62 CE) ▸ Kulasekara Pandyan III ▸ Vira Pandyan III ▸ Jatavarman Srivallabha (1175–80 CE) ▸ Jatavarman Kulasekara Devan I (1190–1216 CE)

PANDALAM (LATER PANDYAS)

Rulers: Parakrama Pandyan II (1212–15 CE) ▸ Maravarman Sundara Pandyan (1216–38 CE) ▸ Sadayavarman Kulasekaran II (1238–40 CE) ▸ Maravarman Sundara Pandyan II (1238–51) ▸ Jatavarman Sundara Pandyan (1251–68 CE) ▸ Maravarman Kulasekara Pandyan I (1268–1308 CE) ▸ Sundara Pandyan IV (1309–27 CE) ▸ Vira Pandyan IV (1309–45 CE)

***

CHERA

Cher is slushy land, so probably 'rulers of the slushy land'. Though this is not commonly agreed upon, it is probably after them that Kerala is named today.

Symbols: The bow and the palm-tree flower.

Start time: At least 100 BCE, maybe earlier.

End time: 12th century CE because of the Cholas, but their distant relatives continued to rule till British times.

Territory: Kerala and south-west Tamil Nadu.

Capital: Early Cheras: Vanchi and Muziris ; Kongu Cheras: Karur; Chera Perumals: Mahodayapuram.

Famous for: Selling pepper and spices through Arab merchants; learning how to use rivers and elephants to protect their country.

Unforgettable: Nedum Cheralatan (sometime before fourth century BCE) because he is said to have expanded the boundary of the Chera kings till the Himalayas – probably did not actually do that but must have fought a successful war there. Kulasekhara Varman is thought to have authored the Sanskrit texts *Mukundamala* and *Perumal Tirumozhi*, compiled as a part of *Nalayira Divya Prabandham*. Sthanu Ravi Varman reign was noted for developments in science.

Preceded by: Villavar tribes.

Succeeded by: Zamorin of Calicut; kingdom of Travancore; kingdom of Cochin.

Must visit: Remains of their ports in Muziris (Kodungallur nearby had an observatory), Kochi and the palace at Padmanabhapuram built by a much later successor. Their cave temples in Vizhinjam, Kottukal and Chihral.

EARLY CHERAS

Rulers: Nedum Cheralatan (or Cheral Athan) ▸ Palyani Chel Kezhu Kuttuvan ▸ Kalangai Kanni Narmudi Cheral ▸ Kadal

Pirakottiya Chenguttuvan ▸ Adu Kottu Pattu Cheralatan ▸ Chelva Kadumko Valia Athan ▸ Kanaikkal Irumporai ▸ Perum Cheral Irumporai Chelva Kadumko Valia Athan Kudakko Illam Cheral Irumporai ▸ Kadummipudha Chera ▸ Ko Athan Cheral Irumporai ▸ Perum Kadungo (Irumporai) ▸ Ilam Kadungo (Irumporai) ▸ Mak-kotai ▸ Kuttuvan Kotai ▸ Kollippurai ▸ Kol-Irumporai ▸ Sa Irumporai

KONGU CHERA DYNASTY (KARUR)

Rulers: Ravi Goda ▸ Kanthan Ravi ▸ Vira Goda ▸ Vira Narayana ▸ Vira Chola ▸ Vira Kerala ▸ Vira Kerala Amarabhujangadeva ▸ Kerala Kesari Adhirajarajadeva

CHERA/PERUMALS OF MAKOTAI (KERALA)

Rulers: Sthanu Ravi Varman (844/5–70/71 CE) ▸ Kulasekhara Varman (Kulasekhara Alvar) ▸ Rama Rajasekhara (Cheraman Perumal Nayanar) ▸ Vijayaraga; Goda Goda ▸ Kerala Kesari ▸ Goda Ravi ▸ Indu/Indesvaran Goda ▸ Bhaskara Ravi Manukuladithya ▸ Ravi Goda; Rajasimha ▸ Raja Raja ▸ Ravi Rama ▸ Adithyan Goda Ranadithya ▸ Rama Kulasekhara

***

CHOLA

The name probably comes from from *chezhipu* or fertile; their other names like *killi* or *valavan* all connect them with ruling a very fertile land.

Symbols: The tiger and the Ficus tree flower.

Start time: At least 100 BCE, maybe earlier.

End time: 13th century CE, because of the Pandyas.

Territory: Primarily the River Kaveri region in Tamil Nadu, but in the 12th century CE, they ruled nearly all of south India, and parts of present-day Sri Lanka, Malaysia and Cambodia (indirectly).

Capital: Pazhaiyaarai; Thanjavur; Gangaikonda Cholapuram.

Famous for: Recording minute administrative details on stone inscriptions in the many grand temples they built; managing water and irrigation systems; building three outstanding temples: in Thanjavur, Gangaikonda Cholapuram and Darasuram.

Unforgettable: Rajaraja Chola never saw defeat in battle. He built massive temples, including the Brihasdisvara Temple, organized the administrative system in the region, and very carefully recorded important information. Sundara Chola encouraged both Sanskrit and Tamil literature, including Buddhist works. He built a 16-mile long and three-mile wide artificial lake. Rajendra I built a new capital, Gangaikonda Cholapuram, to commemorate his victory over Mahipala, the Pala king of present-day Bengal and Bihar. Rajaraja Chola II initiated the construction of the very famous Airavatesvara Temple at Darasuram. In his time, Chola navies dominated both the western and eastern seas.

Preceded by: Pandyas, Pallavas, Cheras, Chalukyas.

Succeeded by: Pandyas, Polonnaruwa kingdom, Kakatiyas, Eastern Gangas, Melayu kingdom, Venad, Hoysalas.

Must visit: The remains of their palace in Gangaikonda Cholapuram, canal networks in the River Kaveri, and their temples, including smaller ones like the Nageswaraswamy Temple in Kumbakonam, with its detailed carvings.

EARLY CHOLAS

Rulers: Ilamchetchenni ▸ Karikala Chola ▸ Nedunkilli ▸ Nalankilli ▸ Killivalavan ▸ Kopperuncholan ▸ Kocengannan ▸ Perunarkilli

MEDIEVAL CHOLAS

Rulers: Vijayalaya Chola (848–71 CE?) ▸ Aditya I (871–907 CE) ▸ Parantaka Chola I (907–50 CE) ▸ Gandaraditya (950–957 CE) ▸ Arinjaya Chola (956–57 CE) ▸ Sundara Chola (957–70 CE) ▸ Uttama Chola (970–85 CE) ▸ Rajaraja Chola I (985–1014 CE) ▸ Rajendra Chola I (1012–44 CE) ▸ Rajadhiraja Chola (1018–54 CE) ▸ Rajendra Chola II (1051–63 CE) ▸ Virarajendra Chola (1063–70 CE) ▸ Athirajendra Chola (1067–70 CE)

CHALUKYA CHOLAS

Rulers: Kulotunga Chola I (1070–20 CE) ▸ Vikrama Chola (1118–35 CE) ▸ Kulotunga Chola II (1133–50 CE) ▸ Rajaraja Chola II (1146–63 CE) ▸ Rajadhiraja Chola II (1163–78 CE) ▸ Kulotunga Chola III (1178–18 CE) ▸ Rajaraja Chola III (1216–56 CE) ▸ Rajendra Chola III (1246–79 CE)

***

AY/AI

Symbol: Elephant.

Start time: Early historic period (pre-Pallava).

End time: 10th century CE.

Territory: Pamba to Kanyakumari.

Capital: Podhigai Malai; Vizhinjam.

Famous for: Many Ay chiefs such as Andilan/Andiran, Thitiyan and Atiyan/Athyan are mentioned in Tamil poetry.

Gunasila, around the eighth century CE, excavated a cave temple dedicated to Vishnu in Namakkal.

***

SATAVAHANA

Symbols: Arched hill or hill symbol, popularly known as the *chaitya* symbol.

Start time: Late 2nd century BCE.

End time: Early 3rd century CE.

Territory: Present-day Andhra Pradesh, Telangana and Maharashtra. At different times, their rule extended to parts of modern Gujarat, Madhya Pradesh and Karnataka.

Capital: Pratishthana, Amaravati.

Famous for: The rulers, especially Satakarni II, significantly repaired and embellished the Sanchi stupa. The gateways and the balustrade were constructed possibly by the Satavahanas. One of the kings, Shalivahana, is said to have changed the calendar system to what is even now used as the Saka calendar.

Unforgettable: Gautamputra Satakarni was the first king who bore a matronym (mother's name). His mother's name was probably Gautami Balashri.

Preceded by: Mauryas, Kanvas.

Succeeded by: Western Kshatrapas, Andhra Ikshvakus, Chutus, Vakatakas, Pallavas, Abhiras.

Must visit: The stupa sculptures of the Amaravati stupas, and at Goli, Jaggayyapeta, Ghantasala and Bhattiprolu.

Rulers: Simuka (100–70 BCE) ▸ Kanha (70–60 BCE) ▸ Satakarni I (70–60 BCE) ▸ Satakarni II (50–25 BCE) ▸ Sivasvati (1st c. CE) ▸ Gautamiputra Satakarni (2nd c. CE) ▸ Vashishtiputra Pulumavi (2nd c. CE) ▸ Vashishtiputra Satakarni (2nd c. CE) ▸ Shivaskanda Satakarni (2nd c. CE) ▸ Yajna Sri Satakarni (2nd c. CE)

***

KALABHRA

Symbols: The coins feature elephant, tiger, horse and fish iconography.

Start time: Third century CE.

End time: Sixth century CE.

Territory: Some or all parts of the Tamil region.

Capital: Kaveripoompattinam, Madurai.

Famous for: Not much verified information is available about this period.

Unforgettable: A 10th-century Jain text on grammar quotes a poem that some scholars attribute to Achyuta Vikranta, a Kalabhra king. They were Jain or Buddhist.

Preceded by: The Three Crowned Kings.

Succeeded by: Pallavas and Pandyas.

***

PALLAVA

Symbols: Lion and Nandi (bull).

Start time: Third century CE.

End time: Ninth century CE, because of the domination of the Cholas.

Territory: North Tamil Nadu, and south Andhra (very small part).

Capital: Kanchipuram.

Famous for: Building fabulous cave temples and early structural temples in Mahabalipuram and Kanchipuram. They developed the Pallava script from which the Grantha script ultimately came and gave rise to several other South-East Asian scripts.

Unforgettable: Mahendravarman (I) Pallava, for excavating many cave temples but also for writing two Sanskrit plays: *Mattavilasa Prahasana* and the *Bagavadajjuka.* Narasimhavarman I was known as 'Maha Malla' or 'Mamallan' (great wrestler), and Mamallapuram (Mahabalipuram) was named after him. Chinese traveller Xuanzang visited Kanchipuram during his reign. Nandivarman II built the Vaikuntha-Perumal Temple and added his plays to dramatized dance worship such as Kutiyattam.

Must visit: Mahabalipuram, their port, where the Shore Temple (built by Narasimhavarman II) is a UNESCO World Heritage Site; and their cave temples in places such as Tiruchirappalli, Vallam and Moghalrajpuram.

Preceded by: Kalabhras, Satavahanas.

Succeeded by: Cholas, Kadambas, Western Gangas.

Rulers: Virakurcha ▸ Vishnugopa I ▸ Vishnugopa II ▸ Simhavarman III ▸ Simhavishnu ▸ Mahendravarman I (600–30 CE) ▸ Narasimhavarman I (630–68 CE) ▸ Mahendravarman II (668–70 CE) ▸ Paramesvaravarman (670–95 CE) ▸

Narasimhavarman II (695–728 CE) ▸Paramesvaravarman II (728–31 CE) ▸ Nandivarman II (731–95 CE) ▸ Dantivarman (795–46 CE) ▸ Nandivarman III (846–69 CE) ▸ Nripatungavarman (869–80 CE) ▸ Aparajitavarman (880–97 CE)

***

WESTERN GANGA

Symbols: Their coins commonly had an elephant on the obverse and petals on the other side.

Start time: 350 CE.

End time: 999 CE.

Territory: Parts of southern Karnataka.

Capital: Kolar, Talakad.

Famous for: Tolerance for all faiths and special patronage of Jainism; construction of monuments in places such as Shravanabelagola and Kambadahalli; patronized Kannada and Sanskrit literature.

Unforgettable: The statue of Gommateshwara in Shravanabelagola built by King Butuga II and his commander and minister Chamundaraya; Durvinita was well versed in arts such as music, dance, Ayurveda and taming wild elephants.

Preceded by: Pallavas.

Succeeded by: Cholas.

Must visit: The monuments and *basadis* of Shravanabelagola and Kambadahalli.

Rulers: Konganivarman Madhava (350–70 CE) ▸ Madhava (370–90 CE) ▸ Harivarman (390–410 CE) ▸ Vishnugopa (410–

30 CE) ▸ Madhava III Tandangala (430–69 CE) ▸ Avinita (469–529 CE) ▸ Durvinita (529–79 CE) ▸ Mushkara (579–604 CE) ▸ Polavira (604–29 CE) ▸ Srivikrama (629–54 CE) ▸ Bhuvikarma (654–79 CE) ▸ Shivamara I (679–726) CE ▸ Sripurusha (726–88 CE) ▸ Shivamara II (788–816 CE) ▸ Rachamalla I (816–43 CE) ▸ Ereganga Neetimarga (843–70 CE) ▸ Rachamalla II (870–907 CE) ▸ Ereganga Neetimarga II (907–21 CE) ▸ Narasimha (921–33 CE) ▸ Rachamalla III (933–38 CE) ▸ Butuga II (938–61 CE) ▸ Marulaganga Neetimarga (961–63 CE) ▸ Marasimha II Satyavakya (963–75 CE) ▸ Rachamalla IV Satyavakya (975–86 CE) ▸ Rachamalla V (Rakkasaganga) (986–99 CE) ▸ Neetimarga Permanadi (999 CE)

***

KADAMBA

Symbol: The royal lion.

Start time: c.345–450 CE.

End time: 550 CE.

Territory: Northern Karnataka and the Konkan.

Capital: Banavasi.

Famous for: The Kadambas patronized both Hinduism and Jainism. They built many temples, Jain *basadis* and monasteries during their rule, including the Jain temples at Kolar, Shravanabelagola and Halebid. Their temple architecture evolved from rock-cut to stone and brick, and contributed to the Dravida style.

Unforgettable: Many Kadamba kings were scholars, including the founding king Mayurasharma, whom an inscription describes as 'Vedangavaidya Sharada' ('master of the Vedas') and Vishnuvarma, who was an expert in grammar and logic.

Preceded by: Chutus, Pallavas.

Succeeded by: Chalukyas.

Must Visit: Hanumakonda and Warangal; many monuments such as Thousand Pillar Temple, Ramappa Temple or Rudresvara Temple, a UNESCO World Heritage Site, Warangal Fort and Kota Gullu.

Rulers: Mayurasharma (345–65 CE) ▸ Kangavarma (365–90 CE) ▸ Bagitarha (390–415 CE) ▸ Raghu (415–35 CE) ▸ Kakusthavarma (435–55 CE) ▸ Santivarma (455–60 CE) ▸ Mrigeshavarma (460–80 CE) ▸ Shivamandhativarm (480–85 CE) ▸ Ravivarma (485–519 CE) ▸ Harivarma (519–25 CE)

TRIPARVATHA BRANCH

Rulers: Krishna Varma I (455 CE) ▸ Vishnuvarma ▸ Simhavarma ▸ Krishna Varma II ▸ Pulakesin I (Chalukya) (543–66 CE)

***

CHALUKYA

Symbols: The boar (Lord Vishnu as Varaha saved Earth and so would the Chalukya kings save it from their enemies).

Start time: Sixth century CE.

End time: 12th century CE, because of the Cholas.

Territory: All of present-day Karnataka and Maharashtra, and much of Andhra.

Capital: Badami.

Famous for: Building fabulous cave temples and structural temples in Badami, Aihole and Pattadakal. During Rajaraja Narendra's reign, two literary works in Kannada, *Vikramarjuna Vijayam* and *Gadayuddam*, popularized the story of the Mahabharata in Karnataka. Tamil translations of the Mahabharata were done during his reign.

Unforgettable: Someshvara III for writing the *Manasollasa*, an exciting text that gives us a detailed picture of what daily life was like at the time, besides covering topics such as polity, governance, astronomy, astrology, rhetoric, medicine, food, architecture, painting, poetry and music; Pulakesin II's victories.

Preceded by: Kadambas, Vakatakas.

Succeeded by: Rashtrakutas, Eastern Chalukyas.

Must visit: Biccavolu, Ambapuram (both in Andhra) and Tilvalli (Karnataka), but most of all, read the *Manasollasa* or its translation.

CHALUKYAS OF BADAMI

Rulers: Pulakesin I (543–66 CE) ▸ Kirtivarman I (566–97 CE) ▸ Mangalesha (597–609 CE) ▸ Pulakesin II (609–42 CE) ▸ Vikramaditya I (655–80 CE) ▸ Vinayaditya (680–96 CE) ▸ Vijayaditya (696–733 CE) ▸ Vikramaditya II (733–46 CE) ▸ Kirtivarman II (746–53 CE)

CHALUKYAS OF VENGI (EASTERN CHALUKYAS)

Rulers: Kubja Vishnuvardhana (624–41 CE) ▸ Jayasimha I (641–73 CE) ▸ Indra Bhattaraka (673 CE) ▸ Vishnu

Vardhana II (673–82 CE) ▸ Mangi Yuvaraja (682–706 CE) ▸ Jayasimha II (706–18 CE) ▸ Kokkili (719 CE) ▸ Vishnuvardhana III (719–55 CE) ▸ Vijayaditya I (755–72 CE) ▸ Vishnuvardhana IV (772–808 CE) ▸ Vijayaditya II (808–847 CE) ▸ Kali Vishnuvardhana V (847–9 CE) ▸ Vijayaditya III (849–92 CE) ▸ Chalukya Bhima I(892–921 CE) ▸ Vijayaditya IV (921 CE)▸ Amma (921–27 CE) ▸ Beta Vijayaditya V (927 CE) ▸ Tala I (927 CE) ▸ Vikramaditya II (927–28 CE) ▸ Bhima II (928 CE)▸ Yuddhamalla II (928–35 CE) ▸ Chalukya Bhima II (935–47 CE) ▸ Amma II (947–70 CE) ▸ Tala I (970 CE) ▸ Danarnava (970–73 CE) ▸ Jata Choda Bhima (973–99 CE) ▸ Shaktivarman I (1000–11 CE) ▸ Vimaladitya (1011–18 CE) ▸ Rajaraja Narendra (1019–61 CE) ▸ Vijayaditya VI (1063–68 CE, 1072–75 CE) ▸ Rajaraja II (1075–79 CE) ▸ Vira Chola Vishnuvardhana IX (1079–1102 CE)

CHALUKYAS OF KALYANI (WESTERN CHALUKYAS)

Rulers: Tailapa II (957–97 CE) ▸ Satyashraya (997–1008 CE) ▸ Vikramaditya V (1008–15 CE) ▸ Jayasimha II (1015–42 CE) ▸ Someshvara I (1042–68 CE) ▸ Someshvara II (1068–76 CE) ▸ Vikramaditya VI (1076–26 CE) ▸ Someshvara III (1126–38 CE) ▸ Jagadhekamalla II (1138–51 CE) ▸ Tailapa III (1151–64 CE) > Jagadhekamalla III (1163–83 CE) ▸ Someshvara IV (1184–1200 CE)

***

RASHTRAKUTA

Symbol: Golden eagle; name from *rashtra* (country) and *kuta* (chieftain).

Start time: Eighth century CE.

End time: 10th century CE due to Paramara and Chalukyan invasions.

Territory: Maharashtra, Karnataka, Madhya Pradesh, Andhra Pradesh and parts of Tamil Nadu.

Capital: Manyakheta.

Famous for: Promoting Kannada and Sanskrit literature.

Unforgettable: Amoghavarsha I, who overcame initial resistance to establish a peaceful and stable empire. He remained friendly with all his feudatories, and is known for his interest in fine arts and literature. Suleman, an Arab merchant, wrote of Amoghavarsha I as one of the four great kings in the world, the others being the Caliph of Bagdad, the King of Constantinople and the Emperor of China.

Must visit: The splendid rock-cut cave temples at Ellora and Elephanta, especially the monolithic rock-cut masterpiece, the Kailasanatha Temple at Ellora. If you see this temple from the top, you will understand what hard work and precision would have gone into converting a hill into a temple!

Preceded by: Chalukyas.

Succeeded by: Western Chalukyas.

Rulers: Dantidurga (735–56 CE) ▸ Krishna I (756–74 CE) ▸ Govinda II (774–80 CE) ▸ Dhruva Dharavarsha (780–93 CE) ▸ Govinda III (793–814 CE) ▸ Amoghavarsha (814–78 CE) ▸ Krishna II (878–914 CE) ▸ Indra III (914–29 CE) ▸ Amoghavarsha II (929–30 CE) ▸ Govinda IV (930–36 CE) ▸ Amoghavarsha III (936–39 CE) ▸ Krishna III (939–67 CE) ▸ Khottiga (967–72 CE) ▸ Karka II (972–73 CE) ▸ Indra IV (973–82 CE)

***

ZAMORIN (SAMUTHIRI) OF CALICUT

Ibn Battuta, the Moroccan traveller, first mentions the word 'zamorin' in his accounts in 1342. Duarte Barbosa (c. 1516), a Portuguese official and writer, also mentioned the Calicut ruler of Calicut as *çamidre* or *zomodri*, with its root in the Malayalam word *samutiri.*

Symbol: Two crossed swords, with a conch in centre and a lighted lamp above it.

Start time: 1124 CE.

End time: 1806 CE.

Territory: The Samuthiri and his feudatory kings from Nilambur Kovilakam established Calicut as a very important trading port-cities of the time. At their most powerful, the Samuthiris ruled over a kingdom stretching from Kozhikode Kollam (Kollam) to the borders of Panthalayani Kollam (Koyilandy).

Capital: Calicut.

Famous for: Establishing the port-city at Kozhikode, which held a strategically significant position on the Kerala coastiline in south-west India. It was the entry point for traders and travellers – the Arabs, the Chinese, the Portuguese, the Dutch, and ultimately the British.

Unforgettable: Gaining from the policies of the Samuthiris, Calicut became a hub for trading in spices in medieval times. The pot was efficiently managed by the port commissioner, who supervised customs services, fixed the prices of items and collected the king's share.

Preceded by: Cheras.

Succeeded by: Company rule in India.

Must Visit: Pazhassi Raja Museum And Art Gallery; Mishkal Mosque; Mother Of God Cathedral; Muchundi Palli; Lokanarkavu Temple; Azhakodi Devi Temple; Valayanad Temple.

Rulers: (*The zamorins are referred to here by their number of the king in the dynastic line*): Mana Vikrama (Manikkan) ▶ 27. Eight-year reign ▶ 65 (1339–47 CE) ▶ 73. (1402–10 CE) ▶ 78. (1442–50) ▶ 81. Mana Vikrama the Great (1466–74 CE) ▶ 82. Manaveda (1474–82 CE) ▶ 84. (1495–1500 CE) ▶ 85. (1500–13 CE) > 86. (1513–22 CE) ▶ 87. (1522–29) > 88. (1529–31 CE) ▶ 89. (1531–40 CE) ▶ 90. (1540–48 CE) ▶ 91. (1548–60) ▶ 92. Vira Raya (1560–62 CE)

***

KAKATIYA

Symbols: Garuda, Varaha.

Start time: c. 800 CE; early rulers ruled as feudatories of the Western Chalukyas. Prola II was the first independent Kakatiya ruler.

End time: 1323 CE.

Territory: Much of the today's Telangana and Andhra Pradesh, and parts of eastern Karnataka, northern Tamil Nadu, and southern Odisha.

Capital: Orugallu (Warangal).

Famous for: Rudramma Devi, who was the first woman ruler of Kakatiya dynasty as well as the Andhra region.

Unforgettable:; Rudradeva encouraged art and literature, authored the *Nitisara* in Sanskrit and built the Rudresvara

Temple in Palempet. The long-reigning Ganapathideva promoted trade.

Preceded by: Eastern Chalukyas, Western Chalukyas.

Succeeded by: Reddi kingdom, Musunuri Nayakas, Delhi Sultanate, Bahmani Sultanate, Vijayanagara Empire.

Must Visit: Hanumakonda and Warangal; many monuments such as the Thousand Pillar Temple, Ramappa Temple or Rudresvara Temple, a UNESCO World Heritage Site, Warangal Fort and Kota Gullu.

Rulers: Betaraja I (1000–52 CE) ▸ Prolaraja I (1052–76 CE) ▸ Betaraja II (1076–1108 CE) ▸ Durgaraja Prola II (1110–58 CE) ▸ Rudradeva (1158–95 CE) ▸ Mahadeva (1195–98 CE) ▸ Ganapatideva (1198–1262 CE) ▸ Rani Rudramma Devi (1262–96 CE) ▸ Prataparudra (1296–1323 CE)

***

HOYSALA

Symbol: Sala attacking a tiger.

Start time: 11th century CE (subordinate to the Western Chalukya Empire until 1187).

End time: 14th century CE, due to attack by the Delhi Sultanate armies.

Territory: Karnataka, north-western parts of Tamil Nadu and parts of western Andhra Pradesh.

Famous for: Attention to detail in their architecture, both the interiors and exteriors of their buildings (even the pieces of jewellery worn by the deities in their temples were intricately carved); Hoysala hero stones; and promoting

Kannada art and literature. Their temple architecture shines in the Keshava Temple at Somanathapura, the Chennakeshava Temple at Belur and the Hoysaleswara Temple at Halebidu.

Unforgettable: Vishnuvardhana built the Keerthi Narayana Temple at Talakadu, and the spectacular Vijayanarayana Temple at Belur; Veera Ballala II patronized Kannada poets such as Janna, Nemichandra, and Rudrabhatta, and built the Kedareshwara Temple at Halebidu, the Veera Narayana Temple at Belavadi, the Amrutesvara Temple at Amruthapura and the twin Chennakeshava and Nageshvara Temples at Mosale.

Must visit: The temples and *basadi* (Jain temple) in Halebidu, Belur, Somanathapura and Hosaholalu. Besides the sculptures, look at the finely and profusely carved ceilings and windows.

Preceded and succeeded by: Western Chalukyas.

Rulers: Nripa Kama II (1026–1047 CE) ▸ Vinayaditya (1047–98 CE) ▸ Ereyanga (1098–1102 CE) ▸ Veera Ballala I (1102–08 CE) ▸ Vishnuvardhana (1108–52 CE) ▸ Narasimha I (1152–73 CE) ▸ Veera Ballala II (1173–1220 CE) ▸ Vira Narasimha II (1220–35 CE) ▸ Vira Someshwara (1235–63 CE) ▸ Narasimha III (1263–92 CE) ▸ Veera Ballala III (1292–1343 CE)

***

REDDI/REDDY

Start time: 1325 CE.

End time: 1448 CE.

Territory: Present-day coastal and central Andhra Pradesh.

Capital: Addanki, Kondaveedu, Rajahmundry (now known as Rajamahendravaram).

Famous for: Blossoming of Telugu literature, with some of the Reddi kings themselves being scholars. Prolaya Vema Reddi had the Srisailam Mallikarjuna Swami Temple repaired.

Unforgettable: Anavota Reddi abolished customs duties and trade taxes, and trade flourished.

Preceded by: Kakatiyas.

Succeeded by: Vijayanagara Empire, Gajapati Empire.

Must Visit: Srisailam.

Rulers: Prolaya Vema Reddi (1325–53 CE) ▸ Anavota Reddi (1353–64 CE) ▸ Anavema Reddi (1364–86 CE) ▸ Kumaragiri Reddi (1386–1402 CE) ▸ Kataya Vema Reddi (1395–1414 CE) ▸ Peda Komati Vema Reddi (1402–1420 CE) ▸ Racha Vema Reddi (1420–24 CE) ▸ Allada Reddi (1414–23 CE) ▸ Veerabhadra Reddi (1423–48 CE)

***

BAHMANI SULTANATE

The name comes from the founder's name, Ala-ud-Din Bahman Shah.

Start time: 1347 CE.

End time: 1527 CE.

Territory: Parts of the present-day states of Karnataka, Maharashtra and Telangana.

Capital: Gulbarga (1347–1425 CE), Bidar (1425–1527 CE).

Famous for: The Persian Indo-Islamic style of architecture, which was later adopted by the Deccan Sultanates. Mahmud Gawan, a Bahmani prime minister, established the world-famous Madrasa in Bidar, which had a library containing 3,000 manuscripts.

Unforgettable: The Bahmani rulers built tombs and mosques in Bidar and Gulbarga as well as forts at Daulatabad, Golconda and Raichur. The architecture was highly influenced by Persian architecture as they invited architects from Persia, Turkey and Arabia.

Preceded by: Delhi Sultanate, Musunuri Nayaks.

Succeeded by: Vijayanagara Empire, Deccan Sultanates, Portuguese India; the Bahmani Sultanate separated into five kingdoms: Ahmednagar, Bijapur, Golconda, Bidar and Berar.

Must visit: The Gulbarga Fort, Haft Gumbaz and Jama Masjid in Gulbarga; Bidar Fort.

GULBARGA PERIOD

Rulers: Ala-ud-Din Hassan Bahman Shah (1347–58 CE) ▶ Muhammad Shah I (1358–75 CE) ▶ Ala-ud-Din Mujahid Shah (1375–78 CE) ▶ Da'ud Shah (1378–78 CE) ▶ Muhammad Shah II (1378–97 CE) ▶ Ghiyas-ud-din Tahmatan Shah (1397–97 CE) ▶ Shams-ud-din Daud Shah II (1397 CE) ▶ Taj-ud-Din Feroze Shah (1397–1422 CE)

BIDAR PERIOD

Rulers: Shihab-ud-din Ahmad Shah I (1422–36 CE) ▶ Ala-ud-Din Ahmed Shah II (1436–58 CE) ▶ Ala-ud-Din Humayun Shah

(1458–61 CE) ▸ Nizam-ud-din Ahmad Shah III (1461–63 CE) ▸ Shams-ud-din Muhammad Shah III (1463–82 CE) ▸ Shihab-ud-din Mahmud (1482–1518 CE) ▸ Ahmed Shah IV (1518–20 CE) ▸ Ala-ud-Din Shah (1520–22 CE) ▸ Wali-ullah Shah (1523–26 CE) ▸ Kaleem-ullah Shah (1526–38 CE).

***

VIJAYANAGARA EMPIRE

Vijayanagara means 'the city of victory'.

Symbols: The Boar, with a push dagger for bravery, and the sun and the moon to indicate their eternal glory.

Start time: 14th century CE.

End time: 17th century CE.

Territory: All of south India, parts of southern Maharashtra.

Capital: Vijayanagara, Penukonda, Chandragiri, Vellore.

Famous for: Creating Hampi, their capital city, one of the richest in the world at that time, and for making Telugu a great language.

Unforgettable: Krishnadevaraya, who was only in his twenties when he expanded the empire, administered it well and still found time to write books such as the *Amuktamalyada*, which tells us what we can do to be rich and famous.

Preceded by: Hoysalas, Kakatiyas, Yadavas, Kampili kingdom, Madurai Sultanate, Pandyasy, Musunuri Nayaks, Reddis, Delhi Sultanate.

Succeeded by: Kingdom of Mysore, Nayakas of Keeladi, Thanjavur Nayaks, Madurai Nayaks, Nayakas of Chitradurga, Adil Shahis, Qutb Shahis, Nayaks of Gingee.

Must visit: Hampi, Tirupati, Kalahasti. In the Virupaksha Temple in Hampi, to the right of the temple, inside a small dark room is a pinhole camera effect of a reverse shadow of the main temple *gopuram* or entrance tower.

SANGAMA

Rulers: Harihara Raya I (1336–56 CE) ▸ Bukka Raya I (1356–77 CE) ▸ Harihara Raya II (1377–1404 CE) ▸ Virupaksha Raya (1404–05 CE) ▸ Bukka Raya II (1405–06 CE) ▸ Deva Raya I (1406–22 CE) ▸ Ramachandra Raya (1422 CE) ▸ Vira Vijaya Bukka Raya (1422–24 CE) ▸ Deva Raya II (1424–46 CE) ▸ Mallikarjuna Raya (1446–65 CE) ▸ Virupaksha Raya II (1465–85 CE) ▸ Praudha Raya (1485 CE)

SALUVA

Rulers: Saluva Narasimha Deva Raya (1485–91 CE) ▸ Thimma Bhupala (1491 CE) ▸ Narasimha Raya II (1491–1505 CE)

TULUVA

Rulers: Tuluva Narasa Nayaka (1491–1503 CE) ▸ Viranarasimha Raya (1503–09 CE) ▸ Krishnadevaraya (1509–29 CE) ▸ Achyuta Deva Raya (1529–42 CE) ▸ Sadashiva Raya (1542–70 CE)

ARAVIDU

Rulers: Aliya Rama Raya (1542–65 CE) ▸ Tirumala Deva Raya (1565–72 CE) ▸ Sriranga I (1572–86 CE) > Venkata I (1586–1614 CE) ▸ Sriranga II (1614–1614 CE) ▸ Ramadeva (1617–32 CE) ▸ Venkata III (1632–42 CE) ▸ Sriranga III (1642–46 CE)

ACKNOWLEDGEMENTS

This book had its genesis in the online sessions I conducted during the summer of 2020 when the COVID-19 pandemic was in full force. Prabhakar Kadavasal, Shanmughapriya Thyagarajan, Ranjith Pillai and Bhargav Raghunathan were all instrumental in making it a success and, of course, so were all the children who logged in ahead of time and were most curious and excited.

Malati Raghunath, Sathya Sriram, Prema Raghunath, Justice Prabha Sridevan (Retd) and Purvi Betai helped me a lot with the initial drafts in various ways, and I thank them for their time and effort. I struggled somewhat with Andhra history for many months till Professor Nagaraj Paturi and Professor Gangadhara Prasad magically appeared and helped me with so much generosity and patience! Dhananjayan Mama for Kerala, Gopu for maths, and Hari Ravikumar for Kannada were also very generous.

Kabir, Shai, Krishna, Navya and Vir looked at the first draft and shared their detailed feedback, and I hope they will like the final product though it has been a while.

Doing this has been a learning for me of the joys of stepping outside the comfort zone of the history of Tamil Nadu. Researching the sources for all of south India was an eye-opening and enriching experience, and I hope parents will enjoy the book as much as children, and perhaps even go on to read the original sources like the *Manasollasa* and the translations of inscriptions, among other historical material.

I am happy I spent the lockdown in this useful way and must thank Vatsala and Hachette India for giving me this opportunity. It was a delight working with her.

My time with my son and other children has always been the moments that I have enjoyed and learnt from the most. I hope this humble offering has given back a little to an age group that I have taken much from!

INDEX

E

F

G

T

U

V

W

X

Y

Z

IMAGE COPYRIGHT INFORMATION

CHAPTER 1: p.5: Map by Syed Salahuddin; **p.7, 8, 9, 10, 12, 13, 15:** Vibha Surya; **p.14:** Mother Goddess figurine from Adichanallur, Tamil-Nadu, c. 800 BCE: © **Sharada Srinivasan**, 2021, 'Goddess worship and the dancing form: Exploring ritual in Indian prehistory and South Indian antiquity', Lietuvos Archaeologija 47: 145-166.

CHAPTER 2: p.20: Wikimedia Commons Public Domain (PD): Plate 5 from Richard Barron's 'View in India, chiefly among the Neelgherry Hills', 1837; **p.21, 22, 23:** Vibha Surya; **p.27:** Statues of King Vishnuvardhana (1108–52 CE) and his queen Santale, in the Kesava temple at Belur, Mysuru, *South Indian Portraits In Stone and Metal* by Aravamuthan, T.G., 1931: Wikimedia Commons PD; **p.31:** 'Cranganore with Dutch East India Company ships in the harbor' (1708) from *Wouter Schouten's travels into the East Indies* (2nd ed): Wikimedia Commons PD; **p.35:** Jewish immigrants in Kerala, India: Wikimedia Commons PD; **p.40:** A chegada de Vasco da Gama a Calicute em 1498 by Roque Gameiro, c. 1900/National Library of Portugal collection: Wikimedia Commons PD; **p.44:** Marthanda Varma: A *History of Travancore from the Earliest Times* by P. Shungoonny Menon, 1878: Wikimedia Commons PD; **p.47:** Ashoka in the Kanaganahalli inscription: Upinder Singh: Wikimedia Commons PD; **p.50:** Vibha Surya; **p.53:** Shutterstock/Vinayak Jagtap; **p.54:** Shutterstock/Denny George; **Page 55:** Malik Kafur, from *Hutchinson's Story of the Nations*: Wikimedia Commons PD; **p.58:** Vibha Surya; **Page 65:** Hero stone, *Pulikuthipattan kal*, Dharmapuri Musuem collection, from Pikkuhalli, 14th century CE: © Arokia Antoniate Priya A; **p.67:** Vibha Surya; **p.70:** Rajaraja Chola: Wall paintings: Author: Junykwilfred; CCA-SA 3.0; converted to black-and-white: https://commons.wikimedia.org/wiki/File:Wall_paintings_depicted_in_the_cloister_Mandapa,_Big_Temple,_Thanjavur_-_3.JPG; **p.71:** Rajaraja Chola: © Pradeep Chakravarthy; **p.73:** Vibha Surya; **p.76:** A model of the Mangulam Tamil Brahmi inscription at Dakshin Chithra, Chennai; Author: Sodabottle: https://commons.wikimedia.org/wiki/File:Mangulam_inscription.jpg; CCA-SA 3.0; **p.77:** © Pradeep Chakravarthy; **p.83:** Gautamiputra_Rajni_Shri_Satakarni by PHGCOM: Wikimedia Commons PD; **p.84:** Veneration of the Buddha as a Fiery Pillar, Cleveland Museum of Art, USA, Purchase from the J.H. Wade Fund; Source/Photographer: https://clevelandart.org/art/1943.72: Wikimedia Creative Commons CC0 1.0 Universal Public Domain Dedication; **p.85:** Los Angeles County Museum of Art, Made in: Nepal Gift of Paul F. Walter (M.70.70) to en:LACMA: Wikimedia Commons PD; **p.87:** Coins of the Pallavas of Coromandel: **Attribution: Classical Numismatic Group, Inc.**

http://www.cngcoins.com; Source: CNG Coins; https://en.m.wikipedia.org/wiki/File:Pallavas_of_Coromandel.jpg; CCA-SA 3.0 Unported; the GNU Free Documentation License, Version 1.2; **p.88:** Shutterstock/ Drishtant Xaxa; **p.89:** Vibha Surya; **p.90:** Shutterstock/ praveenkumar bashaboina.

CHAPTER 3: p.96: Amma II (Eastern Chalukya), Sanskrit language written in Canarese-Telugu script, 10th century CE. Copper plates, exhibited in the National Museum, New Delhi, India; Author: Daderot: Wikimedia Commons PD; **p.98:** (top) A mixed Tamil and Sanskrit inscription. A mix of Vatteluttu and Grantha scripts. Pandya dynasty. 8th century from (1934), *Epigraphia Indica* Volume 22 by N.P.Chakravarti; Author: Ms. Sarah Welch: Wikimedia Commons PD; (bottom) Vibha Surya; **p.100:** Vibha Surya; **p.107:** Srikrishnadevaraya is a well-known king of Hampi kingdom in Southern Andhra Pradesh (a model); Author: IM3847; CCA-SA 4.0 International; Converted to black-and-white; https://en.m.wikipedia.org/wiki/File:Model_of_court_in_Sri_Krishnadevaraya_asthanam.jpg; **p.108 and 110:** Vibha Surya.

CHAPTER 4: p.115, 116, 117, 118, 120, 121, 123: Vibha Surya; **p.126:** Harvesting of Pepper in Coilum in southern India by Mazarine Master; 14th century; Source/ Photographer: Bibliotheque Nationale / Archives Charmet / Bridgeman Art Library (Boucicaut Master); http://expositions.bnf.fr/gastro/grands/076.htm: Wikimedia Commons PD.

CHAPTER 5: p.129, 130, 131: Vibha Surya; p.134: Rajendra Chola in Battle, Kolaramma Temple; Author: WestCoastMusketeer; https://en.m.wikipedia.org/wiki/File:Rajendra_Chola_in_Battle,_Kolaramma_Temple_-_Edited.jpg; CCA-SA 4.0 International; **p.136:** Arjuna_Karna_final_battle,_Kurukshetra_war,_12th-century_Mahabharata_relief,_Hoysalesvara_temple_Halebidu; Author: Ms. Sarah Welch: : CCA-SA 4.0 International; **p.140 and 141:** English: 12th century hero stone (Viragal) with old Kannada inscription from the Tarakeshvara Temple at Hangal, Karnataka, 1855; Author: William Henry Pigou (1817–1858); British Library: Wikimedia Commons PD; **p.144:** A Hero stone (Viragallu) at Panagal Museum in Nalgonda district; Author: Adityamadhav83; **Attribution: Adityamadhav83/**; CCA-SA 4.0 International Licence; **p.149:** Vibha Surya.

CHAPTER 6: p.155 and 159: Vibha Surya

CHAPTER 7: p.169: Dancer's Headpiece in the Form of a Panjurli Bhuta (boar spirit deity), Kerala; Collection: Los Angeles County Museum of Art; released into Wikimedia Commons PD; **p.169:** © Vatsala Kaul Banerjee; **p.175:** bahubali-719922_1920 Image by pudiravi0 from Pixabay; **p.176:** Shutterstock/ RealityImages; **p.179:** Shutterstock/AnilD; p.180: Shutterstock/Zvonimir Atletic; **p.181:** Adi Shankara with disciples; c. 1904; Oleograph: PD; **p.183:** https://archive.org/details/itav_20220707/IrandamThiruvandhadhi-PBA; Author:

Sri PB Annangaracharíar: Wikimedia Commons PD; **p.189**: Shutterstock/ Nesru Markmedia; **p.191**: Shutterstock/Nesru Markmedia; **p.193**: St. Thomas, from Rubens' Twelve Apostles Series; P001654 (Museo del Prado): Wikimedia Commons PD; p.**194**: Shrine Of Saint Thomas At Mylapore,18th century print reproduced in Toynbee, A *Study of History*; Author: Unknown: Wikimedia Commons PD; **p.196**: Shutterstock/Trini Jacobs.

CHAPTER 8: **p.202–03**: Shutterstock/Snap Royce Photo Co; **p.204**: Shutterstock/Jayakumar; **p.206**: (top two illustrations) Vibha Surya; (middle) Shutterstock/ AnithamRaju Yaragorla, (bottom) Shutterstock/ prudhvichowdary; **p.207**: (top left) by courtesy of **SHARAT SUNDER**; (top right) Shutterstock/ECO LENS; (bottom) by courtesy of **SAURABH SAXENA/ puratattva.in**; **p.208**: shutterstock/NG Shutterbug; **p.213**: Shutterstock/ Somnath C; **p.215**: Shutterstock/RealityImages; **p.216**: (top) P.V. Jagadisa Ayyar (1920) *South Indian shrines: illustrated*, Madras Times Printing and Pub. Co., p.282: Wikimedia Commons PD; (bottom) Südindischer Meister um 850, painting; Source/photographer: The Yorck Project (2002) 10.000 Meisterwerke der Malerei (DVD-ROM), distributed by DIRECTMEDIA Publishing GmbH. ISBN: 3936122202: Wikimedia Commons PD; **p.218**: Vibha Surya; **p.220**: (left) Shutterstock/Satish Parashar, (right) Shutterstock/Kathirvelan photography; **p.225**: Bronze, tamil Nadu, c. 1300; Source: Walters Art Museum: Wikimedia Commons PD; © Pradeep Chakravarthy; **p.230**: (left)*Seated Vishnu*, 8th–9th century, granite; Brooklyn Museum, Gift of Alice Boney, 86.133. Creative Commons-BY (Photo: Brooklyn Museum, 86.133_PS2.jpg); (right): Author: Ms. Sarah Welch; https://en.m.wikipedia.org/wiki/File:Vishnu_with_Lakshmi,_13th_century_Keshava_temple_Somanathpur_3.jpg; **p.231** and **233** © Pradeep Chakravarthy; **p.234–35**: Shutterstock/zah108; (inset) © Shubhali Chopra; **p.236**: (top) 2nd-century CE, from Nagarjunakonda; Wikimdia Commons PD; (bottom) © Pradeep Chakravarthy

CHAPTER 9: **p.240**: Part of Muziris from Tabula Peutingeriana, 1-4th century CE. Facsimile edition by Conradi Millieri, 1887/1888: Wikimedia Commons PD; **p.246**: Shutterstock/ Vyas Abhishek; **p.248**: A panorama of Calicut, on the Malabar coast. Georg Braun and Franz Hogenberg's *atlas Civitates orbis terrarum*, 1572: Wikimedia Commons PD; **p.253**: (top) Front and reverse of the 6th copper plate with Pahlavi, Kufic, and Hebrew signatures, Tiruvalla, Kerala, c. 1320; Source: *The Church of the East*: A *Concise History*; Author: Baum, Wilhelm; Winkler, Dietmar W.: Wikimedia Commons PD; (bottom): Augustus Coin found in the Pudukottai Hoard, India; Source: self-made, photographed at the British Museum; Author: PHGCOM; **Attribution: I, PHGCOM**; https://en.m.wikipedia.org/wiki/File:AugustusCoinPudukottaiHoardIndia.jpg: GNU Free Documentation License; CCA-SA 3.0 Unported License; **p.254**: *Vasco da Gama perante o Samorim de Calecute*, painting, 1898; Collection:

Sociedade de Geografia de Lisboa: Wikimedia Commons PD; **p.255:** Mapa mondi (Catalan Atlas of 1375), Majorcan cartographic school, and 14th century Asia". *International Cartographic Association*: 5. Extracted from Catalan Atlas BNF, sheet 10.jpg: PD; **p.257:** Marcio Polo's caravan tgravelling to India; Author: Abraham Cresques, Atlas Catalan: Wikimedia Commons PD; **p.261:** Xuanzang's return to India; c. 8th century; Author unknown: Wikimedia Commons PD; **p.264–65:** Shutterstock/lego 19861111.

CHAPTER 10: p.270: The old Kannada (Hale Kannada) inscription stone (1182 CE) is kept right next to the main entrance. Source: *Epigraphia Carnatica, Inscriptions at Shravanabelgola*, Benjamin Lewis Rice (1889). Chapters: Introduction, p.2. p.57; List of Inscriptions by chronological order, page II, inscription no.124; Author: Ankush Manuja; https://en.m.wikipedia.org/wiki/File:Old_Kannada_inscription_dated_1182_A.D._at_the_Akkana_Basadi_in_Shravanebelagola.jpg: CCA-SA 3.0 Unported License; **p.274:** Vibha Surya; **p.278:** Source: http://postagestamps.gov.in/Stampofyear.aspx?uid=2017; Author: India Post, Government of India. This file is a copyrighted work of the Government of India, licensed under the Government Open Data License - India (GODL); **p.279:** Vibha Surya; **p.282:** Author: Department of Archaeology, Government of Tamil Nadu; Ministry of Culture: This file is a copyrighted work of the Government of India, licensed under the Government Open Data License - India (GODL); **p.286:** Source:http://dbsjeyaraj.com/dbsj/archives/10639: Wikimedia Commons PD.

CHAPTER 11: p.294: Cover page, Pambu Panchangam, 1884; Author: Konnur Manicka Mudhaliar: Wikimedia Commons PD; **p.303:** © Pradeep Chakravarthy; **p.304:** Shutterstock/Satish Parashar; **p.305:** Vibha Surya ; **p.306:** by courtesy of **Ahmad Alugaily, Alugaily Collection - London**; **p.307:** Shutterstock/Jay231985; **p.308:** by courtesy of **Ahmad Alugaily, Alugaily Collection - London**; **p.309:** Shutterstock/AJP; **p.310:** Shutterstock/ RealityImages; **p.314:** by courtesy of Pradeep Chakravarthy.

CHAPTER 12: p.319: Vibha Surya; **p.320:** © Pradeep Chakravarthy ; **p.321:** Shutterstock/DONGSEUN YANG; **p.322, 324, 326, 328:** Vibha Surya; **p.331:** Shutterstock/ explorewithinfo; **p.333:** Vibha Surya; **p.337:** Commemorative stamp of Purandaradasa, printed by Security Printing Press, Nasik; This file is a copyrighted work of the Government of India, licensed under the Government Open Data License - India (GODL); **p.338:** Shutterstock/RealityImages; **p.339:** Shutterstock/ Claudine Van Massenhove; **p.340:** (left) Shutterstock/DONGSEUN YANG and (right) Shutterstock/travel sojourns; **p.342:** Shutterstock/Sammu; **p.343:** Vibha Surya; **p.344:** Shutterstock/RealityImages; **p.345:** Vibha Surya; **p.346:** Shutterstock/Rajesh Kumar Reddy K.

Have you visited these UNESCO World Heritage Sites in south India?

- Group of Monuments at Mahabalipuram, Tamil Nadu
- Group of Monuments at Hampi, Karnataka
- Group of Monuments at Pattadakal, Karnataka
- Great Living Chola Temples (Brihadisvara Temple at Thanjavur, Brihadisvara Temple at Gangaikonda Cholapuram and the Airavatesvara Temple at Darasuram), Tamil Nadu
- Kakatiya Rudreshwara (Ramappa) Temple, Telangana
- Sacred Ensembles of the Hoysalas (temples at Belur-Halebidu and Somanathapura, near Mysuru), Karnataka